EDITED BY

Susan Gottheil &
Clayton Smith

AACRAO®
1910

SEM*IN*CANADA

Promoting Student and Institutional Success in Canadian Colleges and Universities

AMERICAN ASSOCIATION OF COLLEGIATE REGISTRARS AND ADMISSIONS OFFICERS

SEM*IN*CANADA

American Association of Collegiate
Registrars and Admissions Officers
One Dupont Circle, NW, Suite 520
Washington, DC 20036–1135

Tel: (202) 293–9161 | Fax: (202) 872–8857 | www.aacrao.org

For a complete listing of AACRAO publications, visit www.aacrao.org/publications.

The American Association of Collegiate Registrars and Admissions Officers, founded in 1910, is a nonprofit, voluntary, professional association of more than 11,000 higher education administrators who represent more than 2,600 institutions and agencies in the United States and in forty countries around the world. The mission of the Association is to provide leadership in policy initiation, interpretation, and implementation in the global educational community. This is accomplished through the identification and promotion of standards and best practices in enrollment management, information technology, instructional management, and student services.

LIBRARY OF CONGRESS CATALOGING-IN-PUBLICATION DATA

SEM in Canada / edited by Susan Gottheil and Clayton Smith.

p. cm.

ISBN 978-1-57858-097-2

1. College attendance—Canada.
2. Universities and colleges—Canada—Admission.
3. College students—Recruiting—Canada.

I. Gottheil, Susan.
II. Smith, Clayton.

LC148.4.C2S46 2011
378.1'6190971—dc23
2011015852

Contents

13 Case Study: Undergraduate Academic and Career Success at Université Laval 259

by Nicole Lacasse, Patrick Mignault and Johanne Morneau

The emergence of strategic enrolment management among Canadian universities and colleges is rapidly gaining momentum. The growth of SEM in Canada is driven by multiple forces. Proximity to the United States, the birthplace of the profession, is a major factor. Canadian higher education professionals have long availed themselves of ready access to enrolment management conferences and literature promulgated in the U.S. At recent AACRAO SEM Conferences, Canadian participation has reached as high as 20 percent of attendees.

However, the rise of SEM in Canada reflects more than mere geographic opportunity. There are global trends at play. Among highly-developed higher education systems from Canada to the United Kingdom to Australia, major enrolment-related forces are shifting in ways that have sparked interest in SEM concepts. One of these is shifting demographics, involving a decline in traditional college-going populations concurrent with significant changes in student demographics related to socioeconomic status, the latter being strongly correlated with race, ethnicity, and immigrant status. These changes in Canada and their implications for SEM are chronicled in this book by Smith, Gottheil, and Gauthier, as well as others.

Against that backdrop of demographic changes, financial forces have further intensified interest in SEM. As Smith and Gottheil note in their introductory chapter, both the U.S. and Canada have experienced declines in financial support to higher education at the national and state/provincial levels. That fact itself drives institutions toward SEM in multiple ways. It leads to increased tuition rates, which prompts students to exhibit higher degrees of consumerism and comparison shopping. And, institutions are more reliant than ever on the number of students they enrol, and the tuition dollars represented by each student, to balance the institutional budget. These forces have come to the fore in Canada more recently than in the U.S., inviting Canadian institutions to adopt competitive practices focused on marketing and enhanced prospective student communications to a greater degree in the past 10 to 15 years than had previously been the case.

But the rise of SEM in Canada is much more than merely mimicking U.S. trends. Perhaps the most notable aspect of this book is the evidence it provides of Canadian institutions having created not just their own version of SEM, but one that furthers the profession in the U.S. and abroad. Whatever the successes of SEM in the U.S., there have been pitfalls as well, which might be characterized as greater focus on recruitment than retention, over-reliance on marketing hype, questionable deployment of student financial assistance, and, in general, prioritizing institutional interests over those of students. Canadians, and other SEM professionals around the world, have the opportunity to learn from these missteps and help us collectively develop stronger SEM theory and strategies.

It is my sincere hope that this book becomes a milestone for the time when SEM benefitted from a new level of transnational dialogue and sharing of expertise. Thanks are due to Susan Gottheil and Clayton Smith for their leadership in helping this book, and that dialogue, to happen.

Bob Bontrager
Director, AACRAO Consulting
Corvallis, Oregon
February 2011

/ About the Authors /

EDITORS

Susan Gottheil

Susan has several decades of leadership experience in the Canadian post-secondary sector helping institutions to promote and expand academic programs, increase student recruitment and retention, enhance learning and development, improve student and academic support services, and promote collaborative partnerships. With an undergraduate degree from McGill University and an M.A. in Women's History, Susan began her career at Vanier College CÉGEP in Montreal where she spent nine years teaching before moving into senior administrative positions at Carleton University. In 2006, she moved to western Canada to help Mount Royal transition from a college to a university and roll out new undergraduate degree programs. Susan currently serves as Vice-Provost (Students) at the University of Manitoba, and has also helped a number of Canadian institutions develop strategic enrolment plans in her role as a Senior Consultant with AACRAO Consulting.

Clayton Smith

Dr. Smith has 25 years of broad post-secondary educational experience at three institutions in the U.S. and one in Canada. He currently serves as Vice Provost, Students and International, at the University of Windsor (Ontario, Canada). Dr. Smith holds a B.A. from the University of Southern Maine, an M.A. from Drew University, an M.P.A. from the University of Maine, and an Ed.D. in higher education from Florida State University. He has published articles in *CACUSS Communiqué, Col-*

lege and University, SEM Source, the *Journal of College Admission* and the *Journal of College Retention* on such topics as enrolment management, Canadian strategic enrolment management, integrated marketing, inter-institutional joint marketing, student retention and student recruitment. Dr. Smith currently sits on the *College and University* and *Journal of Student Affairs Research & Practice* editorial boards, co-organizes the annual Canadian SEM Summit and serves as a senior consultant with AACRAO Consulting.

Over the past five years Susan Gottheil and Clayton Smith have collaborated on the emergence and implementation of enrolment management in Canada. They have presented workshops at a number of professional conferences in the U.S. and across Canada, published articles, and organized the annual Canadian Enrolment Management Summits.

CONTRIBUTING AUTHORS

Mairead Barry

Mairead is Associate Registrar & Director of Admissions at Dalhousie University. Mairead began her career in Admissions at St. Francis Xavier University, a small, primarily undergraduate university before moving to Dalhousie. As Director of Admissions, Mairead is responsible for all aspects of developing and managing domestic and international undergraduate admissions policies and processes in order to meet the University's enrolment objectives. She also works to develop university-wide best practices for graduate and professional program admission.

Brian Christie

Brian is Associate Vice-President, Resource Planning, at the University of Regina. An economist, he has been a faculty member at universities in Manitoba, Nova Scotia and Saskatchewan, as well as senior policy advisor and coordinator of research at a provincial universities commission. Brian created and directed the institutional research offices at two Canadian universities; at both, he was a member of the strategic enrolment planning committee. Brian has conducted applied research and published articles and book chapters in the areas of university planning and management, government-university relations, program review, and data management. He has prepared and delivered training workshops on strategic planning, and facilitated planning processes for universities and government departments in Canada and the United States.

Sarah Dench

Sarah is the Director, University Curriculum and Institutional Liaison at Simon Fraser University in the Office of the VP Academic. Sarah has responsibility for the development of partnerships between SFU and other B.C. post-secondary institutions, and is the university liaison to SFU's partner pathway college for international students, Fraser International College (a college of Navitas Education Ltd.). She is currently chairing an SFU committee tasked with making recommendations to the VP Academic on how best to improve services and supports to students for whom English is an additional language. Sarah has over 20 years of experience in universities, and has a background in Student Affairs with particular focus on programming for groups under-represented in post-secondary education.

Peter Dueck

Peter has led financial aid and awards offices at two universities and was on secondment for a time with the Canada Student Loan Program in Ottawa. Well known in Canadian financial aid circles, he has served as a two-term president of the Canadian Association of Financial Aid Administrators (CASFAA). Peter is currently the Executive Director of Enrolment Services at the University of Manitoba, where his responsibilities include student recruitment, admissions, financial aid and awards, and the English Language Centre.

E. Jane Fee

Jane is Associate Dean of the Faculty of Arts & Social Sciences at Simon Fraser University and her academic discipline is linguistics. She is responsible for strategic enrolment management within her Faculty, which is the largest at SFU. Additionally, Jane oversees the Faculty's operations at SFU's newest campus in Surrey, located south of the Fraser River in one of the fastest growing communities in Canada. She co-led an institution-wide SEM planning process at SFU in 2009-10, and now represents her faculty on SFU's new Strategic Enrolment Management Council. This

SEM Council is charged with drafting the University's first SEM plan. The Faculty of Arts & Social Sciences has approximately 16.5 percent international undergraduate students and is therefore involved in numerous initiatives to increase the success of international students. Jane will become Associate Vice-President, Academic at Kwantlen Polytechnic University in September 2011.

Gail Forsyth

Gail is the Director of Learning Services at Wilfrid Laurier University where she oversees student academic success services. Prior to assuming this role, she worked in registrarial services specializing in admissions, recruitment and registration activities for undergraduate and graduate programs. Gail has improved Wilfrid Laurier University's transition programs for new students and their families, developed a peer mentoring program, and expanded the student academic success services. She has secured external funding to launch new support initiatives for Aboriginal and first-generation students as well as an outreach and access program for students and their families in "at-risk" communities.

Keith Fortowsky

Keith is Manager, Institutional Research, at the University of Regina, where he leads development, maintenance, and analysis of institutional statistics. His primary goal is to connect institutional data and analysis to the larger "strategic conversation" of the University as a whole. Keith has been "crunching data" in various sectors for 25 years. You can read more about his experience and ongoing adventures by accessing his LinkedIn profile: www.linkedin.com/in/kfortowsky.

Devron Gaber

Dr. Gaber has worked as an Associate Director with the B.C. Council on Admissions and Transfer (BCCAT) since September 2003. Working with the Admissions Committee, he leads work on BCCAT's expanded admissions agenda, which includes conducting a variety of studies on province-wide student mobility. Dr. Gaber represents BCCAT on the Student Transitions Project Steering Committee and currently serves as its chair. He also has lead responsibility for BCCAT's extensive research agenda. Before coming to BCCAT, Devron worked in a number of jobs related to post-secondary education and adult learning in B.C. and Manitoba, beginning in the late 1970s. He has a B.A. from the University of Manitoba, an M.A. from the University of Calgary, and an Ed.D. from Oregon State University.

Larry Gauthier

Larry is a member of the Lac La Ronge Indian Band and grew up on the family's trapline in northern Saskatchewan. Dropping out of school in grade ten, Larry was fortunate to travel the world extensively with the Canadian Armed Forces, serving the required three years. Later, Larry attended the University of Saskatchewan and graduated at the top of his class in 1993. Shortly after graduating Larry began his career in student services as the Native Student Advisor at the University of Alberta. This was followed by an appointment at the University of Saskatchewan as the Director of the Aboriginal Student Centre (where he also taught in the Native Studies Department). Larry's passion for Aboriginal student success took him to the First Nations University of Canada as the Director of Student Success Services. It was at the First Nations University that he developed a successful model of academic support which doubled the success/retention rates of first-year students. In early 2009, Mount Royal University presented Larry another opportunity to design and develop a successful Aboriginal student service model. He holds a B.A. Honors degree from the University of Saskatchewan and an M.S. in Education with a specialization in Enrolment Management from Capella University.

Jody Gordon

Jody is the Associate Vice President, Students at Kwantlen Polytechnic University (KPU), Surrey, B.C. She has worked in post-secondary student services since 1992, beginning her career at Simon Fraser University before joining KPU in 1998. Jody completed a First Class Honours B.A. and an M.A. from Simon Fraser University. She was selected as the recipient of the 2009 Strategic Enrolment Management Award of Excellence in the Canadian Institutions category, an award cosponsored by the American Association of Collegiate Registrars and Admissions Officers and Education Systems Inc. In addition to her administrator role at KPU, Jody teaches first-year criminology students.

Stefanie Ivan

Stefanie is Associate Vice President Student Services at Grant MacEwan University where she leads an energetic team responsible for many facets of enrolment management including the Office of the Registrar and Information Centres, Aboriginal Education Centre, CASE Management, and Graduate School Liaison. Stefanie has the pleasure of chairing both the Student Services Policy Committee and the Admissions & Selections Committee, both standing committees of Academic Governance Council. In her role, she is responsible for student discipline and also is a resource for university appeals. Stefanie was formerly the Registrar at MacEwan, and previously also worked in Student Services and taught upgrading at Red Deer College.

Yves Jodoin

Yves has been Secretary General and Registrar at Bishop's University located in the Lennoxville Borough of Sherbrooke, Québec since 2005. After working overseas for AIESEC International in Belgium, Yves started his university career in 1975 at the Université du Québec à Montréal (UQAM) where he worked for 30 years at various management positions including 21 years in the Registrar's Office. At night, he taught as a part-time lecturer for a few years at UQAM. Yves earned a B.B.A. at UQAM and an M.B.A. from McGill University. From 1997 to 2008, he was a member of the Executive Committee of ARUCC (Association of Registrars of the Universities and Colleges of Canada) including a two-year stint as President of the Association.

Åsa Kachan

Åsa is Assistant Vice-President Enrolment Management & Registrar at Dalhousie University, responsible for strategic direction and oversight of all the activities related to undergraduate recruitment, admissions, registration, scholarships and financial aid, examinations, student records, convocation, and the student information system. Prior to Dalhousie, Åsa served as Director of Admissions and Registrar at the University of Saskatchewan. Well versed in the principles of SEM and their practical application, Åsa has presented on various topics at national conferences including ARUCC and the SEM Summit.

Nicole Lacasse

Dr. Lacasse is Associate Vice-Rector, Academic and International Activities and professor in the Department of Management at Université Laval. She holds a Doctorate in International Trade Law from Université Panthéon-Sorbonne (Paris 1) and has authored and co-authored more than 30 articles in scientific journals, books and colloquium proceedings. Over the course of her career, Nicole has maintained an active presence in Higher Education at the Business School and has served in various positions related to academic administration and international cooperation.

Richard Levin

Richard is keenly interested in evidence-based decision making and has published and presented on issues ranging from accountability to student service. Currently holding the position of Executive Director, Enrolment Services at the University of Toronto, Richard has previously held registrarial and SEM positions at the University of Manitoba, UOIT, Durham College and McMaster University. He began his career with the Manitoba and Ontario provincial governments and also worked as Executive Coordinator, Policy and Planning, with the Ontario Education Quality and Accountability Office.

Steve Marshall

Steve is an Assistant Professor in the Faculty of Education at Simon Fraser University. His research interests fall under the broad umbrella of *Learning Through Transitions*, with a particular focus on Sociolinguistics and Academic Literacy Education. Within these fields, Steve researches the interplay between languages, migration, identities, and literacy in various social and educational contexts. He is currently Principal Investigator for a SSHRC-funded research project into the academic literacy practices of university students in Vancouver, with a particular focus on multilingual students making the transition from secondary to higher education. At SFU, he coordinates and teaches on *Foundations of Academic Literacy FAL X99,* a first-year academic literacy course taken by around 850 students per year. Steve is author of *Academic Writing: Making the Transition*, published by Pearson Education Canada.

Susan Mesheau

Susan joined the University of New Brunswick (Fredericton) in 2001 as its first Director of Student Recruitment & Integrated Marketing. She has spent 35 years working in marketing and directed numerous campaigns within the New Brunswick provincial government that resulted in significant revenue growth. Her breadth of knowledge covers branding, strategic marketing planning and implementation, market research, public relations, product development and marketing consultation. Susan recently assumed the new position of Executive Director of U First: Integrated Recruitment & Retention at UNB Fredericton, with responsibility for domestic undergraduate and graduate recruitment, recruitment marketing and retention.

John Metcalfe

John is the Registrar at the University of Regina. He taught logic and philosophy before becoming an administrator. John held various university positions, including director of recruiting and admissions, registrar, reporting officer, privacy officer and ombudsman, before coming to Regina. He has experience, as both a teacher and administrator, with the introduction in university environments of a number of enrolment-based administrative programs.

Joy Mighty

Joy is director of the Centre for Teaching and Learning and a professor in the School of Business at Queen's University. She is the former president of the Society for Teaching and Learning in Higher Education and has represented Canada on the Council of the International Consortium for Educational Development. Dr. Mighty has an eclectic academic background in English, Education, and Organizational Behaviour, and a wealth of experience as an administrator, teacher, educational developer, researcher and consultant. Her special interests are organizational development and change, as well as equity and diversity issues as they relate to both management and education. A frequent keynote speaker at regional, national, and international conferences, she has published in various conference proceedings, journals, and books, and has provided consulting services to private, public, and not-for-profit organizations in Canada, the Caribbean, England, and the U.S.

Patrick Mignault

Patrick is lecturer in the Department of Management at Université Laval and a doctoral student in law at Université de Montréal. Admitted to Québec Bar in 2002, he holds a Master in Business Administration (finance) and a Master Degree in Actuarial Mathematics. He teaches courses both at the undergraduate and graduate levels in business law, personal finance law and financial risk management. On the research side, he is interested in pension fund governance and risk management, law and economics and business law. Professionally, he began his career with Stikeman Elliott LLP, one of Canada's leading business law firms, in its Montreal office. During his graduate study, he also has been research assistant and project manager at Stephen-Jarislowsky Research Chair in International Business Management (Université Laval). In 2009, he obtained a doctorate scholarship from Fonds québécois de la recherche sur la société et la culture (FQRSC) that ends summer 2012.

Johanne Morneau

Johanne is Assistant to the Vice-Rector, Academic and International Activities at Université Laval. She is a psychologist, specializing in educational and career advising and holds a Master's degree from Université Laval. During her career, Johanne has served in various positions related to academic administration, student recruitment, internationalization of the university and student life.

Dave Morphy

Dave is the former Vice-Provost: Student Affairs at the University of Manitoba where he led the development of a wide range of student affairs programs and cochaired the University's SEM team and the Student Leadership Development Project. He has served as president of the Canadian University College Counsellor's Association (CUCA), on the Board of the Student Affairs and Services Association (SASA) and as President of the Canadian Association of College and University Student Services Association (CACUSS). Dave has also been the Course Director for the Canadian Institute of Student Affairs and Services (CISAS) for 15 years and has recently worked to launch the Institute on the Student Experience.

William Radford

Dr. Radford is Director of Internationalisation at Simon Fraser University. He is in the process of completing a Ph.D. in Education at SFU and has an M.A. in Adult Education from St. Francis Xavier University and a B.A. and PGCE from the University of Leeds. He is also a certified literacy instructor. Bill has lived and worked in Europe, Botswana and Italy and managed international projects from Estonia to Sakhalin Island. He has been employed as a car design journalist, ESL teacher, community developer and international educator. As Director of Internationalisation, Bill is responsible for international services for students and views himself as a roving catalyst to ignite internationalisation across the institution.

Deborah Robinson

Deborah is Executive Director, Enrolment Management Strategy at The University of British Columbia. In her almost 30-year career in post-secondary education, Deborah has worked at a number of Canadian institutions in positions ranging from Manager of Educational Technology and Curriculum Development to Dean of Educational Planning and Development. Prior to her current position, Deborah spent almost a decade as Associate Registrar and Director, Recruitment, Admissions, Financial Assistance and Awards at UBC. In 2010, she received the AACRAO SEM Award of Excellence in recognition of her leadership in strategic enrolment management at a Canadian institution.

Laurie Schnarr

Laurie is the Director, Student Life at the University of Guelph. During almost three decades in Student Affairs, Laurie has overseen and developed innovative programs and services designed to foster student engagement and success. She also led the implementation of the University's first Aboriginal Resource Centre, the Off-Campus Living office, and the Office of Intercultural Affairs, and served on the team that created the Undergraduate Certificate in Leadership. Her teaching background includes undergraduate courses in leadership, the senior year transition and a first-year seminar focusing on the interplay between leadership practice and global citizenship. Her M.A. research explored the facilitators and inhibitors of youth civic engagement in Canada, an area of continued interest. Laurie currently serves as a Civic Engagement Expert with the Talloires Network at Tufts University and on the executive committee and board of a local community organization dedicated to providing housing, supportive services and programs for persons with disabilities and older adults.

Lynn Smith

Lynn has worked in the field of Student Affairs for over two decades. She is currently the Executive Director of Student Services at the University of Manitoba with responsibility for Aboriginal Student Services, Counseling and Career Services, International Centre for Students, Learning Assistance Centre, Student Advocacy, Disability Services, Health Services and the Student Affairs research portfolio, which includes the Canadian University Survey Consortium. Lynn is a member of the University of Manitoba's Strategic Enrolment Planning Committee and co-chair of the Student Retention and Success Sub-committee.

Barry Townshend

Barry is the Manager, Centre for New Students at the University of Guelph. He has also worked in a variety of roles in residence life, with a focus on living-learning communities and the first-year experience. A component of his Master of Social Work degree included practicum placements in hospital settings, where he worked with individuals and families who were facing life-threatening illnesses. He also has experience working with street-involved youth and volunteers as a member of the Board of Directors for a community-based, not-for-profit organization serving the local queer community. Professional highlights include having taught first-year seminar courses and having been a counsellor/therapist. Drawing upon his interest in online technologies, Barry has been the primary architect of a number of innovative strategies for engaging new students.

W. Alan Wright

Dr. Wright holds degrees from Mount Allison University, McGill University, and the Université de Montréal. Before assuming his current duties as vice-provost, teaching and learning at the University of Windsor, he worked for several years as a dean and director of undergraduate studies in the Université du Québec multi-constituent system, as well as for Dalhousie University, where he was the founding director of the Office of Instructional Development and Technology. Dr. Wright is active as a teacher, researcher, and author, and is the former series editor of the Green Guides, a collection of pedagogical manuals published by the Society for Teaching and Learning in Higher Education. Over the past decade, Dr. Wright has participated in a $2.5 million Major Collaborative Research Investigation sponsored by the Social Sciences and Humanities Research Council of Canada, as well as several projects funded by other research agencies.

Clayton Smith and Susan Gottheil

1

INTRODUCTION
MOVING BEYOND
THE AMERICAN SEM EXPERIENCE

/ **Chapter 1** /

Shaping enrolment through a focused approach to student recruitment and re-tention is now acknowledged by many Canadian educators as an essential part of the higher education landscape. Yet some see enrolment management as pri-marily an outcome of the American experience and thus not easily transposed into the Canadian context. Although the emergence of strategic enrolment management (SEM) in Canada has been more recent, the experience of Cana-dian enrolment professionals demonstrates that many of the issues facing Cana-dian colleges and universities are similar to those in American institutions. Yet Canadian history and value systems have also shaped a distinctive approach to SEM that has resulted in different areas of focus and different strategies and tac-tics to influence student recruitment and retention. As our profession reaches maturity we are discovering lessons we can learn from each other, pitfalls to be avoided and innovations to be adopted and adapted on both sides of the border. The difference in approaches to SEM in the two countries is a result of the differing social, political and economic contexts in which it developed. Although Canada and the United States share some of the same heritage, the American break with England in the late 1700s changed forever its cultural focus from being linked to Eu-rope to charting its own course. Canada, on the other hand, remains well connected to both the United Kingdom and other parts of the world through membership in the Commonwealth and la Francophonie. Canada's national commitment to bilin-gualism, multiculturalism and universal health care has helped to shape a different social and value system than its neighbour to the south. These differing factors af-fect the way our post-secondary educational systems operate in the 21st century. With more than 4,300 colleges and universities, the American post-secondary education system is heterogeneous in terms of academic focus, degrees offered, size of enrolments and students served. It is oriented toward providing a holistic student experience where student life is an important part of the college experience. It also operates within the context of decreasing state support of public institutions, increased accountability, increasing tuition levels, significant differences in regional student demand and continuing growth in the not-for-profit institutional sector. This has led to SEM becoming a mainstay at most institutions in the United States. Canada, on the other hand, has many fewer post-secondary institutions (over 300 in total). Despite a recent emphasis on rankings and consequent tiering in the university sector, there is a relatively small quality gap between top-ranked universities and those ranked lower, which results in most institutions being considered of "good quality." Canadian students frequently attend their local colleges and universities as commuters. Until recently there has been less concern for student development and the broader campus experience in Canada than in the United States. Although participation in post-secondary education has continued to increase in Canada, there is a looming decline in secondary school enrolment. Dramatic cuts in provincial grants, a heavier reliance on tuition income and increased public accountability (in the form of key performance indicators and national newspaper and magazine rankings) have resulted in increasing competition between institutions. Although many enrolment practitioners have turned to American colleagues and consultants for "best practices" and ideas for new tactics and strategies, many Canadians still remain uncomfortable with SEM's market orientation.

The rapid increase in attendance at American-based SEM conferences, the Canadian SEM Summit[1] and a number of one-day SEM workshops offered throughout the country is a testament to the importance of SEM on Canadian college and university campuses.

THE CANADIAN HIGHER EDUCATION SYSTEM

Unlike many Western countries, education in Canada does not fall under the auspices of the national government. It is considered a provincial and territorial responsibility, which results in no single national strategy for education, including

---

[1] The Canadian SEM Summit Web site: <www.uwindsor.ca/sem>.

post-secondary education. The Canadian post-secondary education landscape is composed of 12 different educational systems in the 10 provinces and two of the three territories. Nearly a hundred institutions are universities offering bachelor's and master's degrees, with a smaller number offering doctoral degrees. Some provinces support university colleges, polytechnics and institutes. Community colleges, which offer vocational-oriented apprenticeship, certificates and diplomas, are available in all jurisdictions. In Quebec, the College of General and Vocational Education (CÉGEP) system serves a dual function, providing vocational-oriented programs and serving as a bridge between high school and university.

Coordination between institutions of higher learning falls primarily to the provincial and territorial governments who have set up coordinating bodies (such as Campus Alberta), and provincial and regional networks (*e.g.*, Council of Ontario Universities, Conseil des Recteurs et Principaux des Universités du Québec, Association of Atlantic Universities). Additional coordination is provided by two national coordinating bodies, the Association of Universities and Colleges of Canada and the Association of Community Colleges of Canada.

Change across the post-secondary education landscape has been considerable in recent years. We have seen previously non-degree granting community colleges, institutes and polytechnics given degree granting authority; many also now offer post-graduate diplomas for university graduates. More comprehensive and coordinated systems of credit transfer have been developed and are being implemented in most regions. Graduate and professional education is becoming increasingly more available as provincial governments have provided extra funding to grow master's and doctoral programs. Some colleges and universities have entered into partnerships to offer integrated programming and more seamless pathways for students, often in the same locations (*e.g.*, Guelph-Humber, Seneca@York). In response to provincial government encouragement, nearly all institutions are positioning to increase the enrolment of international students.

Provincial governments—partially as a result of the world-wide economic slowdown—are relatively cash strapped and unable to support continuing growth of the higher education sector and are looking to reduce the number of duplicate programs, amalgamate or possibly eliminate institutions, and create new, more differentiated institutions. Governments, however, remain committed to supporting a robust and comprehensive post-secondary education sector. Most grasp the importance of the key Council of Ministers of Education finding (2010) that people with post-secondary education, particularly university education, have higher levels of employment and significantly higher earnings than those with only a high school diploma. Thus all of the provincial governments have expressed concern about the relatively low post-secondary participation of certain student populations (such as first-generation and Aboriginal students). This has led many institutions to develop new programs to widen college and university access.

At the same time, demographic realities are impacting the Canadian higher education landscape. Starting in 2012–13, the echo boom population will start to decrease in size. Because of this the post-secondary education environment in Canada has become nearly as competitive as that in the United States.

SEM DEFINED

A definition that captures the essence of SEM was suggested by Hossler and Bean (1990):

> *Enrollment management can be defined as an organizational concept and a set of systematic activities designed to enable educational institutions to exert more influence over their student enrollments. Organized by strategic planning and supported by institutional research, enrollment management activities concern student college choice, transition to college, student attrition and retention, and student outcomes.* (p. 5)

The traditional enrolment perspective focused on the beginning stages of the student lifecycle. The SEM framework puts forward a more comprehensive view. It stresses the full student success continuum and emphasizes the importance of the inter-relationships between recruitment/marketing activities, in-class curriculum and pedagogy, academic support programs, and the total on-campus student experience (Bontrager 2004b). Figure 1 displays the student success continuum.

Strategic enrolment management is an intentional planning process that involves all sectors of the institution. SEM includes establishing clear goals for the number and types of students needed to fulfill the institutional mission; promoting students' academic success by improving access, transition, persistence and graduation;

and promoting institutional success by enabling effective strategic and financial planning. The SEM goals in an institution can be successfully achieved by creating a data-rich environment to inform decisions and evaluate strategies; improving process, organizational and financial efficiency and outcomes; strengthening communication with internal and external stakeholders; and increasing collaboration among departments across the campus to support the enrolment program (Bontrager and Pollack 2009).

Key to an understanding of SEM is the notion of optimum enrolment. Each institution has an ideal enrolment that is appropriate to its mission. It can be calculated using both qualitative and quantitative measures and by considering such factors as physical capacity, number of majors and program capacity, and preferred student profile (*e.g.*, ethnicity, geographic draw, student quality, and so on). Institutional attributes need to be considered when determining optimal enrolment, including institutional strengths and weaknesses, historic role within the post-secondary system, programs offered, and competition from other colleges and universities. As

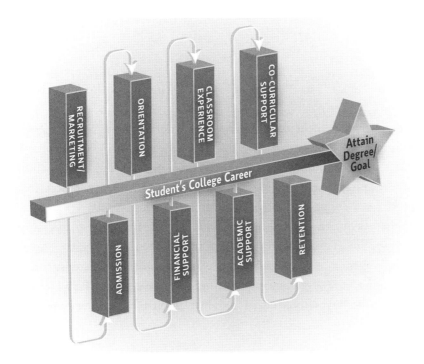

◀ FIGURE 1

The Student
Success Continuum
(Bontrager and
Smith 2009)

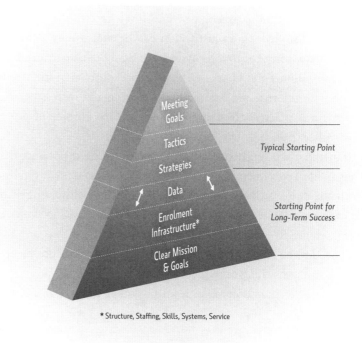

institutions cannot "be all things to all people," institutional differentiation and market niche are key.

While many enrolment managers focus on tactics and strategies as a way of meeting institutional enrolment goals, Figure 2 shows how the SEM planning model endorses first establishing a clear institutional mission and setting enrolment goals, developing the enrolment infrastructure to ensure goals can be successfully achieved, and focusing on data analysis.

Another way to understand SEM is to look how it fits together from a systems perspective. Table 1 provides an example of an enrolment management system. This model is an open system approach that shows how student characteristics and environment impact the development of institutional goals, objectives and strategies. It also shows how the results achieved from institutional activity help to refine future SEM goals and activities.

TABLE I: THE ENROLMENT MANAGEMENT SYSTEM*

Student Characteristics	Environmental Factors	Institutional Goals — Institutional Objectives		Institutional Strategies	Desired Outcomes	Enduring Effect	Enduring Behavior
■ Member of Underserved Student Group ■ Beliefs & Values ■ Academic Preparation ■ Motivation to Learn ■ Educational Aspirations ■ Self-Discipline ■ Adaptability ■ Interpersonal Skills ■ Peer Involvement ■ Ability to Pay ■ Study Habits ■ Family & Peer Support	■ Student Enrolment Behaviour ■ Demographic Trends ■ Competition ■ Public Accountability (Loan Default Rate, Graduation, Accessibility, Retention) ■ Student Geographic Draw ■ Economic Trends ■ Off-Campus Employment Availability ■ Federal & Provincial Policies	Quantitative Goals >>> Qualitative Goals >>> Diversity Goals >>> Persistence Goals >>> Capacity Goals >>> Net Revenue Goals >>>	Student Headcount Admission Average Transfer GPA Visible Minorities, Aboriginal, International Retention Rates, Student Satisfaction, Graduation Rates Classroom Capacity, Adequate Sections, Class Size Financial Aid Discount Rate, International Enrolment	■ Marketing ■ Recruitment ■ Admission ■ Financial Aid/Pricing ■ Orientation ■ Residence ■ Athletics ■ First Year Experience ■ Advising ■ Supplemental Instruction ■ Service Learning ■ Academic Support ■ Peer Support ■ Teaching & Learning Approaches ■ Student Engagement ■ SEM Organization ■ Data Mining	■ Awareness ■ Interest ■ Commitment ■ Enrolment ■ Persistence ■ Satisfaction ■ Education ■ Relationship	Institutional Loyalty	Institutional Image

* Adapted from: Kuh et al, 2007; Black 2008

SEM IN CANADA:
WHAT'S DIFFERENT?

Adapting SEM tactics and strategies that have evolved in the United States may not always be appropriate within the Canadian post-secondary context. One way to explore the uniqueness of how SEM is playing out in Canada is to compare it to the American experience. In a survey of Canadian and American post-secondary education enrolment managers, Smith and Gottheil (2008) provide a comparative view of SEM in Canada and the United States. Some of the survey's findings are outlined below, as well as some more recent information on how SEM is being implemented in Canada.

Public Accountability

Accountability is driving institutions to increasingly focus on understanding and responding to data analysis. In both Canada and the United States there is increasing government interest in loan default rates, accessibility (in general as well as for specific targeted populations), student mobility, and retention and graduation rates. Both countries have seen the introduction, on a limited basis, of performance-based funding. Surveys such as the Canadian University Survey Consortium (CUSC) and the National Survey on Student Engagement (NSSE) are now being used as accountability measures and appear in magazine rankings as proxies for educational quality in the university sector.

Enrolment Planning

Many institutions on both sides of the border equate the use of enrolment management strategies with having a SEM plan. An increasing number of American institutions and a few Canadian institutions have developed comprehensive SEM plans, with a sizable number claiming they are in progress. Many Canadian institutions have integrated some SEM elements into their institutional strategic plans. An important challenge noted by Canadian enrolment managers is that most enrolment data analysis occurs in planning offices by staff that do not always fully understand SEM or cannot commit the time or resources to enrolment research and analysis.

Accessibility

Access to post-secondary education has been a priority in Canada since the 1960s when many new colleges and universities were established. However, access to post-secondary education is unequally distributed across various socio-economic groups with marginalized groups posing significantly lower participation rates on average relative to other groups (Finnie, Childs and Wismer 2010b). Periodic government-mandated freezes of tuition fees have had only limited impact on this trend.

In both Canada and the United States, increasing access to post-secondary education is seen as a key economic, social and moral imperative. Groups deemed to be under-represented, and thus targeted for accessibility programs, differ between the two countries due to historic immigration and colonization patterns. Both countries are interested in more access for first-generation and low-income post-secondary students. In the United States, there is also interest in more access for African-Americans, Hispanics, Asians and Native Americans. In Canada, access is seen as key for Aboriginal, Francophone and Northern Canadian students. SEM practices in each country reflect these differing priorities.

Geographic Draw

In the United States, a considerable number of students choose to live on campus and to go away to school. This is true for a much smaller number of Canadians, who tend to attend their local institutions. This results in little student mobility between provinces and small residence populations on most campuses. There are implications in this regard for student engagement, retention and student life programming in Canada. Transfer agreements with community or technical colleges, 4-year universities or both are relatively common in both countries, although the effectiveness of such agreements varies.

Marketing and Recruitment

There are considerable differences between American and Canadian approaches to student recruitment, although the differences have narrowed in recent years. Whereas American higher education no longer fears the "recruitment" word, Canada is now nearing completion of its transition from a liaison outreach effort to one that includes more strategic recruitment strategies. Historic collegial approaches to recruitment in Canada continue side by side with increasing use of targeted print materials, 1:1 marketing and e-recruiting. The United States makes much more extensive use of current student and alumni ambassadors, tele-counseling and predictive enrolment modeling techniques and strategies.

Canadians, in general, have a more highly developed notion of privacy than our neighbours to the south. This affects marketing strategies. American-based institutions make considerable use of direct mail and target marketing. In Canada, advertising is mostly geared to enhancing the image of institutions rather than specifically targeting student recruitment. Canadian enrolment marketing is also mainly focused toward high school students, whereas marketing in the United States is more broad-based and oriented toward other market segments. Canadian students do not take the Scholastic Aptitude Test (SAT) or the American College Testing Assessment (ACT) and thus Canadian institutions do not purchase names of prospective students and directly market to anyone who has not expressed at least some interest in their institution. This difference extends to approaches to the number of communications sent to students prior to application and post-admission. American institutions communicate slightly more in the pre-application phase and about the same as Canadians in the post-admission phase.

Admission

Canada has seen the development of centralized application centres in Alberta, British Columbia, and Ontario as a way to make it easier for applicants to find information on colleges and universities and to apply for admission.

The basis of university admission in Canada is primarily high school marks, whereas American institutions use a combination of Scholastic Assessment Test (SAT)/American College Test (ACT)/Advanced Placement (AP) test scores, essays, interviews and a variety of non-cognitive factors. Most admission offers in Canada are made between March and June, with some earlier offers made to top candidates. In the United States, offers are made throughout the final year of high school using early action, early admission and rolling admission approaches. Whereas the United States has a May 1 reply date, there is no agreed-upon confirmation deadline in Canada, although many provinces use a late May or June date.

Tuition, Pricing and Financial Support

A key difference between Canada and the United States is the role of financial aid. The financial aid program is still seen primarily as a student support service in Canada while American institutions see enrolment management as the primary purpose of financial aid. This has led to the adoption of differing approaches to student financial support. Leveraging and discounting are SEM tactics used extensively in the American university sector but are not intentionally used in the Canadian environment. Whereas most American financial aid offers are provided to students near the time of their admission offer, in Canada the complete financial aid offer is not known to students until after they make their enrolment decision. Canadian institutions have provided mostly merit-based scholarships to prospective and current students, although there has been some recognition over the past few years of the importance of need-based aid (Junor and Usher 2007).

Both Canada and the United States have seen cuts in public funding of postsecondary education coupled with large tuition increases.[2] This, coupled with resistance from students and their families to incurring debt, may be an indication of an affordability (rather than an accessibility) barrier to post-secondary studies.

In addition, many lower-income Canadians overestimate the cost of post-secondary education and underestimate the return on investment, which ultimately discourages greater access and participation. Many students are taking on higher debt loans than in the past. Between 1990 and 2000, the average debt of a university graduate doubled. By 2009, the average debt for university graduates was $26,680; the average for college graduates was $13,600 (Canadian Council on Learning 2010).

Student Engagement

Student engagement is increasingly perceived as a proxy for quality at Canadian colleges and universities. The whole family of student engagement surveys (*e.g.*, NSSE, CCSSE, LSSSE) is now being administered. This is leading to a shift in pedagogical approaches, with an increasing use of a wide array of technologies (*e.g.*, blended

---

[2] The province of *Québec* has been an exception to substantial tuition increases. The provincial universities are lobbying the provincial government to permit increases to address funding concerns and the impact on the quality of education. Although pricing hasn't been a typical Canadian SEM strategy, Memorial University and the province of Newfoundland and Labrador have used it intentionally to drive enrolment growth by having substantially lower tuition fees than any of their Maritime competitors.

delivery, online learning, "clickers"). There is more wide-ranging discussion of enhancing "deep learning," rather than the traditional "acquisition of facts" approach to post-secondary instruction.

Student Services and Supports

Student services and support are seen as important in both the United States and Canada. Specialized services (diversity offices in the United States and Aboriginal centres in Canada) are providing targeted supports for specific groups. There is a growing realization that the access and retention of many students is dependent on services and supports that are not entirely within an institution's control (*e.g.,* government and band funding, adequate childcare, transportation). American institutions have more access to federal grants (*e.g.,* TRIO) and foundation funding (*e.g.,* Lumina and Gates foundations) to support underprepared students and under-served populations. There are fewer sources of external funding in Canada to help drive the SEM agenda.

Student Retention

There is a great deal of similarity between Canadian and American approaches to retention. First-year experience programs, integration of academic support services, student service consolidations and intrusive academic advising are present in both countries. Many American institutions have formulated retention goals and action plans because retention is an accountability measure in many states. Canadian institutions are beginning to formalize retention plans as a result of the development of key performance indicators, increased public accountability and the impact of student satisfaction and other surveys.

SEM CANADA: A UNIQUE APPROACH

Canada is well on its way to the development of its own brand of enrolment management. Although much remains to be learned from the American experience, Canada has developed a wide array of its own SEM practices. These are now chronicled in the new Canadian SEM resource library, which can be accessed at www.uwindsor.ca/sem. Those interested in Canadian SEM are encouraged to visit the Canadian SEM Web site, submit published work, technical papers and conference presentations, and consider attending our annual Canadian SEM Summit that brings together senior academic, student affairs, institutional research and enrolment managers to discuss emerging SEM issues.

In the chapters that follow, Canadian college and university practitioners describe how the SEM components play out in Canada to create a unique SEM approach. In particular, chapters focus on undergraduate admissions, use of data in SEM decision-making, student financial aid, institutional marketing, student recruitment, student retention, student affairs, SEM planning and student engagement. We have also included chapters that focus on how SEM is used to impact the student experience for Aboriginal, first-generation, international and transfer students. The final chapter provides an overview of emerging SEM challenges and opportunities.

Brian Christie, John Metcalfe, and
Keith Fortowsky

2

USING DATA
FOR STRATEGIC ENROLMENT MANAGEMENT

/ **Chapter 2** /

A veteran enrolment manager has commented that, "It's data that puts the 'S' in
SEM." Experience tells us that strategic enrolment management is very unlikely to
be effective without quality data. More precisely, data to support SEM must produce information (intelligence derived from the data) that is integrated (part of a
coherent information set), shared (available to and understood by the many parties
engaged with enrolment management), timely, accurate, actionable, and relevant
(Moore *et al.* 2010, p. 19).

   This chapter examines how data for strategic enrolment management that meet
these requirements can be generated and employed effectively in Canadian post-
secondary institutions.

A METHODOLOGICAL APPROACH

The first step in any organized process of data provision is to understand how the
data will be used. If the uses are unclear or the questions to be answered are not well
defined, then the data gathered is likely to be extraneous, inaccurate or misleading.
Or, the data will be ignored and the effort that has been put into data collection
and analysis wasted.

   Andreason's (1988, p. 65) "backward marketing research process" can be adapted
to describe the sequence of steps to follow in generating the data needed to support
any decision or planning process, including SEM:

   1. Determine what decisions are to be made, or what issues are to be investigated,
      using the data.
   2. Determine what information will help make the best decisions: ask decision-
      makers how their choices may vary depending on different data possibilities.

③ Prepare a prototype report and ask decision-makers/planners if this form of report will help them make the best choices.

④ Determine how the report will be completed: data sources, data gathering activities and processing, and analysis.

⑤ Examine how others (in your institution or elsewhere) have answered the same or similar questions. Does the data already exist somewhere? Can it be accessed and its accuracy and relevance assessed?

⑥ Design the data collection process.

⑦ Implement the data collection (*e.g.*, data query or survey or market research).

⑧ Organize and analyze the data, including assessment of reliability and limitations of the data.

⑨ Write and present the report.

⑩ Assist decision-makers/planners to employ the data.

⑪ Evaluate the data provision experience and its contribution or impact.

This process is illustrated in an abbreviated fashion in the following case history based on a Nova Scotia campus' experience. The history also illustrates a useful analytical tool in SEM research, predictive modeling, that has a variety of applications.

A university in Nova Scotia was interested in improving the conversion rate from accepted applicants to undergraduate registration and reducing the number of "no shows" (Step 1). Research indicated that predictive modeling had been successfully employed in a variety of countries to identify the characteristics of accepted applicants who are most likely to enrol. The theory maintains that concentrating efforts on the subset of accepted applicants who share these characteristics will produce a higher conversion rate to registrants. Following discussion of this technique, how the results could be employed, and the limitations of approach in the given context, the university's enrolment planning committee endorsed a research project employing this methodology (Steps 2–5).

Predictive modeling uses statistical regression techniques, in this case to estimate the likelihood of enrolment based on the information available about accepted applicants. The difficulty with employing this technique in Canada is the paucity of relevant data collected by institutions about applicants, in comparison with the United States, where standardized testing and application data for financial aid provide many more possible explanatory variables to use in the modeling (Steps 6–7).

In the Nova Scotia case, one result overwhelmed all other possible explanatory possibilities (Step 8). Those accepted applicants from Ontario who also successfully applied for a place in residence were almost certain to attend. Those who did not apply for residence were almost certain not to show up. About one-third of those who applied for a residence place and were wait-listed because their application was too late, also enrolled. This same pattern was not evident in those accepted applicants from the Maritime Provinces who lived at a distance from the home city of the university.

The report was prepared and presented to the enrolment planning committee (Step 9). A number of obvious policy implications were considered with respect to the use of residence accommodation in the university's recruiting efforts (Step 10).

The researchers reviewed the results and considered what additional data might be collected in the recruitment and application process to strengthen the power of this analytical approach (Step 11).

SOURCES OF DATA IN STRATEGIC ENROLMENT PLANNING

In preparing a strategic enrolment plan, it is best to use a different approach, more like exploratory research. This is not to deny that frequently those who come to the planning table have pre-conceived notions about what strategies should be present in the plan; these concepts need to be tested against the evidence that data and analysis can provide.

Data to support strategic enrolment planning can be found, and should be sought, from a wide variety of sources. While not exhaustive, the following list provides a guide to the most frequently used data sources.

- *Student Information Systems:* The institution's own information systems are the source for descriptive data about its student population, including both current students and their recent trends. Data also exists in the institution's databases about graduate and alumni characteristics, spending on financial aid, student employment on campus and in co-op programs, occupation of the residences, and so on. Analysis of the institution's data can yield information about student success (persistence, time to completion, grade distributions), the recruiting process (yield rates), the effectiveness of the student assistance program, net program or academic unit costs, and so on.

If the institution belongs to a collective, like a common application centre, or contributes to a shared regional database, then more data are available to be mined for relevant information.

- *Academic Programs:* A dialogue with the institution's academic administrators will produce estimates of program capacity for the institution's various programs and the key limiting factors, whether instructional capacity (the interaction of faculty numbers, faculty workloads and the curriculum), physical plant capacity (classrooms or laboratories), market demand for graduates of professional or vocational programs, or resources for the experiential learning components of the curriculum.

- *Future Enrolment Projections:* Demographic projections are available from Statistics Canada, while ministries of education and school divisions can provide high school and elementary school enrolments by grade and gender, and often projections of future enrolments.

- *Student Surveys:* Student surveys can provide a wealth of information. The Canadian Undergraduate Survey Consortium (CUSC) gathers information from university undergraduates across the country annually about their satisfaction with their experiences and their use of support services and, on a three-year cycle, about how and why they selected their institution and program, or their post-undergraduate plans and financial situation. The National Survey of Student Engagement and its family of surveys describe the academic activities and experiences of students in universities and colleges, from their perspectives and those of their faculty. Follow-up surveys of graduates, conducted on a regional, provincial, institutional or program basis, gather information about their experiences in the labour market and further education, as well as graduates' debt trajectories. In the college sector, employment surveys of graduates and employers are regularly used for program planning.

An institution may wish to conduct a special-purpose survey particularly geared to issues that arise in its strategic enrolment planning (*e.g.*, number of drop-outs or "no-shows") or undertake an over-sampling of particular student groups (First

Nations and Métis students, students in low enrolment programs) in the CUSC or other surveys. Surveys of faculty and staff should not be over-looked.

- *Student Networking:* Information from surveys can be augmented by the use of focus groups, intercept interviews, or simple observational techniques, including monitoring the institution's social network sites—a new source of intelligence.
- *Institutional Consortia Data-Sharing:* Other data-sharing consortia exist that enable institutions to compare their own data with that from peer institutions. The U15 universities, for example , swap data that allow comparisons of program costing and resourcing. Regional or provincial collectives also have their central data collection utilities.
- *Online Resources:* The Web sites of other institutions (or of their collectives, like the Council of Ontario Universities) can provide information about their strategic enrolment plans, programs offered, enrolment characteristics, tuition and financial assistance, graduation and retention rates, and so on.
- *National Statistics:* Government departments and agencies are a useful source of data and analysis, ranging from census data and other Statistics Canada data bases and reports to labour market information from provincial ministries and Human Resources and Skills Development Canada (HRSDC). For instance, HRSDC has recently published a report entitled *Comparison of College Performance of General Educational Development (GED) and High School Diploma Students in Nova Scotia and PEI* (2011).
- *Market Research:* Market research, most commonly conducted for institutions by consultants in branding exercises, can provide information about the perceptions of the institution and its programs among the general public, influential members of the community, high school administrators, and high school students and their parents. It can identify competitor institutions in various market segments and identify the characteristics on which that competition is founded.
- *Higher Education Resources:* The results of relevant external research can also inform strategic enrolment planning. Reports published by Statistics Canada resulting from analyses of data from its Youth in Transition survey and other data sources, as well as articles in journals such as the *Canadian Journal of Higher Education* or *College and University,* and reports published by think tanks such as the C.D. Howe Institute or the Canadian Centre for Policy Alternatives, can be

very useful in informing strategy. The conference proceedings at events such as the annual conference of the Canadian Institutional Research and Planning Association[3] or presentations at the annual SEM Summits[4] are other sources to be utilized. These reports and papers provide insight into issues as wide-ranging as the major determinants of post-secondary education participation, the impact of distance from an institution on participation, and the effectiveness of programs to improve persistence. They may suggest institutional research projects to be undertaken on the populations particularly relevant to an institution's strategic enrolment planning and management.

THE CLASSICAL SEM MODEL

In the classical SEM model, once the planning process is complete and strategic goals have been identified, two other processes that utilize data are necessary. The first is the translation or "operationalization" of the strategic goals in terms of optimal enrolment. The second is the management of institutional activities to approach or achieve that optimal enrolment.

In SEM, the notion of "new student in a given year" might be operationalized by selecting and counting from a student information database all of the unique registered students in a given set of semesters who have never previously registered in any course at the institution. Operationalizing "student success rate" for a given year could involve selecting from a student information database all the students who have graduated within seven years of the year when they registered in their first course and dividing that number by the total number of unique new students from the year in question.

At this point a few observations about operationalization can be made. First, the notions or concepts that are used in thinking about enrolment are often extremely complex and vague. Notions like "the academic quality of a program" or "the effectiveness of course delivery" are notoriously difficult to assess. Second, there likely will be many competing measurements or magnitudes that can be associated with a single enrolment management concept. For this reason, some colleagues resist the operationalization, in terms of using data, of the concepts in their strategic enrol-

---

[3] *See* Canadian Institutional Research and Planning Association Conference information at <www.cirpa-acpri.ca/page.asp?page=1869>.

[4] *See* University of Windsor's Strategic Enrolment Management Resource Library at <www.uwindsor.ca/sem/overview>.

ment goals. However, if SEM is to succeed in addressing a significant range of institutional goals through the use of data, it must involve all areas of the institution. Thus, in the classical SEM model, it is important that institutions involve all levels and all areas of the institution in the task of operationalization. Both the academic and non-academic sides of the house must participate.

Optimal Enrolment

The central idea of "optimal enrolment" enters into the classical model when we turn from operationalizing enrolment concepts to the operationalization of the strategic goals. For SEM to work, strategic goals must be unpacked or defined as a set of student population segments, each with a defined target enrolment. Many goals of interest to post-secondary institutions can be tied to the number of enrolled students exhibiting some particular property or set of properties. Each group of students exhibiting the particular property or group of properties is an *enrolment segment*. For example, male students constitute one simple enrolment segment. And each segment can have a target enrolment. Thus, having 10,000 male students might be the operationalization of a simple strategic goal related to the diversity of the student population. Or, in a more complicated example, the strategic goal of attracting an academically appropriate student body might be partially defined for a particular institution as having an enrolment segment that has the following properties: first-year students, registered in the Faculty of Arts, and membership in the top 20 percent of their high school's graduating class. And the size of this group should be greater than half of the size of the first-year class entering that faculty or school. These expressions of the goals, frequently called targets, allow data to measure progress towards the goals and to estimate the impact (and the success or shortfalls) of policy initiatives.

Optimal enrolment describes in detail what the institution's student population would look like if all the strategic goals were achieved. In the classical model, optimal enrolment is an operationalization of *all* the institution's relevant strategic goals. Once the strategic goals of an institution are completely unpacked, a fairly detailed picture of the student population should emerge. The optimal enrolment for the institution will be constructed out of the various component enrolment segments that reflect the individual strategic goals identified by the process of generating a strategic enrolment plan. Each of the segments may overlap with others, sharing members. So, optimal enrolment is the integrated sum of the targets for all the enrolment segments for all of the relevant strategic goals.

To utilize this model, institutions need to collect and retain data concerning many properties of their students. To be extensive enough to capture strategic planning goals, the information collected is much more detailed than that usually collected to drive the admissions process. Hence, institutions that wish to make use of the classical SEM model need to develop methods to collect this information from students. However, this needs to be done in a manner that does not make the process of application for admission too difficult or time consuming for the student. It would be counterproductive for most institutions to decrease their ability to attract students in order to track their success in achieving strategic goals.

In practice, institutions rarely formulate an exhaustive picture of their optimal enrolment. Operationalization is perhaps too contentious, too expensive or too difficult for most institutions to complete. But examples of partial pictures abound. A good example is *The University of Saskatchewan Enrolment Plan: Bridging to 2010* (2003) which contained the following goals (among others):

- Undergraduate student enrolment will increase, in selective areas, by approximately 2,600 students, from an average headcount (1997–98 to 2001–02) of 15,900 students to 18,500 or approximately 15,800 FTE by 2010, and measures will be taken to sustain that enrolment for the period beyond 2010. To accomplish this goal, the University will place primary emphasis on the academic preparedness of students (from Saskatchewan or elsewhere), establish aggressive recruitment policies for the best Saskatchewan and Canadian students, and increase its admissions average to direct-entry colleges from the currently advertised 65 percent to 70 percent by 2005 and to 75 percent by the end of the decade.

- The graduate student body will be expected to increase from an average headcount (1997–98 to 2001–02) of approximately 1,790 students to 2,500 or 2,100 FTE by 2010. In addition, to ensure that the University of Saskatchewan continues to be included as a major doctoral degree-granting institution, greater emphasis will be placed on recruiting students into doctoral programs. Funding priority and faculty recruitment will be placed here.

● International student enrolments will increase from 4 percent in 2000 to between 7 and 8 percent of the new overall enrolment targets for the University by 2010.

Surprisingly, the University of Saskatchewan enrolment plan had no goals for the enrolment of First Nations and Métis students.

Another useful example comes from the *Five Year Strategic Enrolment Plan, 2008–2009 to 2012–2013* of Mohawk College of Applied Arts and Technology in Ontario (2007). A sample is shown in the sidebar to the right.

The operationalization of strategic goals in terms of segmental enrolment targets generates - by definition - a clear measure of success in achieving those goals. And this is one of the great powers of the classical SEM model. Once there is agreement on enrolment segment targets as the "meaning" of the SEM goals, there is an obvious and public transparency to the success or failure of achieving those goals. This in turn may be another reason why it is so unusual to see an institution completely operationalize its strategic goals in terms of such easily expressed metrics: failure cannot easily be hidden.

Know Your Enrolment Targets

It should be clear that the classical SEM model requires much more than enrolment targets by faculty or degree program. It requires targets defined to capture every strategically relevant aspect of the student population. And it is through this rich set of targets that the classical SEM model involves almost every academic and administrative part of an institution. Moreover, by measuring every success and failure through

---

SAMPLE FIVE-YEAR ENROLMENT PLAN

GOAL (GUIDING PRINCIPLE) #1— FINANCIAL VIABILITY: Grow post-secondary and apprenticeship enrolment incrementally each year for the next five years.

Objective: Mohawk will grow enrolment each year for the next five years in the following areas

✸ Post-secondary by 2%
✸ Apprenticeship by 5%

GOAL (GUIDING PRINCIPLE) # 2— FUNDING DIVERSIFICATION: Broaden the distribution of College enrolment across other "student types" in order to reduce the College's dependency on post-secondary (funded) enrolment.

Objective: Mohawk College will increase enrolment each year for the next five years in the following areas;

✸ International:
　→ Off-Shore: 5% (Students participating in off-shore partnerships, e.g., China)
　→ On-Shore: 2% (Students participating in programs delivered at Mohawk College)
✸ Continuing Education: 5%, distributed between post-secondary courses offered by Continuing Education and General Interest
✸ Corporate Training: 5%* (excluding Government Contracts;)
　* Corporate Training growth will be reflected in revenue not headcount

CONTINUES ON NEXT PAGE ▶

···
CONTINUED FROM PAGE 27 ▶

GOAL (GUIDING PRINCIPLE) # 3—
COMPETITIVE POSITIONING:
Increase Mohawk's market share by becoming more competitive within the traditional (regional) market as well as expanding beyond the traditional market.

Objective: Increase enrolment by greater penetration of Mohawk's

✸ "core" market by 2% per year over the next five years
✸ "commuter" market (1 hour commute) by 2% per year over the next five years
✸ "relocate" market (Provincial, National) by 1% per year over the next five years

the enrolment behaviour of students, SEM forces an institution to take seriously its commitments to be student-centered.

Poorly defined targets are like poorly defined taxes: they elicit unexpected behaviour! For example, within educational institutions, grade inflation may be driven by the misidentification of high student grades as a measure of the effectiveness of course delivery. And, as discussed above, measuring the perception of the achievement of some goal can draw resources away from activities in support of the goal itself. For example, the inclusion in *Macleans* universities ranking of "innovativeness" has likely resulted in universities advertising more aggressively about their innovations as much or more than actually increasing the amount of innovation itself. That is, the care taken by an institution in operationalizing its strategic goals is no less important than the care taken in identifying those strategic goals.

Data Analysis: Enrolment Targets and Magnitudes

The management of institutional activities to achieve optimal enrolment introduces a new level of complexity with respect to the use of data. When an institution characterizes a set of segmental enrolment targets that embodies its strategic goals, it does so in order to elicit efforts to adjust the actual sizes of these enrolment segments. In order to influence enrolments one must understand the causes of changes in enrolments. This consideration introduces the methods of empirical science into the analysis and use of data in SEM.

Some of the most complex analyses of data within the SEM model are directed at identifying the magnitudes that vary, directly or inversely, with enrolments. These magnitudes are associated with causal factors that influence enrolments. Managers then concentrate their efforts on those causal factors or, put another way, they attempt to affect the magnitudes associated with those causal factors. These causal factors can be specific to certain segments of the population, apply to all applicants or students, or vary in their effect based on some property of the applicants/students, like family income. Managers may also choose to design targeted program enrolments that utilize causal factors that are universal in their effect, so as to influence only segmental enrolments. For example, student engagement is seen to influence persistence or retention of all students, which in turn impacts enrolment in all segments. Managers may, however, choose to concentrate on increasing student engagement only in a particular segment of the student population such as at-risk students, in order to attain target enrolments in certain segments. When direct measures of engagement increase, they can conclude that the activities are likely appropriate to the purpose. When the enrolment targets are approached, they can conclude that the activities are targeted correctly.

Challenges to the Classical SEM Model

It is not an exaggeration to say that this part of the SEM project introduces all of the complexity of empirical science. This is expensive and delicate work that requires the involvement of professionals. Unfortunately, too many institutions depend on mere hunches, accepted wisdom, or common sense to identify the active causal forces that influence enrolment. This has two immediate effects. First, resources are directed to programs that have little positive influence on enrolment, at the expense of programs that would have helped achieve the strategic goals of an institution. Second, the institution's strategic plan is rendered impotent, because programs and innovations that have little or nothing to do with an institution's strategic goals can be introduced and supported by spurious reference to the institution's strategic plan.

In summary, there are significant impediments to the use of the classical model. First, operationalization is difficult and contentious. Second, information about students is usually limited. Third, clear numerical goals are sometimes too transparent for some administrators. And finally, while the scientific investigation necessary to understand how to influence enrolment is expensive and complicated, it is essential to managers tasked with achieving the strategic goals of an institution. These challenges may explain why efforts to generate a rigorous characterization of optimal enrolment for an institution so often fail .

More importantly, the classical model is, in an important sense, backward looking: it analyzes past data to judge the effectiveness of past actions. This simple approach has since been superseded. Data use in SEM has developed into much more dynamic processes that involve real-time analyses and predictive modeling of student behaviour.

ACTION ANALYTICS

A new step in the evolution of the use of data in strategic enrolment management is what is becoming known as *action analytics* (Norris *et al.* 2008). Action analytics employs predictive modeling, data mining of real time processes (such as activity in course management systems), and statistical techniques to produce information that informs action and practice adaptations that in turn improve student access, success and competency acquisition.

Action analytics focuses on processes, practices and behaviour. It aims to develop "new practices and solutions that ensure the alignment of institutional goals, initiatives, interventions, outcomes, and measures in a variety of ways.... [It] develop(s) organizational capacity and change(s) culture to encourage evidence-based *behaviour* (emphasis added) and action-focused innovation to improve performance" (Norris *et al.* 2008, p.44).

For example, monitoring how often students log into the course management system's sites provides a strong indication of their engagement with the courses and their studies in general. Those who connect infrequently are candidates for intervention as potential "at-risk" students. One American university conducts a survey of entering students soon after its compulsory orientation and welcoming event, ostensibly to evaluate the orientation program. The university's research has shown that those students who do not complete the survey are likely already disengaged and at risk. Intervention follows.

TOOLS AND TECHNIQUES TO USE DATA FOR SEM

This chapter now turns to a discussion of the tools and techniques to access and manipulate data. The focus is on internal data, *i.e.*, student registration data, but much of the discussion is equally applicable to the external datasets discussed earlier.

Modern student information systems have created very large datasets. Since they now reside on computers, these datasets are much more accessible than paper records. Essentially, they are available "on demand" to computerized applications. Access via computer also means that the data can easily be sorted and summarized in an almost limitless number of ways. In comparison, paper records were generally only accessible by student name, with limited summary records that had usually been compiled once per term (*e.g.*, student headcount).

However, computerization has also had three other major effects upon student data:

- An explosion of available reports and analyses.
- A large increase in the amount of data collected.
- A large increase in the "touch points" for data, with an associated decline in data quality.

All of these trends work together to, paradoxically, make access to modern student datasets much more difficult than was ever envisaged in the early days of computerization of record systems. And our high expectations of data systems mean that every successful analysis is usually quickly followed by a request for a yet more detailed analysis. However, this trend is far from unique to student data. Every organization that deals with data is trying to deal with these problems. Fortunately, this means that SEM analysts are at least not alone in their tasks, and can draw upon the tools and experiences of a much wider community.

There are four primary hurdles that must be overcome in any analysis using large datasets:

- Access to the data.
- The underlying quality and "fitness for purpose" of the data.
- Creation of a categorizing framework or model.
- Computer tools to manipulate the data.

Access to the Data

SEM analysis of institutional student information deals with the unique pathways of individual students. As will be discussed, analysis requires somehow categorizing and then grouping these individual pathways. But stock reports impose their own categorical structures, and generally do not provide the required level of detail for SEM analysis (*i.e.*, they summarize).[5] The required starting point for most SEM analysis is data at the level of the individual student: at least one "identity" record per individual (containing at least their name and identity number), and generally one additional record for each term in which each individual is recognized (for example, when the student registers for classes). This generally means nine records for a "classic" undergraduate university student who attends and completes in four years at two terms per year. In fact, most students will have more terms and thus more records.

The insurmountable hurdle for analysis in the past was the sheer amount of data that was required for the analysis. The tools capable of handling these volumes of data were the domain of specialized Information Services (IS) staff. Today, however, these volumes of data can be easily handled by individual analysts with simple desktop tools. That said, extremely large datasets may still have to be broken into smaller datasets by being "segmented" by a major divider, such as faculty or time period. It should be noted that segmentation is never ideal and will always create additional problems for the analysis through the cases that "cross" whatever category is used. For example, what should one do with a student who switches faculties? In general, time period is the preferred segmentation from a purely technical perspective.

IS staff are still usually required to create the initial data sets. The data are generally delivered through one of two methods:

- A direct extract from the database, typically using SQL *or*
- An extract via a data warehouse.

In both cases the extracts can then be processed with the desktop tools.

The data about individual students and their activities in the institution are now almost always stored in what is called a "normalized relational database". Relational databases are accessed through a language called SQL.[6] "Normalized" means that the data are stored in a series of linked tables to eliminate duplication within any individual record. For example, if a student has multiple known addresses, rather than physically storing all the addresses in the single student identity record, an ad-

---

[5] Note that existing summary reports do play an important role in auditing data.

[6] For an explanation of SQL, *see* <http://en.wikipedia.org/wiki/SQL>.

dress table is created with one record per address. These records are then linked to the identity record of the student.

Fortunately most demographic information, such as age, gender and citizenship at birth, exists only once for a given student and thus has what is called a "one to one" relationship. This means that it can either be directly stored in the student identity record, or easily linked to it.

However, most student activity, such as enrolling in classes and receiving grades for those classes, occurs many times for a single student. These data are said to have a "many to one" relationship to the student record. The fundamental computational difficulty for most SEM analysis is that it is conceptually and technically difficult to analyze student activity data in its original "many to one" form. Somehow the many activity records must be transformed into a single "one to one" activity record for each student. Conceptual decisions must be made about how this transformation will occur.

It is beyond the scope of this chapter to discuss data warehouses in depth, but it is useful to note that what we have described as the "single activity record" (one to one) is, in a data warehouse, called an "accumulating snapshot".[7] Such snapshots are the product of a very intensive design and implementation process. They thus generally would not be created until an analysis drawn from the relational tables is performed as a proof of concept to demonstrate the usefulness of the snapshot.

As a technical note, a relational database can, through SQL, take multiple tables and build a "virtual table." Such a table is called a "view." A view has two major advantages. The first is that other applications, such as desktop tools, can easily access the view as if it were a simple table, rather than having to link to and manage multiple relational tables. The second is that no separate process must be run to retrieve updated data. Queries or analyses using the view are automatically accessing the most up-to-date data, extracted directly from the source database.

The Underlying Quality and "Fitness for Purpose" of the Data

As discussed previously, computerization has had three major effects upon student data. Each of these effects has created substantial data quality problems. First, there

---

[7] For explanations regarding data warehouses and related terminology, *see* <http://en.wikipedia.org/wiki/Fact_table>.

has been an explosion of available reports and analyses, which is not a problem in and of itself. However, every report performs some sort of categorization and/ or calculation that is typically designed by an IS staffer and embedded within the report. The rules or logic used are rarely accessible to the end user and often inaccessible or at best inconvenient to other programmers. As rules or logic change over time and reports are not updated, or as programmers use different rules or logic in creating a new version of a report, reports become inconsistent. It is the rare organization that cannot produce examples of reports which were designed to report upon the same thing but produce conflicting results.

The second effect of computerization is a large increase in the amount of data collected. Since new processes that add data are relatively inexpensive once a system has been computerized, there is almost inevitably a growth in such processes. More data collection is required to support these new processes. And often new data are collected "just in case" they might be needed for future analysis or processes. The problem is that the data of rarely used processes, and particularly "just in case" data, are rarely actually used in the organization. Without any "eyes" upon the data, comparing them to other data and the "real world," these data quickly become obsolete. Definitions and usage change, but nobody sees that the data are now out of date. Sometimes these data stop being entered at all, simply because they are seen to have no purpose or to be confusing, and thus a waste of time. In many ways, this is the preferable outcome since it at least prevents the data from being mistaken for "quality" data in some future analysis.

The third effect of computerization is significant increases in the "touch points" of data. Since computerized data can be much more easily shared and distributed than paper, processes can easily be decentralized, with perhaps the ultimate example being student self-registration via the Web. The difficulty is that every person brings their own interpretation of what each field means. Process training has difficulty keeping up with staff who regularly enter data, given the explosion of new processes. The training problem becomes more acute once de-centralized staff, with only casual acquaintance with the process, begin to enter data. And, the final level of dysfunction is reached when anybody can create a record via the Web.

Note that none of these problems is addressed by IS organizations' usual definition of data quality. The IS definition of data quality usually includes only two things. First, that a value in a field is not lost or accidentally changed once it is entered. Second, that only a defined list or type of a value can be entered in the field. However, ensuring that for example, only "FT" or "PT" can be entered in a field, and that this value is subsequently not changed or lost, in no way ensures consistent understanding among those entering the data of whether or when "FT" or "PT" should be entered in the field.

The intent of the above discussion is not to create the impression that data quality will always be so bad that analysis is simply not possible. However it is important to realize that a large part of the work in most analyses will involve resolving or at least accounting for these inevitable quality problems. The discussion is also meant to describe the context in which our data have been created.

Thus there is a strong interrelationship between error and meaning. With data systems that disallow "illegal" entries, most errors are simply due to lack of knowledge regarding the meaning of the fields in use—either by those entering the data or by those attempting to use it for analysis.

In summary, the key to understanding data is that it is collected as part of administrative processes, *not* for SEM analysis. A student will encounter many administrative processes as they move through the University. Each of these processes will record information about the student that is pertinent to that process. But the student's pathways through these processes can be remarkably complex. SEM is concerned with understanding the overall pathways (and administrative processes are not). There follows from this three fundamental principles of data that must be considered in any use of data for SEM analysis:

- The meaning of the data comes from the administrative processes for which it was collected;
- Data quality depends upon the familiarity of users with the administrative process for which it is collected; and,
- Data that are not used regularly in an actual administrative process (*i.e.* only collected "just in case") are highly unreliable.

These principles are fundamental not just to evaluating the quality of data. They are also key considerations in understanding the data in order to create categorizing frameworks.

Creation of a Categorizing Framework

The essence of analysis is to create a picture of "the forest," not just the trees. For example, student paths to graduation are highly individual, but to use this path for analysis, it must be grouped with similar paths. Then the individual path can either be assessed in terms of deviation from the norm, for possible intervention, or simply become part of a larger statistic that indicates such things as progress towards strategic goals. A less obvious implication of seeing "the forest" is that the forest must also be seen by others, *i.e.*, the groupings must be based upon shared understandings.

A categorizing framework is what turns a large number of unique records into a much smaller number of groups that can be quantified. One or more attributes of the individual records are used to create groups of "like" records. We take the best categorizing frameworks for granted, because they are so effective that they are "obvious." But there are almost limitless possible categorizing frameworks, and only a few of them will lead to insight, much less to actionable insight.

Creation of a categorizing framework starts with a question. Then we explore the theory and the available data to see how we could answer the question. We modify the question to fit what we think we can answer, and we create a categorizing framework that links theory and data to the question. Finally, we summarize the data according to the framework, and look for significant differences.

Categories often need to be reassessed as the analysis is repeated in subsequent years. The "low hanging fruit" found by the analysis is "plucked" and the significant differences begin to fade away. Or, larger conditions begin to change such that originally powerful categories are no longer significant. For example, female representation is no longer an issue in many fields of study.

The most basic demographic category in SEM analysis and planning, and often the most important, is the selection of the overall population for the analysis. For SEM metrics in particular this is a key issue. Population selection strongly interacts with the analytical results. For example, retention is an ambiguous term. Should a student who never planned to stay be considered "not retained"? The solution to such complexities is too often assumed to be the elimination of all ambiguous cases from the population. But, if the goal is analysis that leads to actions that improve retention, then the population selection has often eliminated the very cases where intervention is desirable (for example, part-time students).

The most common cohorts for SEM analysis are students' year of study, major academic unit (*e.g.*, faculty), and degree program. All of these categories have always been somewhat ambiguous and are becoming more so. "Year of study" used to be both a measure of time in program (*i.e.*, years since the start) and of progress to completion (*i.e.*, as a fraction of completion in the normal period, *e.g.*, 4 years for an undergraduate degree). The rapid rise of part-time studies has broken this link. But "year of study" is still often used without clear definition of whether it is a measure of time (years since start) or progress to completion (perhaps based upon credit hours completed). What should happen to these definitions when a student "restarts," *e.g.*, through switching programs, or after a "stop-out" period? And how should we categorize those who have started post-secondary studies before they have arrived at the university or college (*e.g.*, in high school)?

Beyond the issue of changes in program, an even tougher situation to categorize is the student simultaneously pursuing multiple programs ("duplicated headcount"). The most common solution has been to somewhat arbitrarily select a single "first major" or similar categorization. But the steady rise in multiple programs (in many respects, accelerated by our computer systems that make them more possible) is making this approach less and less feasible.

Admission and graduation are points of particular difficulty in using the data for SEM analysis and planning. There are often not clear procedural links between admission, a program, and graduation. Many students are admitted multiple times. Some may have taken classes before admission (*e.g.*, in high school). Although graduation is typically considered an end point, many students proceed to, or pursue simultaneously, other degrees, or simply a few more classes. In other words, an admission or graduation may occur for the student, but might not be linked (other than accidentally) to the program under study.

Computer Tools to Manipulate the Data

When the manipulation of data was a slow and labor intensive process, it was very difficult to modify the categorizing framework after the data had been summarized. Now, the situation has changed dramatically. The initial "signature" records are still generally created by Information Services staff through SQL queries (or extracted from an "accumulating snapshot" in a data warehouse). But the power of modern desktop tools, notably relational lookup tables and pivot tables, allow categories to be changed literally with the click of a mouse button.

A relational lookup table supplies a value for a field based upon a value in another field. These are also often called cross-match tables, or simply cross tables. This allows repeatable groupings that are both easy to implement, and easy to modify. An example is a table that links subjects to a department.

The central feature of pivot tables is the ability to very easily create and modify cross-tabulation tables. "Cross-tabs" have always been a fundamental and extremely effective tool to display data, but creation of cross-tabs used to be highly laborious and was thus usually done at the end of analysis. Now, a properly structured dataset allows a trained user to create cross-tabs virtually instantaneously, through pivot tables. This is very useful for rapid "ad hoc" analysis. And once the analyst has found useful pivot table views, they can be readily repurposed as the equivalent of reports, which can be easily "filtered" by end-users to show only the user's desired portion of a large dataset (*e.g.*, a filter by Faculty). Both lookup tables and pivot tables are available in Excel and many other desktop products.[8]

As a result of these tools and the products (such as Tableau) that yield much easier user access to results, creation of a categorizing framework can now be a rapid iterative process. Results—or more often lack of results—from a given framework feed back into the question, theory, and data. And the process repeats, until either the analyst moves on to more productive lines of enquiry or effective categories are found.

CONCLUSION

Problem identification and problem solving are important tasks for educational administrators and other administrators. When problems become clear, most institutions take action to resolve them.... [I]t takes time and effort to gather the most useful information and come to a decision. Before undertaking the process, decision makers should take pains to identify the "right" problem, and take seri-

---

[8] *See also* these resources:
- Pivot table illustration: <http://en.wikipedia.org/wiki/Pivot_tables#Explanation_of_a_pivot_table>.
- Pivot table video example, Excel 2007: <www.youtube.com/watch?v=7zHLnUCtfUk>.
- Excel example of data layout required for pivot tables: <http://spreadsheetpage.com/index.php/tip/creating_a_database_table_from_a_summary_table/>.
- A recommended book about pivot tables for Excel (pre-2007 and post-2007 versions available) is *Pivot Table Data Crunching* by QUE Publishing.

ously the results of data-gathering and market research in coming to a decision (Kotler and Fox 1995, p. 65).

This observation is particularly apt in enrolment planning and management, where pre-conceived solutions to ill-defined problems abound. Data can be used to challenge these pre-conceptions, provide clearer definition of the problem, and illuminate the possible solution and/or actions.

While lacking the richer data environment of our neighbours to the south, Canadian institutions do have access, as has been illustrated, to considerable information and analysis that can inform and improve our SEM outcomes.

As this chapter has emphasized, clarity of purpose is a paramount condition for effective enrolment planning and management. Specification of the issue, or of the planning goals (through objectives and targets), provides direction to effective data collection, analysis, presentation and use.

Finally, the tools for data manipulation and analysis, and visualisation of the results of these processes, are becoming increasingly refined, accessible, and easy to employ by analysts and their audiences.

If anything, happily, the challenge is now to select from among the many opportunities for data use and from the new tools that monthly become available that are most "fit for purpose."

Deborah Robinson

3

STRATEGIC ENROLMENT MANAGEMENT
PLANNING AT UBC

/ **Chapter 3** /

The University of British Columbia (UBC) comprises two campuses and a total enrolment of 54,400 students, making it one of the 15 largest universities in North America. Founded in 1908, The UBC Vancouver campus hosts a total student population of 47,304 — 36,652 undergraduates and 9,652 graduates. The UBC Okanagan campus was founded almost 100 years later in 2005 as part of the Government of British Columbia's 25,000 post-secondary full-time enrolment (FTE) expansion. Starting with fewer than 3,000 students in 2005, at full capacity UBC Okanagan will enrol a maximum of 7,500 FTE, graduate and undergraduate combined.

While the campuses share a vision statement and a set of values, they are very different as a result of size, maturity and location.[9] Each campus has its own Senate and is autonomous, though the two campuses are coordinated. The enrolment challenges that each campus faces are likewise very different. UBC Vancouver has enjoyed full enrolment for almost a decade and is looking to rebalance the mix of local, national and international students. UBC Okanagan, in contrast, continues to grow at an accelerated pace, aiming to reach maximum enrolment within the next few years.

THE IMPORTANCE OF PLANNING

Faced with an urgent enrolment problem, the tendency at many institutions is to skip the planning process and go right to strategies and tactics. Resist that temptation. The chances of success are low without an understanding of what the insti-

---

[9] "As one of the world's leading universities, The University of British Columbia creates an exceptional learning environment that fosters global citizenship, advances a civil and sustainable society, and supports outstanding research to serve the people of British Columbia, Canada and the world," *Place and Promise, The UBC Strategic Plan:* <http://strategicplan.ubc.ca/the-plan/vision-statement/>.

tution is trying to achieve for the long run, an honest assessment of institutional strengths and weakness, a frank acknowledgement of challenges and opportunities, a clear understanding of the environment in which the institution operates, and an agreed upon set of goals and objectives. The value of planning, according to the Society of College and University Planners, is "to provide decision-makers with a kind of road map for understanding what it will take for goals and objectives to be met; for their institutions to be successful, distinctive, and to survive in a rapidly changing environment" (Rose 2003). By itself, planning doesn't guarantee success, but it minimizes failure by fostering the alignment of strategies and tactics with agreed-upon goals and objectives.

THE CONTEXT FOR STRATEGIC ENROLMENT MANAGEMENT AT UBC

The University of British Columbia is nationally and internationally recognized as ranking among the world's leading public universities with diversified programs that support provincial priorities and a strong record of achievement in research and teaching. Attracting a student body that is provincial, national and international is key to UBC maintaining its global reputation. In 2007, 75 percent of undergraduate students on the Vancouver campus came from British Columbia (B.C.) primarily from the Lower Mainland; under 13 percent were international and 12 percent came from the rest of Canada. Increasing the proportion of international and out-of-province students, and finding ways to attract B.C. students from right across the province are considered critical to UBC's continued success.

Even more critical, the competition amongst top-tier Canadian universities for the best and brightest students continues to grow fierce. Between 2001 and 2004 virtually every province responded to crowding in universities and colleges by dramatically increasing the number of seats. In Ontario, the situation was especially significant due to the double cohort that led to the introduction of 73,000 new post-secondary seats within two years. At the same time, provincial governments in both Alberta and British Columbia announced significant increases in FTE funding: 50,000 new seats over five years were added in Alberta and 25,000 new seats over five years in British Columbia. The irony is that these increases were announced just as the number of students graduating from high school was starting to decline. Demographers predict that the number of students graduating from secondary schools in Canada will continue to drop until at least 2016 and in some jurisdictions even longer.

By 2007 UBC had already begun to see some disturbing signs in enrolment as a result of this demographic shift. For the first time since 1989, the number of applications from Vancouver secondary school students was down. This reflected both the smaller graduating class and the increased competition from universities outside the province. Surprisingly, the yield rate—the proportion of admitted students who register and attend classes at UBC—for B.C. secondary school students dropped from 62 percent in 2006 to 57 percent in 2007. Furthermore, the Faculty of Science yield rate for students from secondary schools in the Lower Mainland dropped more dramatically from 73 percent in 2006 to 62 percent in 2007.

The link between student enrolment and university funding at UBC was also becoming clear as a result of an unanticipated budget shortfall in 2007. In addition to tuition, the university receives government funding in direct proportion to the number of students it enrols. It quickly became apparent that neglecting future enrolment issues would only exacerbate budget problems.

The University of British Columbia's share of the new 25,000 post-secondary seats announced by the government in 2004 came in the form of 7,500 new FTE spaces at a campus 400 kilometers away in Kelowna, B.C. UBC was not simply being funded to add new seats to existing programs, but instead to open an entirely new campus in a different part of the province and to grow enrolment as quickly as possible.

Together these factors convinced the senior leadership of the University that it needed a more systemic and integrated approach to enrolment management at UBC.

THE HISTORY OF ENROLMENT MANAGEMENT AT UBC

In its earliest iteration, the term *enrolment management* referred to what Maguire (1976) called a sort of "grand design" aimed at bringing about synergies among functions such as recruitment, admissions, financial assistance and retention—functions that too often were viewed as independent and working at cross purposes—in order to better serve both students and the institution. Enrolment management institutions were typically born out of an urgent need for change, usually in response to fluctuations in student enrolment—under-enrolment and over-enrolment are both equally challenging—and/or budget reductions (Hossler 1986). In most cases, the desired change was effected by realigning responsibilities across student services and the introduction of committees focused on student enrolment and student retention.

Thus UBC has been an enrolment management institution since the late 1990s. An Enrolment Management Committee was formed in 1998, comprised of representatives of all direct-entry undergraduate programs, the registrar and the directors of admission and registration. A comprehensive review by students, faculty and external stakeholders in 1999 identified a number of deficiencies that resulted in a restructuring of the student services area into two groups: Enrolment Services and Student Development & Services. Within Enrolment Services, recruitment and advising, admissions, financial assistance and awards were aligned under one senior director, while registration, tuition, records and graduation were aligned under another, both of whom reported to a single vice president. Student Development & Services remained a series of separate units: student development, counselling, access & diversity, student exchange programs, health services, and career services, each with its own director.[10] A related development was the creation of the International Student Initiative in 1997, which gave UBC a strategic focus on the recruitment of international undergraduate students. Under the watchful eye of the Enrolment Management Committee, UBC enjoyed full enrolment and incremental improvements in student services for the better part of a decade.

Professor Stephen Toope's arrival in 2006 as the 12th President of UBC changed everything. A former Dean of Law at McGill University, President Toope's vision of a national university is "one that aspires to contribute productively to the great national debates, that attracts students, staff and faculty members from across the country, that links fruitfully with researchers at other Canadian institutions and around the world." (Toope 2006) He was surprised to discover that, in the entering class of 2006, 12 percent of the students came from outside Canada, but only 8 percent from provinces other than British Columbia. "If we do not do a better job amongst Canada's universities in furthering inter-provincial student mobility," he said in his installation address, "we will reap the consequences: regions that do not understand each other; provinces that perceive themselves to be isolated; the lack of those personal connections that make a truly national politics and society pos-

---

[10] More recently, the separate units within Student Development and Services have been aligned under the leadership of a Senior Director.

sible." Although applauding UBC's enrolment success over the years, especially the growth of international student enrolment, and acknowledging the ethnic diversity of UBC's student population (largely a reflection of Vancouver's ethnic diversity), President Toope explicitly asked the University to change the composition of the student body, while simultaneously respecting UBC's reputation for academic excellence and maintaining full enrolment. A task like this required the commitment of Enrolment Services and other student service units, the academic community and the whole campus as well.

Meanwhile in the Okanagan, the need for a more comprehensive approach to enrolment management was obvious. Based on the assumption that UBC Okanagan was "inheriting" 2,900 FTE from the former Okanagan University College, the Government of British Columbia's goal was for the campus to grow by 900 FTE annually in order to reach optimum enrolment of 7,500 FTE in five years. All of the financial assumptions of the new UBC Okanagan campus—new faculty hiring, new program development, capital investment in residences and buildings, and the growth of student services—were predicated on achieving these enrolment goals. Four factors added to the challenge: first, the Okanagan Valley had one of the lowest post-secondary participation rates in the province; second, the number of students graduating from high schools in the Okanagan had already peaked and begun a downward slide predicted to continue well into the 2020s; third, the University of British Columbia itself, although among the top 40 research-intensive universities in the world, did not have a strong affiliation with the Okanagan region; and fourth, the number of FTE transitioning from Okanagan University College to UBC Okanagan was not 2,900 but more like 2,500 or less.[11]

STRATEGIC ENROLMENT MANAGEMENT AT UBC

Michael Dolence defines *strategic enrolment management* as "a comprehensive process designed to help an institution achieve and maintain the optimum recruitment, retention and graduation rates of students where 'optimum' is defined within the academic context of the institution. As such SEM is an institution-wide initiative that touches almost every aspect of an institution's function and culture." (Dolence

---

[11] It was difficult to ascertain the exact number of FTE transitioning from Okanagan University College to UBC Okanagan. Students enrolled at the University College could straddle upgrading programs and degree programs in ways that UBC could not support.

1993) Inherent in this definition is the need for integrated planning, systems thinking and long-term strategies—all difficult but necessary to achieve at large, highly-decentralized institutions like UBC with its enrolment challenges at both campuses. Strategic enrolment management looks to involve the entire university community—academics, students, administrators, alumni and professional staff—in planning and delivering a university environment that attracts the right kinds of students in the right numbers, and provides them with the right learning and support environments to be successful.

In short, SEM at UBC is about deciding what kind of university it wants to be, figuring out what it needs to do to get there, and then evaluating the costs and benefits before going further. It is about matching goals and aspirations with capacity—physical, human and financial. The goals of strategic enrolment management include: (1) enabling institutional mission; (2) increasing academic quality and student success; (3) optimizing financial resources and opportunities; and (4) ensuring and encouraging campus-wide collaboration. (Gottheil and Smith 2010)

Implementing SEM at UBC: The Planning Council, Steering Committees and Working Groups

As a result of the changes described above, both UBC campuses are well on their way to developing a strong strategic enrolment management culture epitomized by collaborative leadership and problem solving. The culture begins at the most senior levels. Members of the Executive of both campuses sit on a system-wide UBC SEM Planning Council. (*See* Sidebar on page 49.) The council's job is to ensure development of a strategic enrolment management plan that represents an integrated and systemically coordinated effort to connect mission, current state and the changing environment to long-term enrolment and fiscal health. In recent years, the Planning Council has tackled difficult issues related to the balance between undergraduate and graduate enrolment, the right mix of international, out-of-province and in-province undergraduate students; the proportion of direct entry to transfer students; Aboriginal access; the role of UBC in higher education in B.C. and across the country; student mobility between the two UBC campuses; academic quality and assessment; admissions reform; and predicting future student demand. An explicit component of the Council's mandate is to engage the University community in identifying, prioritizing, implementing, evaluating and modifying enrolment management strategies and goals in order to realize the University's mission. One way in which the council does this is through the SEM Steering Committees.

The SEM Steering Committees—one for each UBC campus—are responsible for resolving campus-specific issues related to admission, retention and graduation; achieving the annual enrolment targets for each campus; and advancing the long-term enrolment strategy developed by the Planning Council. The steering committees are co-chaired by the provost and the senior executive responsible for students (a deliberate, overt example of collaborative leadership) and include key senior administrators, Faculty deans and the directors of related units. (*See* Sidebar on page 50.) Faculty deans and associate deans use the Steering Committee to reinterpret high-level goals in light of specific campus or Faculty constraints and opportunities. For example, if a key goal of the Planning Council is to increase the number of international students year after year, different faculties will likely adopt different strategies: one Faculty may choose to increase enrolment by addressing problems of retention, while another may choose to expand capacity in programs especially popular with international students.

Each of these two committee levels meets four to five times each academic year (approximately every six weeks, excluding Christmas Break and Reading Week), and the Planning Council has an annual full day retreat where it reviews progress, reaffirms or revises goals and strategies, and identifies priorities for the coming year. At its most recent retreat, for

MEMBERSHIP AND MANDATE OF THE UBC SEM PLANNING COUNCIL

The SEM Planning Council is a system-wide committee responsible for long-term (5-10 years) enrolment planning. It is specifically tasked with:

* Developing long-term enrolment plans and identifying the resources required to support their achievement;
* Ensuring the development of a strategic enrolment management plan that represents an integrated and systemically coordinated effort to connect mission, current state, and the changing environment to long-term enrolment and fiscal well-being; and
* Engaging the campus community in identifying, prioritizing, implementing, evaluating and modifying enrolment management strategies and goals in order to realize the University's mission.

Membership

* Vice President, Students, Chair (appointed by members of the Committee)
* Deputy Vice Chancellor and Principal, Okanagan
* Provost and Vice President Academic, Vancouver
* Vice President, Finance, Resources and Operations
* Provost and Associate Vice President, Academic, Okanagan
* Associate Vice President, Academic Affairs, Vancouver
* Associate Vice President, Academic Resources, Vancouver
* Associate Vice President, Students, Okanagan
* Associate Vice President, Enrolment Services
* Director, Planning and Institutional Research
* Executive Coordinator, Enrolment Strategy

MANDATE AND MEMBERSHIP OF THE SEM STEERING COMMITTEE

The Strategic Enrolment Management Steering Committees—one for each campus—are responsible for translating the SEM Planning Council's high-level goals into campus-specific plans. Typically, these committees focus on short- and medium-term goals and strategies. The SEM Steering Committees have decision making power over a specific set of enrolment issues or can more broadly recommend to the Senate on matters such as:

* Defining UBC's distinctive advantage
* Strengthening linkages across campus to better support students
* Promoting student success by improving access, transition, persistence and graduation rates;
* Promoting policies, procedures and practices that facilitate experience learning opportunities for students.

Membership (Vancouver Campus)*

* Provost and VP Academic/Vice President Students, Co-Chairs
* Vice President, Finance, Resources and Operations
* Associate Vice President, Academic Affairs
* Associate Vice President, Academic Resources
* Associate Vice President, Enrolment Services
* Director, Planning and Institutional Research
* Deans of all Faculties
* Senior Director, Student Development and Services
* Chair, Senate Academic Policy Committee
* Chair, Senate Admissions Committee
* Director, Public Affairs
* Director, Student Recruitment and Advising
* Executive Coordinator, Enrolment Management Strategy

* Membership of the SEM Steering Committee at the Okanagan Campus is similar but not identical, reflecting the different organizational and decision-making structure of that campus

example, the SEM Planning Council listed admissions reform, including universal broad-based admission; 1st to 2nd year retention for international students; time to completion; the first year experience; and redevelopment of summer session as its top priorities for the coming year.

In between Steering Committee meetings, specific issues are advanced through ad hoc working groups or through a recently formed committee of associate deans. Ad hoc working groups, comprising both Steering Committee members and key resource people from across campus, were formed for multiple purposes including to: recommend a new strategy for scholarships and awards better aligned with the University's strategic plan; articulate the role of UBC within the changed B.C. post-secondary landscape (five new universities were created in 2008 and many more institutions were given expanded degree-granting capabilities); and develop guidelines for student mobility.

To coordinate all of these committees and working groups, the University created a senior position titled Executive Coordinator, Enrolment Management Strategy. The Executive Coordinator is a system-wide executive position with responsibilities at both campuses, and strong ties with the Office of the Provost and VP Academic (Vancouver) and the Office of the Deputy Vice Chancellor and Principal (Okanagan). The position reports directly to the VP Students and has three overarching responsibilities: (1) to drive the SEM agenda through the timely identification of issues and opportunities; (2) to serve as an in-house consultant or resource to senior administrators, faculty and staff involved with enrolment management; and (3) to stimulate and support a SEM culture. By instituting a position with thematic rather than functional responsibilities, the University deliberately created a position that could easily cross organizational boundaries and that was positioned to bring together groups of diverse people to resolve problems in mutually beneficial ways.[12]

A particularly successful strategy aimed at stimulating a SEM culture at UBC was the introduction of a SEM Colloquia Series, which brings global thinkers on post-secondary education to the campus to meet with members of the various SEM committees and other campus partners. The speakers' lectures and seminars challenge members of the campus community to think in new ways about issues of critical importance to higher education and UBC's future within it. SEM leaders at UBC chose speakers whose areas of expertise overlap with aspects of the University's strategic plan, and have been able to demonstrate the breadth of strategic enrolment management (it isn't just recruitment and admissions) and jumpstart thinking on new initiatives. For example, a highlight of the 2010 SEM Colloquia Series was having Dr. Carol Twigg, Executive Director of the U.S. National Centre for Academic Transformation, lecture on the issue of academic quality and fiscal constraint. Her presentation inspired the integration of UBC Vancouver's Office of Technology and Learning with the Office of Teaching and Academic Growth into the new Centre for Teaching, Learning and Technology as part of a renewed emphasis on improving teaching and innovative pedagogies.

The comprehensiveness of the strategic enrolment management process came as a shock to many on campus who did not at first see the connections between the structure of an academic degree program and time to completion or between retention and financial aid programs. There was a tendency at first to think of strategic enrolment management as solely focused on student recruitment and admission, but in Vancouver the introduction of a new SEM-inspired budget model explicitly linking Faculty budgets with enrolment and teaching soon changed that. Under the new budget scheme, two sources of funding were identified: revenue from the provincial government and revenue from student tuition. Each Faculty's budget would

---

[12] Jay Goff's and Jason E. Lane's 2007 SEM conference paper, "Building a SEM Organization: The Internal Consultant Approach," was very helpful in shaping the roles and responsibilities of the Executive Coordinator position.

include an allocation from the provincial grant in direct relation to the Faculty's enrolment target as a proportion of the University's overall enrolment target. Additionally, student tuition dollars would be distributed to Faculties based on service teaching. For example, the Faculty of Arts would receive a portion of the provincial grant equal to the annual enrolment target agreed upon by the Faculty and the Provost's Office and a portion of student tuition based on teaching FTEs, including the teaching that Arts does for students enrolled in Faculties other than Arts. If Arts were to underachieve on its enrolment target, its budget would be cut, and if Arts exceeded its enrolment target, the Faculty would receive more tuition dollars but no additional funding from the government grant. All of this gives Faculties a huge incentive to manage enrolment strategically, to coordinate cross-Faculty teaching requirements, and to resolve process and policy issues that negatively impact student retention.[13]

In the Okanagan, the situation differed. From the beginning, the campus's entire development plan was tied to aggressive enrolment growth (900 new FTEs annually for five years) with no need to introduce budget models explicitly linking enrolment and funding. The challenge in the Okanagan was to keep capacity and enrolment growth in line. Because of relatively low post-secondary participation rates in the local communities, enrolment growth at UBC Okanagan is dependent on attracting students from other parts of B.C. and Canada. However, bringing students from outside the Okanagan region meant having enough student housing to meet demand. As one of Canada's premier resort destinations, affordable student rental housing in Kelowna is non-existent. It was soon clear to everyone: reputation and academic quality alone were not enough to attract students in sufficient numbers to meet enrolment targets.

Another challenge at UBC Okanagan has been aligning FTE spaces with student demand. The original academic plan for UBC Okanagan envisioned about half the students enrolled in Arts and Science and the other half in professional programs ranging from engineering, business management, nursing, social work and human kinetics to education. But demand for professional programs has far outstripped

---

[13] Stan Henderson's article in *College and University* (Winter 2005), "Refocusing Enrollment Management: Losing Structure and Finding the Academic Context," argues persuasively that, to be successful, enrolment management needs to go beyond the traditional SEM realm and connect to the academic side of the institution.

demand for Arts and Science; one of the difficult questions facing both the SEM Planning Council and the Okanagan SEM Steering Committee is whether FTE should be redistributed to reflect student demand.

EXPERIENCE TO DATE

Challenges

The first and biggest challenge to strategic enrolment management at UBC was resistance to what many viewed as an imported—American—ideology, too market-driven and corporate to serve the purposes of an internationally recognized, publicly-funded, research-intensive Canadian university like UBC. Previous campus visits from respected SEM gurus, like Michael Dolence and Jim Black, are positively regarded by senior staff in enrolment services, but did little to persuade influential academic administrators that SEM had anything to offer UBC. In the eyes of many, SEM merely reinforced the trend toward the commodification of higher education and seemed to ignore the larger societal role of universities in contributing to the public good. SEM appeared to be all about advertising, recruitment tactics, tuition discounting and remedial programs aimed at boosting retention rates.[14] In fact, resistance was initially so strong that we deliberately avoided using the phrase "strategic enrolment management" or its acronym until SEM planning was fairly far advanced and we could clearly demonstrate the utility of strategic enrolment management thinking to faculties.

A second challenge was the fact that UBC Vancouver did not have an enrolment "problem." For almost a decade, UBC Vancouver had operated at full enrolment; if there was a problem, it was that demand far outstripped supply, which was driving admission cut-offs higher and higher. But no professors ever complained about students who were "too good." What helped in this regard was the new President who viewed enrolment somewhat differently. He believed that the composition of the student body went a long way in determining the quality of the educational experience and that being part of an intellectually diverse student body better prepared students to lead productive lives, thus it was important to bring together the right

---

[14] For a Canadian perspective on the commodification of higher education, see Pocklington and Tupper (2002).

mix of students. Another influential factor was Canada's shifting demographic and a growing recognition that UBC would need to become more intentional about recruiting and retaining students if it wanted to maintain its high standard of excellence in the face of a declining high school population.

In contrast, on the Okanagan campus, where the enrolment challenges were enormous, the urgency of the situation at first worked against the idea of taking time to develop an integrated, strategic approach. From the day the government announced the creation of UBC Okanagan to the day when students first set foot on the campus, less than a year and a half had elapsed. Who had time to be strategic about enrolment? Ironically, what helped change peoples' minds about strategic enrolment management in the Okanagan was the sense of deep disappointment when UBC Okanagan opened its doors in September 2005 to 250 FTE fewer than expected. Since that first year, and following the introduction of SEM planning processes, strategies and tactics, enrolment has grown at a rate of 12–15 percent annually.

A third significant challenge had to do with governance and committee mandate. Prior to the advent of the various SEM committees on both campuses, there were committees, including a number of senate committees, that by default included enrolment management or enrolment planning as part of their mandates. None of them had a mandate broad enough to represent an integrated approach to enrolment management or to cross campus boundaries. Rather, each of these committees tended to look at aspects of enrolment—the recruitment of international students, priority placement in housing, academic policies—in isolation from all the rest. Often, this resulted in the inadvertent adoption of contradictory policies, of practices that served narrow special interest groups, and of processes that unintentionally worked against what others were trying to achieve elsewhere. The challenge was how to acknowledge the existence of these committees and their mandates while at the same time wanting to give ownership of university- and campus-wide strategic enrolment planning and management to the new SEM committees. This challenge is one of the most difficult to resolve and is still a work in progress. A good starting point, however, was to invite the Chairs of those pre-existing committees to become members of the campus-based SEM steering committees. In this way, they became part of a larger discussion on enrolment and could take back to their committees information about the kinds of integrated systems thinking about enrolment that was taking place elsewhere at the university.

Accomplishments

THE MATRIX: ONE FOR EACH CAMPUS

The first big achievement of the SEM Planning Council was the articulation of a strategic enrolment management matrix. The matrix identifies different target student populations—domestic undergraduates, B.C. students and out-of-province students, international undergraduates, graduate students in research programs, graduate students in professional programs, transfer students, Aboriginal students and summer students—and assigns to each a long-term enrolment goal. There is a matrix for the Vancouver campus and another for the Okanagan campus; the two are quite different and reflect the scope, size and maturity of each campus, as well as their different aspirations.

In the course of developing the SEM matrix, the Planning Council realized four important things: (1) that intentional, sustained conversations about long-term enrolment planning had not taken place previously; (2) that definitions of student populations varied depending on context (Does "international student" refer only to students on study permits or does it sometimes also refer to students—independent of citizenship—who have been schooled outside of Canada? Similarly, does "national enrolment" refer to students who are Canadian citizens coming from outside of B.C. or does the term include any student schooled in Canada but outside of B.C., regardless of citizenship?); (3) that establishing long-term enrolment goals is an iterative process that needs constant refinement and correction in response to changes in capacity and external events; and (4) that communicating these enrolment goals to the campus community is critical if collaboration across and between units is to take place.

UBC'S ROLE IN B.C. HIGHER EDUCATION

The second big achievement was the development of clarity about the role of UBC—both the Vancouver and the Okanagan campuses—in the B.C. post-secondary landscape. Over the past three decades, a very sophisticated and robust post-secondary transfer system has evolved in B.C. Careful alignment of college programs with degree programs at UBC, SFU and the University of Victoria facilitated almost seamless student transfer from B.C. colleges to universities. UBC has always taken its responsibility to the larger B.C. post-secondary system seriously, reserving a significant portion of each year's new student intake for transfer students.

The expansion of degree-granting status across different types of B.C. institutions throughout the 1990s and 2000s (virtually every B.C. post-secondary institution now offers one or more degree programs), coupled with the announcement of five new universities in 2008, forced UBC to rethink its role within the B.C. post-secondary system. Could UBC best serve the higher education sector by continuing to recruit transfer students, or would the post-secondary system be better served if UBC focused on direct-entry students, thereby allowing the new regional universities to grow their own degree programs more rapidly? Again, the answer differed for the two campuses.

As an internationally recognized research-intensive institution already boasting a student population of over 50,000, UBC Vancouver decided on a course to reduce the total number of undergraduate students and to focus more on first-year students, gradually limiting its intake of transfer students. In contrast, UBC Okanagan, as one of the newest B.C. universities, is still establishing its reputation for excellent students and quality research and is dedicated to growing its enrolment—first-year, transfer and graduates—as quickly as possible.

THE DATA CONSOLE

The third and very significant achievement was the development of a data-rich environment in order to support informed decision making. Critical to this was the launch of a data "console." Bigger and more comprehensive than the more familiar "dashboard," the data console is an easy-to-read, easy-to-access repository of data on key performance indicators related to both annual and long-term strategic enrolment management. The data console also contains UBC-specific discussion papers and research briefs on issues related to student recruitment, retention, academic success, productivity and graduation at UBC. By creating a single source of data for the whole campus, we were more easily able to resolve discrepancies, correct errors, refine definitions, and identify problems related to strategic enrolment management.

FACTORS CRITICAL TO THE SUCCESS OF SEM

Commitment of Leadership to SEM

One of the single most critical factors in the success of strategic enrolment management at UBC has been the active engagement and support of the Executive at both UBC campuses. Their intentionally open and collaborative leadership style allows for constructive debate at SEM meetings and has fostered an especially productive approach to problem-solving. Without the Executive's willingness to take joint ownership of problems whose boundaries cross organizational lines, SEM at UBC would probably be nothing more than an improved approach to enrolment or student services, and while that might serve the immediate needs of the institution, it would not contribute very much to improving students' educational experiences or to ensuring the institution's long-term success. The importance of senior leadership in the advancement of strategic enrolment management at the institutional level cannot be over-estimated. When all of the vice presidents take time out of their busy schedules to attend SEM meetings or to participate in a SEM Colloquia Lecture, it sends a very strong message to the campus community about the significance of the initiative.

Mechanisms Reinforcing SEM

A second critical factor in the success of SEM at UBC has been the timely introduction of "facilitating mechanisms" that continue to reinforce the link between strategic enrolment management and long-term institutional health. The new budget model at UBC Vancouver is one such facilitating mechanism, as are the government enrolment targets for UBC Okanagan, the SEM committee structure, the further development of our data systems, and the university's new strategic plan.

Continual Evaluation

A third and final critical factor has been the idea of creating and maintaining a sense of urgency. Canada's changing demography, the decline in the number of students in the traditional university-going age range, creates an imperative for universities like UBC to constantly re-evaluate what they do and who they do it for. Fluctuations in enrolment from year to year are difficult to manage and compromise an institution's ability to realize its full potential. An over-enrolment one year takes several years to work its way through the system, and for that cohort of students compromises the quality of the educational experience throughout. Conversely, an under-enrolment can have serious negative impacts on the financial stability of an institution as provincial grants and tuition revenues are cut for years to come. Continuing to make tangible connections between strategic enrolment management and the fiscal (and therefore academic) well-being of the institution is an important aspect of strategic enrolment management.

LESSONS LEARNED

The most important lesson is that, notwithstanding all of the advice and helpful hints from SEM experts, successful SEM planning needs to acknowledge and honour the culture of the institution. UBC considered a number of different SEM structures before settling on the idea of creating both a SEM Planning Council and two SEM steering committees. This planning structure works at UBC because it respects the academic independence of each campus while at the same time acknowledging that the futures of UBC Okanagan and UBC Vancouver are inextricably tied. Likewise, membership on these committees reflects the fact that at very large institutions like UBC, accountability for key issues is often distributed over several senior portfolios. For example, at UBC Vancouver, annual enrolment planning—that is, negotiating with the deans how the overall enrolment target is divided amongst the faculties—is the formal responsibility of the Office of the Provost and VP Academic. Responsibility for achieving those targets, however, belongs with the VP Students in collaboration with the faculties. Given their respective roles, it makes sense that the UBC Vancouver SEM Steering Committee is co-chaired by the Provost and VP Academic and the VP Students.

Another important lesson is that SEM planning is more organic than linear; you can start anywhere—with retention, recruitment or alumni engagement—and still be successful provided you have a defined vision or mission and clear goals. In the first instance, SEM efforts need to be focused on what is of immediate concern to an institution's well-being. For UBC Okanagan, that meant enrolling as many new students and retaining as many continuing students as possible; for UBC Vancouver, where retention is consistently above 90 percent, the goal was to attract more top-quality students from across the country and around the globe. Moreover, although the intention of the SEM plan is long-term, the plan needs to be constantly reviewed, assessed and revised as the environment changes, the metrics no longer work and the priorities shift.

UBC does not have, and is likely never to develop, a single comprehensive SEM planning document. Rather, UBC has a series of plans related to different aspects of strategic enrolment management: an institutional vision and strategic plan; a recruitment plan; a plan for improving student advising; a plan for internationalizing the campus; a business process redesign of admission; Faculty academic plans; a campus development plan; a plan for enhanced alumni engagement; etc. At an institution the size of UBC, it is inevitable that at any one time different units or combinations of units will be at different stages in their planning processes. In these cases, what becomes important is that members of the various SEM committees, both as individuals with formal institutional responsibilities and as members of a collective responsible for the overall enrolment health of the institution, work together to integrate and reconcile these plans with the institution's strategic enrolment management goals.

CONCLUSION

Strategic enrolment management planning is less about a prescribed approach to enrolment and more about an attitude that recognizes the importance of campuswide integrated planning. SEM can and does work within a very broad range of organizational frameworks. It has been commonplace in the SEM literature to measure an institution's SEM maturity in terms of its organizational structure. In its infancy, a SEM institution will have a committee or a coordinator responsible for strategic enrolment management, while at maturity that same institution will have a division of enrolment management. If strategic enrolment management increasingly moves beyond enrolment and student services and into the academic realm, the model becomes less effective and the less desirable. At UBC, the last thing the SEM professional wants is to be perceived as competing with deans and academic units for resources.

UBC's particular success in strategic enrolment management planning comes largely from recognizing that responsibility for student recruitment, admission, retention and graduation is shared and that collaboration between and amongst academic, student service and operational units is critical to institutional success. Becoming a SEM institution means that across the campus, faculty and staff have internalized SEM principles so that every decision consciously takes into account the potential impact on the student experience and consequently on student enrolment.

As case studies, the two UBC campuses represent very different applications of strategic enrolment management principles. While there is a need for system-wide coordination (government reporting, for example, is joint), SEM has developed and progressed very differently on the two campuses, partly as a result of their different histories and sizes, but also as a result of different organizational structures and decision-making processes. What the examples of UBC Vancouver and UBC Okanagan show is how SEM can work at both large and small institutions and in the face of very different enrolment challenges.

At UBC Okanagan the challenge was to grow enrolment as quickly as possible. While the government target of 7,500 FTE has not yet been achieved, enrolment at UBC Okanagan has more than doubled in six years. UBC Vancouver, in comparison, has managed to hold domestic enrolment steady while rebalancing the mix of B.C. and out-or-province students and increasing the number of international students. Going forward, the focus will continue to be on recruiting and retaining international and out-of-province students in an increasingly competitive environment, on recruiting and graduating more Aboriginal students, on rebalancing the mix of direct entry and transfer students, and on better understanding as to how strategic enrolment management principles can be applied at the graduate level.

Susan Mesheau

4

MARKETING AND BRANDING

/ **Chapter 4** /

"I prefer that you not use that word." "That's not what we do."

Ten years ago, these were typical responses when one mentioned "marketing" or "branding" within a post-secondary education setting.

My, how times have changed! In a 2007 survey on integrated marketing in higher education conducted by the Council for the Advancement and Support of Education (CASE), 97 percent of respondents indicated that branding and marketing were part of their institution's operations and regular vocabulary (CASE/Lipman Hearne 2007).

In Canada, post-secondary educational institutions are facing economic and marketplace challenges. We are seeing declining demographics in some geographic areas and increased competition from other higher education institutions and from the variety of other credible options available to high school graduates. Student profiles are changing—student mobility is increasing while loyalty is not, and students have higher expectations of their university or college experience and outcomes. In addition, most of us will have to adapt to receiving less government support and fewer domestic students.

We will need to create compelling brands that will differentiate us from our competition. Branding and marketing are not only integral to the development and execution of our institutions' strategic plans—increasing the number of active alumni, donors and partners, and growing research funding—they are fundamental to planning and achieving strategic enrolment management goals.

The power of marketing and branding is beginning to be recognized on Canada's campuses; we will discuss in this chapter how these dynamic initiatives can be used to favourably impact higher education institutions.

BRANDING: THE PROMISE, THE PROCESS AND THE PAY OFF

Often one hears that a university or college has re-branded itself by launching a new logo or tagline. A brand must provide a means of identification, but beyond that it also encompasses a unique set of values, attributes and associations that offer a functional and emotional benefit to the customer.

Although there are as many definitions of branding as there are books on the topic, two stand out as particularly relevant to higher education. According to LEVEL5 Strategic Brand Advisors (2010):

> *"A brand represents the promise made to all audiences regarding the unique experience they have whenever and however they come into contact with the organization and its services. This unique experience should drive all audiences' preference for the organization over its competitors."*

The brand promise is more important in higher education than almost anywhere else. The promise must be authentic, have value to the customer, and be consistently delivered in all areas of the institution. Our product is "intangible," because we promise an outcome through an experience. Experiences and services, unlike goods, are made tangible only by the people who deliver them. It involves a considerable amount of trust on the part of our customers and a considerable amount of responsibility on our part to deliver that experience.

Who better than Michael Eisner, former Chairman and CEO at Disney, therefore, to say that "a brand is a living entity—and it is enriched or undermined cumulatively over time, the product of a thousand small gestures" (LEVEL5 2010).

Brand is built from the foundation of an institution's strategic or business plan, and marketing plans are built from the brand plan. Though the four P's of marketing—product, price, place and promotion—are commonly known, the emphasis when conducting branding or marketing efforts is typically on promotion alone. Dr. Tom Hayes (2009) says that in the case of a service industry such as post-secondary education, there are an additional three P's: physical evidence, process design, and participant.

There is a process to branding and marketing, with each step built upon solid market research. Often, market research is dismissed as too expensive or time consuming and the plan immediately drills down to tactics alone, which is in fact one of the last steps in the process, not the first. The person who said that the greatest obstacle to progress is not ignorance but the illusion of knowledge probably sat around a committee table listening to everyone's opinion of what they thought their customer was thinking.

Goal setting and objectives are an absolute necessity in order to demonstrate the return on investment to the groups or individuals who have a stake, financial or otherwise, in the branding and marketing efforts.

THE CORPORATE AND THE ACADEMIC WORLDS

The corporate world has embraced marketing and branding for many years. The corporate approach is "top down", where the products are clearly defined and the organizational infrastructures are set to accommodate branding and marketing work. Everyone's role is clear.

In the academic world, on the other hand, an institution operates like a small town, or, as one dean put it, as *"a community of scholars"* where all opinions are equal. It is highly decentralized with silo organizational structures and attitudes, resulting in multiple agendas and an internal focus. In some institutions, there may be a history of planning without implementation (or vice versa), which may not necessarily be connected to the bottom line. Furthermore, branding and marketing may still be seen as too corporate or retail and not necessarily trusted. Although marketing professionals are often hired from outside the higher education sector, in some instances public relations employees are being asked to assume marketing functions with little experience or understanding of it.

BRANDING AND MARKETING IN AN ACADEMIC SETTING

"Branding doesn't increase the quality of our academics. I can hire more professors in my faculty with that money." — University Dean

Any talk of branding or marketing in higher education typically defaults to a focus solely on recruitment, which—although important—means that all other areas are often ignored. Done properly, a focused and clear university brand will bring the tide in so that all the boats can rise. Communicating the institution's story and promise in a differentiated and engaging way, and delivering on the promise, will help to not only attract but also retain students and faculty; increase media attention, and donor, alumni and media support—all of which will enhance the quality of academics.

Although results are proven, branding and marketing work is very complex and difficult in an academic setting. It requires logical thinking, an integrated marketing approach and a step-by-step process.

THE INTEGRATED MARKETING APPROACH

Integrated marketing is simply strategic thinking. One of the best definitions of integrated marketing was penned by Larry Lauer (2002), who said that this type of strategic thinking is not to commercialize an organization but to make it recognized for its inherent value, build its reputation and make it continually competitive in the face of ongoing marketplace changes. It is about the clients' needs, the organization's strengths, the experience it provides, and how it is packaged and communicated. It is about establishing organization-wide processes that engage everyone in the organization, get them on the same page and plan coordinated steps to move it ahead. In order to make this approach function in an academic setting, several things have to be in alignment.

First, the will has to be there. Folks in senior administration must recognize the challenges their institution is facing; they must understand that strategic, comprehensive marketing efforts can be a solution to those challenges; and they must take a leadership role in addressing the challenges on an ongoing basis.

A champion, or several champions, must be appointed and supported from the top, and given a clear mandate and accountability. With the way universities and colleges operate, it is too easy to rely on collective accountability, which in fact is no accountability at all. The champion(s) must understand marketing and its processes, have enough experience and success to be credible, appreciate teamwork, and be good facilitators and educators. Because championing is constant and never-ending, they must be patient and persistent relationship builders...in other words, charming bulldogs!

The solicitation and gathering of external advice is crucial. This can take the form of hiring a marketing agency of record for the institution as a whole, if possible, or the use of individuals or groups from outside the institution, not necessarily in the higher education field, who can provide information or viewpoints that wouldn't necessarily be reflected within the institution.

The importance of buy-in to branding and marketing work cannot be overstated, so the organization and use of key internal and external stakeholder groups is fundamentally important. Vital groups to engage include Board members, alumni, deans, faculty members, faculty advisory groups, and senior administration. This approach allows for two-way communication and integration across the institution, and provides a forum for key people to provide input and receive information.

The silo orientation of higher education institutions is not naturally conducive to marketing work. Appropriate working infrastructures must be developed in order to override the often curious organizational infrastructures, and allow for integration, pervasiveness, collaboration, and persistence. The beauty of using working infrastructures is that they can easily change depending upon the type of project, they can foster teamwork and they can cross organizational barriers between and within the academic and administrative sides of the institution. They also allow for the opportunity to bring in appropriate skills from outside the institution.

Advancement cooperation is imperative. If folks in this area align themselves and work together, the ability to create teamwork and buy-in from other internal and external groups and individuals is much easier and the bottom-line success has greater leverage and impact.

Accessing resources for branding and marketing is always a challenge. Success cannot be achieved without ongoing and appropriate human and financial resources. There must be recognition that marketing is an investment that has a return that can add significantly to the bottom line, and provides solutions to external challenges. External challenges or crises can ensure that the institution's leaders take a serious look at branding and marketing, but this can be a double-edged sword and cause senior administration to look at marketing as a silver bullet. If, for example, the crisis happens to be in the enrolment area and, through the use of good branding and marketing efforts that challenge is addressed, the money that was budgeted to enhance enrolment goals may then get diverted in order to address a different challenge in another area.

Finally, significant discipline is required to follow a process that, at times, can seem like grunt work instead of tactical progress.

THE PROCESS

There are many processes used to develop brand and marketing plans, but the good ones all contain similar elements. In sum, the trick is to keep it simple—and follow through with it!

The foundation of the process is that it builds from—or with—the institution's strategic plan.

It is hoped that the two case studies that follow will provide enough theory and practical examples to give a good feel for the process, both in theory and in practice.

Case Study: University of New Brunswick

"Are you ready for this challenge?" That was the headline of the ad seeking a director of student recruitment and integrated marketing at the University of New Brunswick (UNB) in Fredericton that piqued my interest.

The ad indicated that the institution, one of the oldest public universities in North America, had decided to take integrated marketing seriously. With a new mandate to build a stronger reputation and identity for UNB, senior administrators created a new position reporting directly to the president and a new office devoted to developing and marketing a consistent and focused brand.

Ah, I thought, a university that recognizes the power of marketing—and has commitment from the top and the impetus to do something about it. I was eager to undertake that challenge, and began my work with UNB in January 2001. In September 2002, UNB launched its first multi-year fully integrated marketing program to create recognition and awareness of the university.

We used a five-phase process, with each phase built on solid market research and based on the tenets of the university's existing strategic plan: UNB must remain a national calibre institution; the university is critical to the economic, social and cultural prosperity of the province of New Brunswick and its people; and the university needs more resources from government, business, alumni, and friends.

PHASE ONE: STRATEGIC REVIEW

Marketing isn't really as sexy as folks think. It's mostly grunt work starting with the gathering and analysis of lots and lots of data. I spent my first several months at UNB solely focused on conducting a strategic review that included a thorough understanding of the existing strategic plan, vision and goals of the university; its current customers (not just students!) and partners; its products; and its operational and financial business model. This phase was by far the most time consuming.

With the help of the UNB advancement director, the driving force behind the creation of the integrated marketing office and a person highly respected by the university community, we implemented an internal working infrastructure by assembling a marketing committee made up of other advancement directors from UNB's two campuses to support the development and adoption of a UNB brand and future marketing initiatives. We also assembled key stakeholder groups, including other university administrators, deans, directors, students and a committee of the Board, to act as reporting and input audiences.

A marketing firm was hired to work alongside us as a partner in the development and implementation of this work. With the firm's help, qualitative market research was conducted with a significant number of internal and external key stakeholder groups and individuals.

PHASE TWO: BRAND COMMUNICATIONS AUDIT

A communications audit reviewing markets, audiences, current positioning, competitors, needs and communication materials was undertaken. A SWOT (strengths, weaknesses, opportunities and threats) analysis was completed. We discovered that the university had as many looks as it had publications; there was no main message and no compelling or focused brand. Quantitative market research involving internal and external audiences was conducted to not only help us understand our perceived strengths and weaknesses but to also set performance benchmarks.

The university needed a strong foundation for its image- and brand-building efforts, something that would demonstrate the strength of its connection to the community, the province, the country, and alumni, donors and prospective students.

PHASE THREE: BRAND COMMUNICATIONS DEVELOPMENT

Based on the work of the first two phases, the team was able to develop a brand vision, positioning, pillars in support of the positioning, a key promise, a slogan, key brand messaging and strategic imperatives. These were all validated through market research with key stakeholder groups.

A brand statement evolved from this work: *UNB is a national university committed to making a significant difference through quality learning and contributions to the community*. Each of these components communicated the institution's goals and direction. As part of the brand, a direct communications connection to that vision was established. The term "committed," used as part of the brand statement, provided a tone for communications. The focus was on the people of UNB, their passion, desire and drive. The phrase "making a significant difference" provided the theme for all communications—that is, UNB's programs and research are effective, relevant to people's lives and make significant differences.

Like many institutions, UNB was not focused on its communications, attempting to tell all of its stories all of the time to every audience. From the key brand messages of being a national university, providing quality learning and contributing to the broader community, a series of brand pillars was developed that indicated *why* UNB was a national university, *why and how* we provided quality learning and *how* we contributed to the broader community.

Focused communication does not just mean having a distinct brand positioning or repeating messages; the message details have to be focused on key proprietary areas of the institution and be of importance to the target audience. We needed to be rigorous in determining the most powerful main messages for each audience by leading with UNB strengths as determined by audience interest. Even though the messages focused on particular strengths, they created a "halo effect" over the entire university. Main messages shifted from one marketing program to another but all were derived from UNB's overall brand statement.

PHASE FOUR: CREATIVE DEVELOPMENT

Time was spent developing the brand looks, designs, slogan, development of graphic standards and guidelines. This work was tested through many interviews and focus groups with internal and external stakeholders and audiences.

Because UNB has two main campuses and folks on each campus wanted to ensure that each were "differentiated," it took quite a while to gain consensus on a family of cohesive "looks" that would be used on all UNB communications—a main corporate look for multi-campus initiatives and individual related looks for the two campuses. The standardized look created a cohesive image while still allowing for flexibility of photos and messaging needed for tailoring to the variety of marketing programs in which it would be used.

PHASE FIVE: IMPLEMENTATION OF MARKETING PLANS AND EVALUATION

The first four phases provided a foundation from which to develop a variety of marketing plans, each with its own purpose. Although several were developed, we began with brand awareness and, concurrently, student recruitment. We also targeted other revenue-generating areas, including UNB's College of Extended Learning and the Office of Research Services, in order to develop plans to help them achieve their aggressive business objectives. A fundraising campaign, based on this process, was later developed and became the most successful campaign in the university's 225 year history. At the time of writing, student retention is being targeted.

Every marketing plan must build on the institution's strategic and brand plans and include a number of components: an analysis of the current external and internal environments, competitive situation analysis; a communications strategy with quantifiable objectives, target audiences and markets; positioning and key messaging rolling out the brand, aimed at a specific audience; action plans listing tactics, activities, responsibilities and timelines (both short-term and long-term); budget/resources; and measurement. Each component requires its own market research and analysis.

The first marketing plan developed was a brand awareness program, which we called the *Making A Significant Difference* campaign. Initial market research found that awareness of UNB within New Brunswick was high, but specific knowledge was lacking. Perceptions of the institution were neutral to positive, but people in the province did not see the university as connected to their lives. The research also indicated that our audiences considered jobs, health care, education, research, technology, and the environment important to their daily lives. We realized that we could leverage UNB's strengths in these areas in our brand communications to create a halo effect over the entire university.

Two-thirds of UNB's operating revenue comes from the taxpayers of the province in the form of government grants. Cognizant of this business model and using the results of the research conducted in phases one and two, the committee developed the main goals of UNB's image-building initiative: to create a cohesive brand image, to demonstrate to the people of New Brunswick how UNB is fundamental to their daily lives, and to make the provincial population more predisposed to support the university in a variety of ways. We also needed to foster pride among alumni and internal constituents—faculty, staff and students—to mobilize them to advocate on UNB's behalf.

We developed an initial program strategy that outlined target audiences (internal and external), key messages and preliminary tactics.

In our advertising, we decided to use the real stories of UNB graduates, faculty, and staff members who were improving the quality of life of people in New Brunswick in those areas which our audience told us were important. For example, 75 percent of educators in the province are UNB graduates, 70 percent of our nursing graduates practice in the province, 80 percent of the province's university research is conducted at UNB and of the 65,000 alumni worldwide, 28,000 UNB graduates live, work and create jobs in the province. We used this information and compelling visuals to demonstrate—not tell—how UNB was connected to the economic, social, and cultural prosperity of New Brunswick.

After extensive focus group testing, the committee finalized the creative program and marketing plan. Image-building tactics included television, print ads and a new Web site. Relationship-building efforts included sending general information kits to stakeholders and the general public; hosting a tour around the province for the president to meet with alumni and government, business and media representatives; sending regular targeted emails to key audiences and the internal community about the awareness-building program and its results; and establishing a UNB spokespersons group, which provided advocacy support.

One of the main goals at the outset of this endeavour was to generate pride in and around UNB. We therefore developed a special component of the plan aimed at UNB alumni, titled *Proudly UNB*, with its own complementary initiatives. Building on the same themes of how connected UNB is to the New Brunswick community and using the same look, we sent electronic newsletters and emails to alumni, placed ads in the alumni magazine similar to those we were running in major media outlets, provided postcards for alumni to send to the provincial government in support of the university, and mailed information kits to alumni about our efforts.

Because successful integrated marketing relies on mobilizing the entire university community, we conducted pre-launch information sessions about our image-building campaign—its rationale, plan and benefits—and held a well-attended public and media marketing launch event concurrently on both campuses. These activities helped ensure public awareness and buy-in for what was essentially a new approach to university marketing.

Similar to initial market research and testing, formal post-implementation measurement is a critical component of a marketing plan and is too often overlooked. We made sure to devote time and effort to assessing the effectiveness of our efforts. After the first full year of the *Making A Significant Difference* brand awareness effort, our marketing firm conducted an extensive quantitative survey with our audiences to compare awareness and current perceptions of UNB against benchmark data collected before the initiative started. The program exceeded first-year expectations. Perception of UNB measurably increased with the public and particularly with alumni. Seventy percent of all respondents—and 90 percent of alumni surveyed—could recall the ads, where they saw them, and what the ads said without being prompted. Seventy-one percent of respondents said UNB was relevant to New Brunswickers, and 66 percent felt it made a difference in their lives. The program had a number of other positive indirect outcomes, including a government funding increase of four percent, and a four percent increase in first-time donors. We also saw a two percent increase in active alumni involvement, a six percent increase in student enrolment and an overall increase in regional and national media attention for UNB. The program also caught the attention of our peers, earning a CASE (Council for the Advancement and Support of Education) Circle of Excellence Gold medal.

This program ran successfully for about four years. Performance measurement was conducted each year and reported to the UNB community and its key stakeholders, including the citizens of New Brunswick.

The *Making A Significant Difference* brand awareness program was augmented by the first annual student recruitment marketing plan. Bringing the same process and marketing principles to bear on the "sales" unit, we were able to meet our five-year enrolment objective in one year. This plan had an in-depth focus on product (that is, academic programs), as well as customer behaviours, market trends, use of media and so on. The fact that our tactics were based on solid market research, or as one dean said, *"evidence-based activity,"* gave us credibility with deans and faculty members.

We now work quite closely with many of our academic colleagues on specific market research and resulting recommendations on programs and program development.

Building on the success of the two initial marketing programs, we turned our attention to the Office of Research Services at UNB. Knowing that they were given an aggressive target to increase research funding, I approached the Vice-President responsible for that portfolio to discuss how marketing could be used to help achieve their business objectives. Another marketing plan was developed and implemented following the same process, and contributed to their goal achievement.

An interesting project then followed. Hearing about the marketing work that we were doing in other areas, we were approached by the Director of the College of Extended Learning, the former Department of Extension at UNB. Because of their reorganization from a department to a college and also because they were a revenue-generating arm of the university, we spent considerable time developing a marketing program for them that started with an in-depth review of their products and customers, as well as their organizational and business model. This resulted in recommendations on re-positioning, the development of a new organizational structure that aligned with their products, sales and markets, and a promotional component to raise awareness while generating increased revenue.

A marketing opportunity on the horizon in Canada in post-secondary institutions is student retention. Like many colleges and universities, UNB is now focusing more on this area of student success as part of its strategic enrolment management agenda. As we begin the work of marketing to retain students, we will focus on the student experience and the delivery of that "intangible" through all seven P's of service marketing.

Case Study: Mount Royal University

There are a number of other institutions across Canada doing fine work in marketing and branding. The following case study from Mount Royal is just one example.

In September 2009, Calgary's Mount Royal College became Mount Royal University, the culmination of years of concerted effort. Mount Royal's pursuit of university status was also the catalyst for the college to undertake a formal branding exercise. Although the college was not experiencing a crisis of any kind, there were a number of reasons why the institution engaged in this exercise. Mount Royal College operated in a province with four universities, the second largest of which (the University of Calgary) was located in the same city. In this environment, Mount Royal thought it was important to carve out a specific niche for themselves and to explain to all their audiences who they were and what they stood for.

The institution's positioning and branding focus was broad-based. Audiences that needed to be addressed included government, corporate and individual donors and employers, as well as prospective and current students, faculty, alumni and staff. Each of these audiences had particular considerations. For example, employers needed reassurance that Mount Royal would maintain its commitment to preparing workplace-ready graduates, as the institution broadened its outcomes to focus not only on jobs but also on higher education.

The process that the marketing team used was very similar to that used at the University of New Brunswick.

The Director of Marketing at Mount Royal, Lucille Gnanasihamany, came from the private sector. She had worked in marketing and advertising agencies and corporations where she was expected to make decisions quickly and implement them effectively. Already armed with knowledge of the branding process, Lucille discovered that post-secondary education and marketing did not always mix well (the phrase "the outrage of branding" still resonates in her memory). She quickly came to understand the importance of support from the top, internal buy-in, and driving brand success from the inside out.

An institutional positioning development committee, formed prior to Lucille's arrival, played a major role in the process. The committee's membership represented academics, administration and students. Working closely with internal groups such as the executive and Dean's Council, as well as student, staff and alumni groups, the committee's mandate was to develop a brand plan or, as they called it, an institutional positioning development plan. The plan became the essential foundation and road map for all subsequent positioning and branding initiatives, summarizing Mount Royal's past context and history, current realities and future aspirations.

The college hired two outside firms to assist them. Working in close partnership, one firm conducted quantitative and qualitative market research with external and internal audiences for perception and comparative positioning purposes, and the other helped to develop the positioning statement and creative concept.

The committee organized a day-long positioning summit with leaders from all areas of Mount Royal. This provided a forum for discussion and helped to determine the level of buy-in for various positioning directions. The outcomes of the summit mirrored the results of the market research. It appeared that the institution, for the most part, was ready for the branding exercise and felt the timing was particularly appropriate, given its pending move from college to university status. This group provided the opportunity for internal stakeholders to provide input and feedback—some of it critical. This included some uncomfortable conversations that needed to happen both before and as the process unfolded.

The discipline to follow the process—the research, the situation analysis, the testing, validation and so on—allowed for the development of brand pillars for the institution (quality teaching, personalized learning, being outcome focused, and community responsive) and highlighted an overall tone for communications and marketing (personal, approachable, responsive, and authentic).

A brand tool kit was developed which included creative templates, graphic design standards, core brand messages and photographic imagery. A powerful student awareness campaign became the initial marketing program undertaken. The slogan for the campaign—"Face to Face"—crystallized the brand pillars and overall tone. A variety of internal and external tactics were implemented, beginning with an internal launch of the brand. Traditional media, including newspapers, were used. Ads were developed which demonstrated how people affiliated with Mount Royal "put a face on education." Their personal stories showcased one or more of the four brand pillars. Mount Royal also developed a new Web site, on-campus banners, display materials, new recruitment publications and an inventory of faculty experts who could speak about their areas of expertise in the media as well as at venues such as museums or corporate office building lobbies.

Particularly relevant and unique were the tactics used to help their internal community live the brand. Mount Royal provided an online forum for faculty, staff, current students and alumni to provide "living testimonials"—stories and photos about what "Face to Face" meant to them individually and why they thought the brand reflected their experience with Mount Royal. Interactive "Living the Brand" workshops were delivered to virtually everyone on campus, over the course of 14 months. The workshops (each 1 or 2 hours) showed how each person in the institution could live the brand both personally and professionally, both within their own department and within the institution.

A tactic that has worked very well for Mount Royal is the "brand ambassador" program. Brand ambassadors were amassed from every department and major institutional group. They either volunteered or were appointed by the department head. The brand ambassadors are expected to undertake activities to encourage faculty and staff to live the brand. This has included such things as employees introducing themselves to a student while standing in line for coffee and talking about their experience at Mount Royal, or professors engaging their students in conversation while waiting for a classroom to empty. These have been simple yet powerful ways to demonstrate the face-to-face personalized learning environment. In attempting to make the ambassador position a coveted role, professional development training is provided on a regular basis and meetings are held quarterly.

In 2009, four months after Mount Royal achieved university status and 18 months after the brand launch, the institution engaged a research firm to test the effectiveness of the brand work by measuring message resonance and entrenchment with audiences locally and further afield. The research report was received in December 2010. Once analysis is complete, the results will be used to help Mount Royal University develop and evolve their strategic marketing planning going forward.

One of the biggest initial successes, however, was demonstrated in the 2010 *Globe & Mail* University Report card. The significant increase in positive response from Mount Royal students in the survey prompted a *Globe & Mail* editorial commentary: "Mention should be made of two of Canada's newest universities, Mount Royal and Grant MacEwan, who make their debut in the survey with a splash. Both of the former colleges from Alberta score in the 'A's' on the important categories—including overall satisfaction, quality of education, student-faculty interaction and campus atmosphere. That's an amazing performance" (Usher 2011).

SUSTAINING THE BRAND

A good brand has significant power.

It's in the promise. The unique experience that you offer—and deliver—to your audiences makes them choose you over your competitor(s).

It's in the process. Understanding and following the branding and marketing processes takes knowledge, discipline, champions, collaboration, patience and persistence. (A generous supply of humour won't go amiss either!)

It's in the pay-off. A good brand builds reputation, making your institution recognized for its own inherent value; it ensures differentiation, keeping you competitive in a rapidly-changing world; and it generates return on investment.

We've seen examples of institutions that have used this power to positively impact enrolment, academics, fundraising, alumni involvement and more.

Don't think of this as the end, however.

R. J. Wrigley, the founder of the Wrigley chewing gum empire, is said to have been asked why he continued to advertise so extensively when his company was already the most successful distributor of chewing gum in the world. His response was that he kept on marketing for the same reason a pilot keeps the engines running after the plane is already in the air.

Branding and marketing can too easily be seen as a quick fix for an immediate problem or crisis, as opposed to an ongoing investment with return. This often means that there is no sustainable commitment to ongoing marketing work with the devastating effect of sporadic, limited or one-time funding. This may be a result of the lack of understanding and practice and the limited measurement of return on investment. The need for continuity, ongoing commitment, support, and champions are vital to the progress and continued success of what is becoming an integral part of higher education.

Richard Levin

5

STUDENT
RECRUITMENT

/ **Chapter 5** /

If one were to chart the series of encounters and experiences that students have in relation to a college or university, student recruitment activities would be present at the very beginning. School visits, campus tours, open houses, fairs, Web sites and other forms of recruitment messaging are very often the first point of contact between students and post-secondary institutions and play an important role in shaping a student's choice of institution. Beyond simply attracting learners, colleges and universities also want to manage the number and characteristics of students who choose to attend the institution, goals which must inform recruitment practices.

Student recruitment employs strategies and tactics from the broader discipline of marketing. Terms like *recruitment funnel, segmentation, communication stream, prospect* and many others are borrowed or adapted from public relations, marketing and sales. Classic marketing texts, *e.g., Positioning* (Ries and Trout 2001), will therefore be of interest to those developing student recruitment strategies and tactics. There are, of course, highly distinctive features of student recruitment relative to marketing in general.

This chapter focuses on strategic considerations that should be considered by those engaged in student recruitment. It reviews the Canadian context and common recruiting tactics and touches on the key elements of the recruitment cycle. It also discusses recruitment as part of the larger post-secondary organization and engages in some speculation about the future.

A DIVERSE LANDSCAPE

Canada is a diverse country in almost every respect; geographically, demographically, culturally and economically. These dimensions of diversity are reflected in the array of Canadian post-secondary institutions. Add in the various mandates and cultures of the colleges and universities themselves and the landscape is far from homogeneous. For this reason, any consideration of student recruitment in the world's second largest country cannot be narrowly prescriptive and is unlikely to be fully comprehensive.

Consider, for example, the different missions of three recruiters; one in a B.C. college working to attract greater numbers of Aboriginal students; one in a research-intensive Ontario university which has decided not to expand undergraduate enrolment; and one in a small Atlantic university, focused on maintaining enrolment in the face of a declining local 18- to 24-year-old population. These are all very different challenges. Yet there are common principles to consider in establishing recruitment programs and activities. Before considering what these might be, it is worth a further look at the dimensions along which institutions can vary.

In Canada, education is a provincial responsibility. Educational policies, priorities, funding and tuition levels are set provincially; this tends to foster provincial post-secondary communities focused on local issues. It also creates provincially-oriented information sources for students. For example, an applicant in British Columbia or Ontario will access a common application service that lists only institutions in that province; her counterparts in other areas of the country will not have a similar prepared menu from which to choose.[15]

The varying sizes and populations of each province also result in particular recruitment environments. A high school graduate in Manitoba has five universities and four colleges to choose from; each can claim a relatively unique position in the marketplace. A prospective student in Ontario can choose among 21 universities and 24 colleges, many of which offer similar value propositions. Funding is enrolment-driven in Ontario but not in Manitoba. These factors create a highly competitive environment in Ontario but they have also resulted in co-operative recruitment

---

[15] Despite this, Canada, unlike the U.S. (and with the exception of Quebec), does not have different in-province and out-of-province tuition levels. Pricing is therefore not normally a key factor in decision making (at least within type of institution), although scholarships can have some impact on institutional choice (Dooley, Payne and Robb 2008; Drewes and Michael 2006). Professional programs such as law and medicine can be an exception to this principle because more flexibility in tuition levels tends to be permitted. One therefore generally sees cost considerations as general information provided in the recruitment process, not as part of the marketing strategy.

programs in that province such as the University Information Program and the College Information Program, both of which sponsor common recruiting events.

Institutions themselves also vary greatly in size, mandate and structure and on dimensions such as student population; certificate, diploma and degree offerings; open vs. closed-enrolment programs; percentage of graduate students; and research-intensiveness. These characteristics result in different organizational cultures. A recruitment department in a smaller college may have very considerable autonomy in designing and producing recruitment materials and programs. In a large research intensive university, academic units may expect at least to be fully consulted in these activities and frequently produce their own materials or organize and conduct independent campaigns.

A CHANGING CONTEXT

In addition to diversity, change is an ever-present feature of the Canadian enrolment context. Today the "echo boom" generation is entering colleges and universities. This effect, along with increasing post-secondary participation rates, is fuelling growing enrolments in some, but certainly not all, parts of Canada. We can already see the tail end of this demographic in shrinking elementary and secondary school enrolments. There are varying predictions of the extent to which Canada's low birthrate will be offset by immigration and increasing participation rates in sustaining post-secondary growth but it seems clear that this will happen unequally across the country.

Universities are also experiencing a steady increase in the ratio of female to male students. Statistics Canada reports that women made up 57.5 percent of the university population in 2007–08, and 56.6 percent of the college population in 2006–07. Although high school dropout rates are decreasing generally, the male share of dropouts is increasing (63.7 percent in 2004–05). With the exception of certain programs such as engineering and business, recruiting men to post-secondary programs is becoming a greater challenge, though thus far few initiatives have been directed towards this imbalance.

Another factor affecting student recruiting is public policy. Increasingly, governments are mandating that post-secondary institutions serve particular audiences. In Canada, Aboriginal and first-generation populations (*i.e.*, students whose parents did not attend college or university) may be identified as high priority groups by governments. In some cases, funding is available for special initiatives to serve these populations. Recruitment units may have an opportunity to be part of, or even to lead, institutional proposals in these areas.

Finally, the context of student choice is changing. Parents are significantly more involved in post-secondary decisions (see, for example, Somers and Settle 2010). The influence of guidance counsellors in the decision process is declining while the role of friends is increasing. All those involved in the choice process now rely to a large extent on digital sources of information to make their decisions.

INSTITUTIONAL GOALS

Because standard activities of the recruitment cycle are so widely accepted across Canadian colleges and universities, it is entirely possible for a recruitment unit to be kept busy by simply managing existing cyclical tasks. Well before each cycle begins, however, recruitment managers and teams should regularly review their objectives and activities by asking some critical questions:

- What are the institution's broad enrolment goals? Increased (or decreased) headcount? Higher admission averages? More international students? A larger first-generation or Aboriginal population? How do these goals get defined?
- Have academic units thought about the characteristics of students they are trying to recruit? Is it as simple as anyone with an admission average over, for example, 75 or 80, or is there a specific profile of student that programs are looking for? Do programs have single targets or are targets divided among population segments?
- Where should resources be focused? Schools may spend $100,000 or more on a viewbook and almost nothing on their Web site, or vice-versa. What evidence exists for the efficacy of past efforts or the expected impacts of new ones? How will return on investment be demonstrated?
- Are recruiting efforts and messages aligned with institutional marketing/branding initiatives? Have the recruitment responsibilities of central recruiting units been defined relative to those of other academic and administrative areas?

Institutional recruitment goals should be part of a strategic enrolment management plan or an institutional strategic plan. Some schools will target maximum growth to fill excess capacity and/or generate additional revenue; others may freeze undergraduate enrolment or aim for higher admission averages. Sometimes these goals are precise and explicit; sometimes they are implicit, or even absent. Recruitment managers should advocate for institutional conversations designed to lead to explicit goals. Laurence J. Peter, the Canadian-born originator of the "Peter Principle," phrased it well: *If you don't know where you're going you'll probably end up somewhere else.*

The creation of an institutional recruitment plan has the secondary benefit of ensuring conversations take place among all the areas involved in some form of student recruitment. If an institution does not already have explicit enrolment goals, some form of consultative structure may need to be established to create a plan. Nothing is more critical to an institution's future than defining enrolment plans; this must be endorsed at senior levels of the organization, with the resulting plans disseminated broadly.

RECRUITMENT TACTICS

Student recruiters have a fairly standard arsenal of tools at their disposal. These include school visits, recruitment fairs, viewbooks and other publications, campus tours, telephone campaigns and open houses. In the past 15 years or so, the Internet has become an essential vehicle for informing prospective students; Web sites, email campaigns, virtual tours and more recently social media vehicles have been added to the mix. It is not difficult to fill the recruiting season, or to spend the budget. What is more challenging is focusing the time and resources available on value-added practices. A salient quote (attributed to various sources) goes: *I know half of my advertising budget is wasted, I just don't know which half*! Evidence-based decision making is discussed further later in this chapter.

Once application deadlines have passed, recruiters will find themselves preparing the viewbook for next year's cycle, booking school visits and organizing open houses. Tour guides will be hired and trained for the upcoming recruitment season. There may be fall fairs to book and international and out-of-province schedules to plan. In Toronto, the September Ontario Universities' Fair draws about 100,000 visitors over three days.

At these early stages, a broad audience is being addressed. Tactics change as the cycle progresses and the audience narrows; this will be discussed later in the chapter, as well.

CASE STUDY:
THE POST-SECONDARY CLUB AT
THE UNIVERSITY OF MANITOBA

In 2008 the team of Guidance Counsellors from R.B. Russell Technical Vocational High School, led by Kim Deeley, approached Peter Dueck (Executive Director, Enrolment Services at the University of Manitoba) about establishing a program that would allow the University to work with a group of high school students over an extended period of time for the purpose of creating an awareness of post-secondary opportunities and eliminating barriers in the achievement of such opportunities. R.B. Russell is an inner city school with a large Aboriginal first-generation population. The program was launched in January 2009 with a group of twelve Grade 10 students. Eight of these students have just begun their Grade 12 year of studies.

The first phase of the program consisted of group-building activities, career awareness games, and several visits to the University of Manitoba campus for tours, presentations, and hands-on activities. The second phase of the program allowed the students to gain volunteer experiences in a number of different settings and events. As well, students were given tours of two other post-secondary institutions to ensure a broad range of scope. The year ended with cultural awareness activities that allowed greater bonding and empowerment through identity. The third phase of the program will include career mentoring, leadership enhancement, preparation for applying to post-secondary school (including a session on accessing scholarships and bursaries), and stronger cultural development.

CONITUES ON NEXT PAGE ▶

Segmenting

Market segmentation divides the audience for recruitment communications into smaller groups, allowing messaging and strategies to be more finely tailored. Various audiences for recruitment efforts include high school students, mature students, stopout (or *gap year*) students, previous attendees, international students, and out-of-province students. There are also many other levels and types of segmentation (*e.g.*, geography, gender and program(s) of interest). Parents, teachers, guidance counselors and other opinion leaders may also represent potential audiences for recruitment messaging.

One audience segment of growing importance in universities consists of graduate students. Recruitment of graduate students is often the responsibility of Graduate Studies itself and recruitment strategies are very different. Graduate students tend to come from more varied geographic sources including other countries. They are also much more interested than undergraduates in faculty members, research strengths and program details.

Many post-secondary institutions also see international students as a key enrolment objective, and governments are becoming active in mobilizing international student recruitment. International students are featured in Chapter 14, "Internationalization and SEM at Simon Fraser University," on page 289.

Segmenting audiences allows for more precisely crafted messages and tactics. A student coming directly from high school will have very different information needs and sources than a student returning to university after working for several years. With greater segmentation, content and timing of messages can be more sensitive and responsive to the audience. It is common for schools to develop a viewbook for domestic and international students, as well as program-specific brochures. Often there are Web pages dedicated to certain audiences. However, segmentation remains to a large extent less than fully exploited in many Canadian schools.

Social Media

There is no question that social media and other elements of Web 2.0 are having an impact on student decision making, and for that matter on all forms of marketing. Typing the name of a school into a blog search engine like Google or Technorati will yield hundreds or thousands of results. The word-of-mouth phenomenon enabled by various Internet media is having a considerable impact on marketing. Students can now easily post an experience to the whole world on a blog, or make a video. Consider the amount of attention paid to a customer of United Airlines who posted a YouTube video called United Breaks Guitars, after a bad baggage experience. That video has now had over 9 million viewings. Within four days of the first video going online, United stock dropped 10 percent according to *The Times* Online (July 22, 2010), though the extent to which that drop can be attributed to the video, and the long term impact on the airline, can certainly be debated.

Social media platforms give students and parents a very public voice for their opinions and diminish the level of control that marketers have over messaging. This implies that the interactions that applicants and students have with a college or university, what marketers sometimes call *moment of truth* interactions, will influence prospective student choices. Such interactions need to be seen as part of the spectrum of recruitment efforts, and highlight the importance of considering the full strategic enrolment management continuum in shaping the recruitment agenda.

CONTINUED FROM PAGE 86

The results of the program? Students repeatedly say that they love being part of the Club. They have bonded as a group and many have developed close friendships that didn't exist before. The group has bold career aspirations (and plans on how to achieve those goals).

The group has also become very familiar and comfortable with the large University of Manitoba campus. One student who had virtually dropped out of school now excels and has multiple internship offers and an excellent attendance record and grades to match. Finally, the program has gained the interest of other schools/school divisions in Winnipeg, including two very large 'feeder' schools that are close to campus, and plans are underway to expand the program to these schools as well.

Reasons cited for the success of the program include committed guidance counselors, faculty, staff and students; a regular meeting schedule and program consistency; continual review by program leaders; and, food for the students at each meeting!

Social media is an unparalleled way for students to connect with others and create a community of common interest. What is less clear is how institutions can use social media as an effective marketing force. Social media strategies are complex and subject to unforeseen events. Companies as large and sophisticated as Coca-Cola and Nestlé have had very controversial experiences with the medium. Ask students and they are likely to tell you that Facebook pages are their own medium and they do not necessarily welcome the presence of marketers, and certainly not censorship in any form. Nevertheless, many or most colleges and universities have Facebook pages, post YouTube videos and have Twitter feeds.

Adopters of social media marketing must live with the fact that the message is not neatly controllable. Here is an example of a student-posted comment on a Canadian university site, which was wisely left unedited:

> *Yet I bet you anything, that in a few months, they will be announcing tuition hikes. What a double standard that this great University receives such enormous funding, yet insists at the same time, that students going into debt is more important than the University keeping tuition low and affordable. The right to learn and be educated shouldn't be so costly to us prospective students.*

Institutions working with social networks must be tolerant of such submissions or risk negative publicity and backlashes. Understanding the institutional level of tolerance for such material will help define the boundaries of social media usage. In addition, the institution must define in advance how offensive posts will be treated, and whether posts will be monitored proactively or reactively.

Other digital recruitment tactics involve chat rooms, live chat with an admissions counselor or other front-line representative, QR (quick response) or AR (augmented reality) codes embedded in publications which students scan to activate a Web site, text message subscriptions and smartphone apps. Technology will continue to evolve quickly and today's leading edge efforts may fast become stale. Keeping up with emerging technology trends, and ensuring appropriate staff resources are available to implement them and keep them up to date, will be significant challenges for student recruitment units.

Communication Plan

Once enrolment goals, target markets and communication/marketing strategies have been identified, a communication plan should be built. The plan should identify the nature and timing of each communication to each segment of the market. A key principle here is to balance the number of communications and try to optimize the timing. Too many or ill-timed messages can turn a prospective student off a university as easily as too little communication. Table 2 (on page 91) shows a portion of a hypothetical student communication plan at the suspect/prospect stage.

The table maps out simplified communications to two market segments. A real plan would contain many more rows and columns.

For each communication, recruiters should define an objective or goal, a *call to action* (*e.g.*, a suggestion that students visit a Web page, apply, attend an open house, etc.) and where possible a means of assessing the effectiveness of that communication (*e.g.*, Web site hits, replies, event registrations). There is a balance to achieve between too little and too much communication. This balance can be unique to institutions and to groups of applicants; it is worth monitoring and evaluating this and other elements of the communication plan on an ongoing basis.

RECRUITMENT AND THE SEM FUNNEL

The concept of the marketing funnel is straightforward but very important in planning recruitment efforts. At the top of the funnel is the largest popu-

CASE STUDY:
RECRUITING DISPLACED WORKERS AT LETHBRIDGE COLLEGE

In response to the global economic downturn in 2008, Lethbridge College identified a unique recruitment opportunity that would also build on its institutional reputation within the community. Charting Career Change, explains Natasha Buis, Manager Academic Advising & Recruitment Services, was a program that Lethbridge College developed to target recently laid off or unemployed members of the Lethbridge community. A cross-functional team, comprising various service areas on campus, was pulled together to develop a 'non-credit' program that would provide an opportunity to support individuals who had recently been laid off as they transitioned into new careers or who, more specifically, were looking to re-enter the classroom. Charting Career Change was open to any individual who felt that they would benefit from the program.

In February and March of 2009 Lethbridge College ran two intakes for this two-week program. Capacity was set at 15 for each intake; each had wait lists. Services provided included career advising, inventory testing, financial awareness, interview skills, resume writing, components of the College's traditional Student for a Day program, academic advising and assessments, as well as a number of traditional recruitment activities. Very little promotion or marketing was driven by the institution with this program as it was a popular story in local and regional news and media outlets. Lethbridge College enjoyed an added benefit as the program was well received and reinforced the College's commitment to its community.

At the completion of the first two-week program, the Charting Career Change team was pleased to see that of the 15 prospects registered in the course, 12 had applied to programs that

CONTINUES ON NEXT PAGE ▶

CONTINUED FROM PAGE 89

were starting that fall. This, combined with the initial waitlist, led to the decision to run the program again in March of the same year. At the end of the second session, the College captured 10 of the 15 prospects that participated. Of the 22 participants that chose to consider applying to programs on campus, four have completed their certificate programs and the remaining participants are still registered as students within their individual programs.

By providing a recruitment activity that was meaningful, valuable and timely, Lethbridge College was able to maximize return on investment with very little time and energy. The prospect group was clearly defined and the program tailored to their goals. This clear prospect definition was essential to the success of the program. By the time the fall term of 2009 was underway the local economy began to recover and demand tailed off, so the program was suspended.

Using a strategic enrolment management approach and pulling together an effective cross-functional team of on campus service providers allowed Lethbridge College to reap the rewards from a public relations standpoint, meet enrolment targets and begin to build a culture of SEM on the campus.

lation of interest. Through the recruiting process, the numbers narrow until only students enrolled in a particular institution are left (*see* Figure 3).

In 2006, the Canadian population was about 30 million. The population of 15- to 19-year-olds was just over 2.1 million (Pan Canadian Education Indicators Project 2007). Continue to narrow that figure down to, for example, 700,000 secondary students in Ontario. Of these, about 94,000 enrolled in an Ontario college and a fraction were enrolled in any one college. Clearly, a college in a particular province would find it very expensive to target the entire Canadian population, at least by conventional advertising means, and extremely inefficient. Resources should be allocated to populations that are likely to result in applicants. That is where the concept of a marketing funnel, or SEM funnel in the recruitment context, applies.

Suspects

The first stage in recruiting prospective students occurs before there has been much narrowing of the target audience. These efforts involve broad outreach to possible future students, sometimes called *suspects*. Suspects are individuals whose potential to attend an institution has not been qualified, *i.e.*, their likelihood to attend has not been evaluated or confirmed. At the broadest level, these efforts can involve marketing campaigns such as magazine ads or billboards, which are often the purview of marketing or public relations offices. Such campaigns may not narrow the possible audience at all, or marginally. For example, an advertising campaign carried out at a movie theatre may tend to be seen by more 15- to 19-year-olds than members of other age groups, but it remains a very broad population. Student recruiters have usually refined their suspect population to a greater extent, at least by educational status. School visits

TABLE 2: SIMPLIFIED SAMPLE STUDENT COMMUNICATION PLAN

Student Stream	October	November	December
Local High School	Open house postcard for school visit ■ **Goal:** Maximize open house attendance ■ **Call to Action:** Register for open house ■ **Metric:** Percent of contacts who register for the open house	Famous alumni email ■ **Goal:** Link to brand ■ **Call to Action:** Visit Web site ■ **Metric:** Click-throughs	Application deadline reminder (domestic)
International	Residence information email ■ **Goal:** increase awareness of residence possibilities ■ **Call to Action:** Visit student housing Web site ■ **Metric:** Hits on housing Web site	City tourism info email ■ **Goal:** Emphasize appeal of destination ■ **Call to Action:** Visit Web site ■ **Metric:** Click-throughs	Application deadline reminder (international)

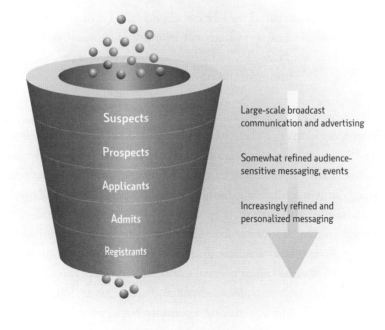

◄ FIGURE 3

SEM Enrolment Funnel

Suspects

Prospects

Applicants

Admits

Registrants

Large-scale broadcast communication and advertising

Somewhat refined audience-sensitive messaging, events

Increasingly refined and personalized messaging

and college or university fairs target secondary school students who may be potential applicants to their institution. However, attendees at these events are not often well qualified in that recruiters have little sense of their likelihood to attend the institution they are representing.

Canadian institutions are at a disadvantage relative to their American counterparts when it comes to building a database of suspects. In the U.S., universities and colleges may purchase contact information for subsets of students who have taken written admission tests such as the SAT. These subsets may be refined geographically and by SAT score, or by a variety of other variables. Considerable effort is directed at communicating with these individuals and qualifying them as prospects. Such lists are not as widely available or as comprehensive in Canada. Some Canadian companies with prospective student Web sites will send, on behalf of a school, recruitment communications to their contact lists at a piece rate, or provide other forms of leads. In general, Canadian high school students will not, unlike their U.S. counterparts, receive copious volumes of mail from universities and colleges looking to recruit them.

As indicated, investment at the suspect stage can be expensive because many or most recipients of the message will have little or no interest in it. Nevertheless, the aim of such efforts is to transform a suspect into a prospect, someone who is now considering attending your institution.

Prospects

The suspect stage is an opportunity to begin narrowing the target audience. A student who fills out an online form or a contact card requesting more information has indicated initial interest in a school. The same is true of attendees at an open house or campus tour. It is critical to capture information about these students because, once they have reached this stage, they become *prospects* and are far more likely than a random visitor to a booth to end up enrolling in that particular school. A much greater share of recruiting resources should therefore be directed to this group as the return on investment will be higher. Schools that do not capture contact information from open house attendees or have no mechanism to collect visitor information from the Web site are missing a considerable opportunity to increase the efficiency of their recruitment efforts. The messages delivered at this stage can also be tailored, since prospects have had an opportunity to provide some degree of information about their status or interests. A student who attends a fair and fills out a contact card indicating an interest in science programs can be sent a viewbook with a science brochure. Examples of initiatives that are commonly directed at encouraging prospects to become applicants include viewbooks and other publications, campus events, campus tours and digital communication.

A number of Canadian schools have implemented a prospective students' portal on their Web site. A portal may be obtained from a commercial provider or built internally. A prospective student portal allows a student to sign up by providing some basic information; the portal then creates a customized Web page based on that information and allows the school to initiate a communication stream with that student. Portal information can provide a rich source of data for modeling prospect and applicant behavior (*e.g.*, what percent of students who sign up with the portal and attend an open house eventually become enrolled). Portals also provide a highly qualified prospect database and may offer additional functionality such as campus tour booking and inventory management.

Note that some recruitment funnels identify "inquiries" as the second stage of the funnel. This indicates that once a student has made some contact with the school they are of greater interest than suspects, but not quite prospects. It is worth noting, however, that the incidence of *stealth applicants*,

CASE STUDY:
A NEW APPROACH TO OPEN
HOUSE AT DALHOUSIE

Dalhousie University offered its first Open House in recent history in 2004. The event opened up the campus to the community and offered hundreds of activity options across the campus. Using signage, individuals and groups found their own way across campus and to a variety of activities, including public lectures, a pancake breakfast and opportunities to explore activities and academic options.

Although considered a general success, it was hard to measure the impact of the event on the university's recruitment effort. There was no registration process and therefore no way to know who had attended. This limited the university's ability to follow up with attendees or to measure the impact of the event on a prospect's likelihood to enroll. Programs at the event were aimed at all ages, rather than being specifically focused on the interests and needs of prospective undergraduates. Although attendance was strong overall, some departments expressed frustration that attendance had been poor at their particular displays/sessions. Some visitors had a hard time finding their way around campus and there were some buildings that were closed when they tried to enter. Since supporting recruitment was deemed the key objective of the Open House, the Open House Committee set about revamping the event for 2005.

Asa Kachan, Dalhousie's Registrar, describes several changes that were made to enhance the impact of the Open House. Online pre-registration of participants captured the interests of participants so that the experience could be personalized. This also allowed the recruitment team to contact students before and after the event. Sessions were revamped with the interests of prospective students in mind.

CONTINUES ON NEXT PAGE ►

CONTINUED FROM PAGE 93

Participants received a tailor-made program of activities for the day based on the interests they identified through the registration process. Participants became members of student cohorts with other prospects who had identified similar interests. Student cohorts are now assigned to a current Dalhousie student who volunteers to be a guide for the day. Student guides are given training to answer general questions and build a strong team among their cohort.

A special parents' program was set up to provide parents with information on university support services, admissions and awards, transitioning their son/daughter to university, and the range of program offerings. Parents were also given opportunities to eat lunch in residence and meet senior members of the university's administration.

A defined start and end to the day was established. Participants start on Wickwire Field to kick off their day with a welcome from the University President and Student Union President, with draws for some prizes. This is where participants meet their student cohort guides. As part of their schedule, each participant attends three information sessions based on their expressed interest; an Expo featuring information booths and displays from over 60 faculties and services on campus; and lunch at a residence cafeteria. At the end of the day, students have the opportunity for residence tours and onsite admissions.

Faculty and staff have become very engaged in the day's events, with over 100 serving in key roles (registration, information booth, parent host, etc.). As well there are volunteers across academic departments offering approximately 75 program sessions (often several in a day) and working at 64 booths at the Expo. A 15-member

CONTINUES ON NEXT PAGE ▶

those that make no contact with the institutions before applying, is increasing (Hoover 2006).

Applicants

The decision to apply to an institution indicates a significant step forward; the student has now defined a limited choice set. Communication from the institution is now less likely to be regarded as spam or nuisance messaging, since the student will be seeking information about her or his status and likelihood to receive an offer. It is essential to acknowledge the student's application and to design an effective communication stream that continues from the point of application to the point of decision.

As mentioned earlier, some provinces—specifically B.C., Alberta and Ontario—offer common application services. Students must apply to colleges and universities in those jurisdictions through provincial web-based services. This represents a convenience both to the student and the institutions. It also creates a unique dynamic around application choice, as students in these jurisdictions select institutions from a menu. In Ontario, students receive three choices for a base application fee (additional choices are available) and institutions are informed of where their school ranks among student choices. That ranking may inform recruitment efforts and predictive models.

Efforts to turn applicants into enrolled students may be referred to as *conversion* tactics (although conversion may also be the term applied to moving prospects to the applicant stage). Such efforts typically include direct communication (digital, voice and/or paper), campus events such as open houses and tours and Facebook pages and chats. Web technologies that allow students to check their application status and access or upload additional information have become common.

Elements of the admission process must also be considered integral to student recruitment. Maintenance of communication, the design of the offer package, adherence to brand standards and service levels are all part of the conversion effort. The applicant stage may involve a structural handoff from the recruitment unit to admissions. This transition should appear seamless to the student.

Conversion efforts normally begin before offers are made and continue after offers go out. The institution must decide how much effort to put into conversion prior to offers being made and how much after the offers are made. Conversion efforts aimed at applicants prior to the offer stage should be clarified so that students do not mistake them for offers, or the promise of offers.

CONTINUED FROM PAGE 94

event steering committee, comprising staff volunteers from across the university, works for several months in advance. Nearly 100 current Dalhousie students serve as hosts for student cohorts and as leaders of end-of-day residence tours. Many of these Dalhousie student volunteers are attendees of previous Open House events and are eager to assist with the event.

The Open House has become a key part of Dalhousie's recruitment efforts. With efficiencies in the registration process, it has become a much tighter event, with less chance for individuals to feel lost or disconnected. Exposing students to sessions and activities that best suit them helps keep their attention and interest. This fits well with the overall goal of successfully engaging both prospective first-year students and their parents through the delivery of an insightful and educational on-campus program, and thereby increasing the likelihood that the students, with their parents, will select Dalhousie University as their final university of choice in subsequent years. The event has also met a secondary objective, which was to engage current Dalhousie students and the Dalhousie community.

Admitted Students

The group of students to whom offers have been made represents the penultimate point in the recruitment funnel, preceding the decision to enrol. It is the last opportunity to influence decision making, but also a very efficient one as the probability of these students attending is much greater at this point in the funnel. It is important to have a defined strategy for converting admitted students after offers have gone out and before decisions are made.

Attention also needs to be paid to the communication flow that occurs once an applicant has accepted an offer of admission. This often involves another structural handoff, this time to a records and registration department and/or an academic unit. Though acceptance deadlines may have passed, in reality applicants still have opportunities to change their minds. Student loyalty to the institution should not be taken for granted at this stage.

The funnel is a highly useful concept in crafting recruitment strategy. It provides a framework around which to conceptualize communication with prospective students and build effective and efficient communication plans and tactics.

EVIDENCE-BASED DECISION MAKING

It is still common for Canadian universities and colleges to invest significant sums into recruitment efforts with no systematic evidence supporting their probable effectiveness. It is similarly common to launch those efforts without defining a means of evaluating their success. Very often a Web site or viewbook is developed based on the instincts of those responsible, while the target market is receiving and processing information in very different ways. It is tempting to believe that students will view a Web site the same way that we do; that the same pictures, ideas and information that appeal to administrators or faculty will appeal to them. This is a risky proposition when substantial resources are at stake. Communications technologies, and therefore sources of and attitudes towards information, change rapidly. Recall that the iPod didn't exist until 2001 and the smartphone was introduced even more recently!

Canadian recruiters do not have a wealth of publicly available research on student recruitment; the reference list for this article is evidence of that. Unlike the u.s. where college choice has been a subject of many publications, *e.g.*, Hossler, Schmit and Vesper (1999), nearly all research on the subject is proprietary. There are rare exceptions, including Drewes and Michaels (2006) and Dooley *et al.* (2008), both of which relate variables to choice based on data from the Ontario Universities Application Centre. Research on choice of colleges in the Canadian context is even sparser.

One of the more comprehensive sources of research on student recruitment efforts in Canada is the University and College Applicant Survey (ucas). Though the results of the survey are generally proprietary to the participating institutions, the data below are presented courtesy of Academic Group Inc.

Figure 4 and Figure 5 (on page 98) depict a subset of the key influencers of institutional choice reported by students in 2010, by both degree of influence and percent of the sample using those sources. A wide variety of information sources are of at least some value to prospective post-secondary students. Web sites are rated as highly influential and widely used as they have been for some years, and print publications continue to be highly valued. Campus tours and visits, though used by fewer students than online sources, are also important. College and university students rely on similar information sources, though university students in general make greater use of most sources. This may be because many colleges are seen to have more local catchment areas and students, and for economic or other reasons, may default to the local option.

Institutions often undertake their own research efforts, not only because public data are so rare but because recruiters are interested in the factors that influence their unique set of applicants. Findings in one context may not generalize well. For example, a campus visit can be a powerful conversion tool if the campus is attractive and friendly; if it is not, a visit may do nothing for enhancing yield.

Individual colleges and universities use a range of tools to evaluate the effectiveness of their recruitment initiatives. One of the most common of these is a focus

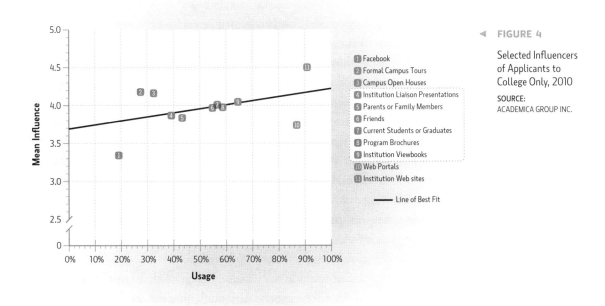

◄ FIGURE 4

Selected Influencers of Applicants to College Only, 2010

SOURCE:
ACADEMICA GROUP INC.

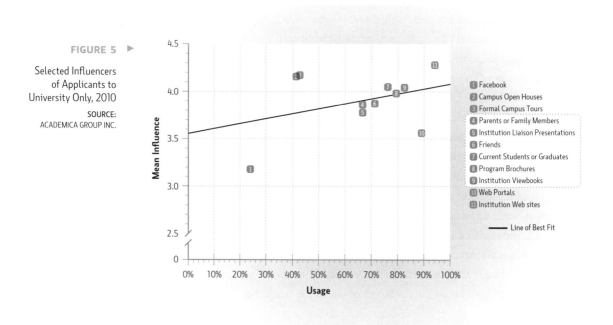

FIGURE 5 ▶

Selected Influencers
of Applicants to
University Only, 2010

SOURCE:
ACADEMICA GROUP INC.

group (or groups) of students who will review a potential Web site or publication. Focus groups provide interesting and detailed information, but the results cannot be generalized to a larger population because the number of participants is too small; yet we do precisely that with regularity. In addition, there are group dynamics that can contribute to inaccurate information.

In research cited by Zaltman (2003), over 60 percent of focus group members said they were likely or very likely to purchase a particular appliance in the next three months. Six months later only 8 percent had actually made such a purchase and participants were unable to explain why. Morais (2001) in a strong critique said "Never, never should focus groups be used as a basis for decision making." Clearly focus groups must be used with caution and the results taken as only suggestive.

Survey data can provide more statistically reliable results because larger populations can be involved. For example, a Web site concept could be displayed and users asked to complete a short online survey. Alternatively, visitors may be asked to rate the features of an existing Web site, before redevelopment is undertaken. Students attending fairs or open houses often register or fill out contact cards; this information can be used to send out satisfaction surveys after the event. Some institutions carry out *decliner surveys* in which students who declined an offer of admission are asked why they made their decision.

Web sites and other online recruitment tools have the advantage of allowing data called *Web analytics* to be gathered. These may be as simple as counting hits on a Web site but can also be used to assess the geographical source of visitors, 'stickiness' (*i.e.*, how long students spend on the site), and the pages visitors have come from.

Beyond opinion-based data, institutions may have at their disposal behaviourally-based evidence. An institution that has an online portal for students to request information can determine the probability of those students applying, accepting an offer and eventually registering, relative to the overall student population.

Predictive Models

Most college and university admissions departments have some form of predictive model for determining the number of offers to make to achieve desired enrolment. The model may range from simple yield ratios to an elaborate regression equation. Such models may be the domain of admissions or enrolment management departments, or of institutional research units, but they have applicability to recruitment. A model that predicts likelihood to enrol based on factors such as grades, geographic location and other variables can better inform the focus of recruiting efforts as well as assist with admissions forecasting. A more elaborate model that extends to predicting factors such as graduation or

CASE STUDY:
EVIDENCE-BASED RESOURCE ALLOCATION AT THE UNIVERSITY OF ONTARIO INSTITUTE OF TECHNOLOGY (UOIT)

At UOIT in Oshawa, Ontario, the SEM team has been making data-driven decisions by measuring the impact of student 'touch points' and augmenting initiatives with a high return on investment. Using various unique identifiers, SEM staff track incidences when students initiate a connection with the university, e.g., in-bound phone calls, email, attending an event or taking a campus tour, as well as tracking incidences where the university contacts the student, e.g., phone, email, social networking or mail, for the purposes of recruitment. According to Joe Stokes, Assistant Registrar of Recruitment at UOIT, these touch points between UOIT and prospective students are then evaluated to identify an event or combination of events that have the highest impact on application numbers or enrolment. For instance, if a student who attended an on-campus event had a greater chance of applying than a student who did not, UOIT will spend more effort and resources on ensuring higher attendance at the event. Other touch points that had a lower probability of generating an application, in-bound phone calls for example, are not abandoned. Rather, the university evaluates the ways in which they can address the type of service—response time, or answer fulfillment—and gauge if the adjustment had a positive or negative impact on yield.

engagement can help schools recruit students who will ultimately be successful or even fit the profile of desirable students for particular programs.

ORGANIZATIONAL DYNAMICS

Acceptance of Student Recruitment Within the Institution

Student recruitment is generally a well-accepted function in colleges and universities. Occasionally, some members of university communities may look askance at certain kinds of strategic marketing since university faculty, more often than their college counterparts, may not support the view of academic institutions having commercial interests. More sophisticated marketing techniques may therefore be somewhat controversial in universities.

Organizational Models

Canadian recruitment offices typically fall into one of the three organizational models. The dominant model, particularly in universities, houses recruitment functions along with admissions in the registrar's office. A second model, which is prevalent in the u.s. but less common in Canada, sees recruitment and admissions as a separate department from records and registration. Finally, recruitment is sometimes an independent function reporting to a senior marketing official or another Vice-President or Assistant President/Associate Provost. This last model is more often seen in colleges than in universities.

There are advantages and disadvantages of each of these models. For example, a joint recruitment and admissions unit can combine elements of both of these portfolios within single staff positions, with individuals recruiting in the fall and doing admissions in the winter. On the other hand, a separate recruitment portfolio with a strong leader may be seen more persuasively in the institution. Regardless of the structure of the organization, student recruitment must maintain strong relationships with admissions, financial aid, student housing, and communications/public relations so that students experience coordinated and complementary communications from the organization.

Decentralization

Some universities, particularly large research intensive and/or medical-doctoral institutions, can be extremely decentralized, with academic units operating many of their own administrative functions. This level of decentralization may include several aspects of student recruitment. Although recruitment activities such as school visits and campus tours can be challenging in a decentralized model, academic units can and do manage their own telephone, letter and email campaigns and campus events. This can lead to tensions between the recruitment office and academic units over consistent and coordinated branding and messaging.

Recruitment departments in decentralized institutions may also experience far less autonomy than their counterparts in centralized environments. A recruitment manager in a small centralized institution may design Web sites and publications with minimal consultation. In decentralized institutions, committees may be established to vet such outreach activities. Autonomy has many positive attributes associated with it, such as greater speed, creativity and flexibility. Too much committee work can result in excessive compromising: a publication that doesn't offend anyone but at the same time is not particularly creative or inspiring; messaging that is acceptable but not bold. However, if academic areas are not brought into the recruitment agenda, they are much less likely to support and augment it. Even a very centralized school will want to be able to depend on the good will of faculty and academic staff to attend fairs, talk with prospective students, and represent the organization effectively.

In a decentralized institution, it is important for recruiting offices to have open avenues of communication and to understand and support the goals of academic units. If academic areas are dissatisfied with central efforts or find themselves challenged with respect to their enrolment goals they are more likely to seek even further local control. Rather than seeking to centralize or maintain tight control, recruitment offices should work to foster coordinated efforts and share best practices. Sometimes simply cataloguing all the central and local recruitment efforts will demonstrate the need for streamlining and coordination. Sincere interest in the agenda of each academic area, clearly expressed, goes a long way to build good will and support.

In larger organizations, a coordinating committee will probably be necessary. This could be a SEM committee or subcommittee, or a stand-alone recruitment committee. It is important to have the right people at the table. A key challenge for such committees is to be inclusive without becoming unwieldy and ineffective. Much of the coordinating work will be tactical, and therefore involve administrators from academic units as well as other administrative functions. However somewhere in the organization, discussions need to be held at more senior levels to establish the overall strategy and approach to coordinating recruitment efforts.

Another key relationship is that between the recruitment office and public relations/communications/marketing. Recruitment officers spend many hours talking with thousands of students and may feel that marketing departments do not understand the dynamics on the ground. On the other hand, marketers may feel that recruiters do not understand larger scale awareness campaigns or buy into the brand fully. This relationship needs to be nurtured. There is nothing more dysfunctional than having a recruiter deliver a message to hundreds of students in a high school, only to have them hear a different message via a radio or TV ad later that day. Good communication and relationships between leaders of these units will go a long way to avoiding these situations. In addition, the roles and responsibilities of each area should be well defined to avoid the kind of scenario just described.

Future Directions

Research in marketing continues to evolve rapidly. One of the most interesting areas of advance is in behavioural economics and behavioural decision making, which study behaviour in relation to real world factors and conditions. It seems increasingly clear that decision-making is not nearly as rational as we might think, and that often our explanations for behaviour, no matter how reasonable, do not describe the real causes of it. One of the more popular expositions of this field is the book *Predictably Irrational* by Dan Ariely (2008). Ariely cites a number of studies which demonstrate that consumers frequently do not understand the factors driving their decisions.

A relevant example in the post-secondary context is provided by Uri Simonsohn, an Assistant Professor at the Wharton School in Pennsylvania (Simonsohn 2010). While intuitively one might think that a nice sunny day is the best circumstance for a campus visit, Simonsohn determined that there is a positive correlation between cloud cover on the day of a campus visit and likelihood to enrol. He provides evidence to support the idea that scholarly pursuits are given more positive consideration if they are not coping with more attractive alternatives provided by nice weather! Institutions that employ current research techniques will always have a competitive advantage.

As discussed at the beginning of this chapter, demographics and public policy play a role in setting the context for recruiting and are likely to continue to do so. Governments are adopting more activist agendas in the post-secondary arena, and institutions may come under pressure to recruit students who help achieve certain goals. The decline of post-secondary age populations in many areas of the country will continue to result in intense competition for students in areas of growing population.

Finally, we are unlikely to see any decline in the pace of technological advancement, nor is the shape of this change predictable. New technologies may transform post-secondary student recruitment in ways as fundamental as those first introduced by the Internet. The phenomenon of social networking may profoundly alter consumer decision making, including college and university choice. On the other hand, it may also fade in popularity as other technologies become dominant.

Effective student recruitment requires constant scanning of the relevant environment, understanding the needs and decision making processes of prospective students, effective communication, relationship-building and evidence-based decision making. Regardless of changes in social, economic and technological circumstances, a commitment to these principles will serve student recruiters well.

Åsa Kachan and Mairead Barry

6

ADMISSION PRACTICES
THAT SUPPORT SEM

/ **Chapter 6** /

At Canadian institutions, unlike those in the United States, the term admission is used separately from the recruitment process. Directors of admission at Canadian colleges and universities are focused on admission requirements, managing the intake, application processing and relationship building with applicants. Responsibilities may be highly centralized in the admissions or registrar's office, or decentralized in programs and faculties.

The admission phase is a critical one from a SEM perspective. Hard work has been done to create interest in the institution and its academic programs, and prospective students face their first formal interaction with the institution. How we communicate admission requirements, how we serve applicants through the process, and how we select those students who will succeed academically and shape our institutions are all critical to each institution's ability to meet its enrolment objectives.

ADMISSIONS CRITERIA

Traditionally, grades have been the primary basis for admission into college and university programs in Canada.

For vocational or community college programs, where access has been the highest priority, achievement of the minimum grades in required subjects is the base criteria, after which those who applied earliest are admitted first until the program capacity has been met.

At universities, competitive admission has been commonly used when the number of applicants has exceeded the spaces available. The strongest qualified applicants have been more successful in securing admission to their preferred programs at their preferred institutions. Canadian universities have overwhelmingly used grade information in the assessment of one applicant against another, particularly for undergraduate programs. Some standardized test scores have been used in place of grades for students who were home schooled. Reference letters and test scores are more common at the professional and graduate level.

Assessing the majority of applicants on the basis of grades and subjects is easy to automate and thereby allows institutions to streamline and improve services. As programs become increasingly competitive and secondary level curriculums more varied, more universities are asking whether this simple formula results in the students who are the best fit for our institutions. Average high school grades have risen dramatically over the years and the line between students admitted and those not, or students offered scholarships and those not, is very fine.

More universities, particularly in western Canada, are moving to a broader-based admission process. Based largely around noncognitive variables identified by William Sedlacek (2004), institutions such as University of British Columbia, Simon Fraser University, and University of Calgary have implemented the use of broad-based admissions questionnaires, in addition to grades and test scores, to better predict which students will succeed and engage at university. In some programs this is used across the entire applicant pool. In others it is used for non-traditional students. Sedlacek identifies eight key noncognitive variables to success that include: positive self-concept; realistic self appraisal; ability to successfully handle the system; preference for long-term goals; availability of strong support person; leadership experience; community involvement; and knowledge acquired in the field. Through questionnaires, applicants are asked to provide background information on themselves and their experiences, and to reflect on their learning through their experiences. Assessing the students on this basis is much more time-consuming, but allows institutions to better select applicants on the basis of leadership, team-work skills and other requirements, which are not always reflected in high school grades.

HELPING APPLICANTS THROUGH THE PROCESS

Applicants don't enjoy being refused admission any more than admission officers like spending their days refusing admission to applicants who don't meet the minimum qualifications. Giving students all the information that they need about the admission requirements and processes upfront will allow them to plan appropriately to ensure they meet admission requirements or to avoid applying for programs for which they do not hold minimum or competitive qualifications.

Interactive web-based interfaces with the capability for prospects to filter admission requirements based on curriculum and program are becoming more common across Canada. Technology makes it easy for applicants from different provinces to hone in on admission information that is customized to the curriculum they are studying. Most of us have visited automobile Web sites, checking out price, delivery date, financing options and features before we visit the dealership. We put aside models that are too expensive or not well suited to our lifestyle before we get serious. Removing the mystery around the admissions process in a similar way for applicants will result in a higher proportion of serious and admissible applicants and a more efficient and effective admissions office.

Although the enrolment funnel in the United States had traditionally been modeled on securing vast numbers of prospects of which a portion will apply and a smaller portion will be selected in order to yield the right enrolment for an institution, the Canadian funnel looks a little different. A truly efficient admissions process looks more like a cylinder, where from the application phase onward the majority of applications received are from the strongest, best-fit applicants, who are highly committed in their intention to attend the institution.

SMOOTHING THE PROCESS

The traditional approach to admissions processing has always had some inherent bottlenecks. Every year it seems like students submit their application just before the deadline. We need to wait for transcripts to be received from high schools before assessments can be completed. And one piece of information can hold up an application that is otherwise complete. Many institutions in Canada have undertaken business improvements at key points in the process to help ease some of these delays. More institutions are offering admission as early as 12 months ahead of the term start. Decisions can then be made on a rolling basis to strong candidates, extending the admissions cycle and stretching out the demand for processing and review of applications across the year.

Conditional offers of admission are often granted to strong candidates who self-report their grades. This alleviates the need to wait for paper records from schools, allows institutions to give offers earlier and then follow up once the official documents have been received. By moving these decision points forward in the admissions process we are able to achieve increased efficiency and timeliness or response.

In contrast to our American counterparts, Canadian admission offices have an opportunity to become extremely efficient in the processing of applications, particularly at the undergraduate level. In a survey of American and Canadian chief enrolment officers in January 2008, 95 percent of Canadian institutions surveyed indicated that they primarily used high school grades/marks as the basis of admission compared to 63 percent of post-secondary institutions in the United States (Smith and Gottheil 2008, p. 33). By using a grades-based assessment system, Canadian admission offices can use automated processes to improve response time to applicants, reduce the need for staff intervention, and reduce the likelihood of human error in assessments. The time spent manually evaluating applications can be used toward better outreach to applicants or counseling of incoming students. This frees up human resources that personalizes the admissions experience and not the admissions decision.

Automated admission processes work well for strong candidates that clearly meet the institution's academic criteria; however, automated processes don't translate well for those students who may not meet the standard admission requirements but might be admissible under alternative admission policies and practices, and, most importantly, have attributes that will make them successful. These candidates need special attention to transition to post-secondary education. Following an assessment of their circumstances they may get an offer of admission or they may be at the point where additional skill development is required before they become competitive for admission. Under both circumstances, it's important that the professional admissions officer spend more time advising and reviewing these applicants. Devoting time to individuals not yet qualified and mapping out a path for them improves the likelihood that there will be more qualified applications in the following admission cycles.

COMMON APPLICATION CENTRES AND ELECTRONIC TRANSCRIPT TRANSFER SYSTEMS

With the creation of the Ontario Universities' Application Centre (OUAC) in 1971 and the Ontario Colleges Application Service (OCAS) a few years later, Canada's most populous province moved to a system of common application centres that were intended to find efficiencies and improve service to prospective students. Today the OUAC and OCAS not only process applications but also collect and distribute academic grades, distribute application material, administer surveys, and produce statistical reports and publications. In recent years, other regions in Canada have also implemented (B.C. and Alberta) or started to explore the idea (Nova Scotia) of a common application centre.

In 2005 a joint project between the Government of Alberta and its public postsecondary institutions saw the creation of ApplyAlberta. With the goal of facilitating the application process to colleges, universities and technical institutes, ApplyAlberta offers a web-based application process and electronic transcript transfer system. With the first application received in the fall of 2009 through ApplyAlberta, there are now 21 institutions using the system.

Several other regions have thus far chosen not to adopt a common application system. For example, when the issue was raised in Nova Scotia, institutions investigated the cost and practicality of the model and concluded that the creation and operation of a common application centre for a relatively small number of institutions would place a serious financial burden on member institutions.

Even when common application centres are in place, each institution operates their own independent internal admission office and student information system. These internal systems receive application data transferred from a common application centre as well as supplemental information directly from applicants. They also support applications from returning students and internal transfers. Nova Scotia institutions did not anticipate that the development of a common application would result in any reduction of the staff required in each registrar's office.

What's lost to provinces without common application centres, however, is the ability to do cross-institutional reporting. Understanding the proportion of applicants that positioned your institution as their first choice compared to others within the province or region is difficult to capture otherwise. Getting clear statistics and trends with respect to applicant behaviour and market share across programs can help inform good SEM decision making.

In the absence of a common application centre, Atlantic Canadian institutions have instead focused on the development of an electronic network to share academic records. The electronic exchange of academic transcripts among post-secondary institutions will provide notable improvements in the quality of service to applicants moving between the secondary and post-secondary levels and amongst post-secondary institutions.

ASSESSING ADMISSIONS REQUIREMENTS

Admission officers get comfortable mastering the fine details of admission requirements. Looking beyond those requirements is critical to ensure your admission processes are meeting your SEM objectives. Here are some questions you might ask when you undertake a self-audit of the appropriateness of your admission requirements:

- What are the provincial and federal laws that might impact admission to your programs?
- Are affirmative action seats being designated for groups identified within the human rights code? How are you identifying special populations? How successful has your program been in encouraging applications among underserviced populations? How many of those applicants are admissible? What is the success rate and experience of those students?
- Have there been secondary-level curriculum changes or are there new English language proficiency tests that need to be reviewed? Are the current subject requirements adequate?
- What does each admission requirement contribute to the selection of students for the program? Evaluate how the applicant pool would look different if certain elements, such as questionnaires or essays, were included or excluded.
- Do you have 'special admission' seats set aside for individuals (often mature) who don't meet the standard admission requirements? If so, are the criteria well laid out for these seats? How successful are students admitted on this basis?
- What personal information are you requesting and storing? Is it required for the delivery of the academic program?
- Do you have a data retention policy to ensure compliance with privacy laws?

Programs which lead to a particular trade or profession may need a special review, as institutions occasionally confuse admission requirements to the academic program with the skills and attributes required to practice the profession.

Take the experience of Grant MacEwan University. The Associate Vice-President and the University's legal counsel undertook an institution-wide audit of all the admission requirements to programs and admission processes to ensure that they were defensible and bone fide. The reviewers wanted to ensure that what was needed for entry into a program was actually related to the curriculum (Ivan and Kernahan 2010).

For example, a student in a program within the health professions might be required to complete an internship following his studies. Most hospitals and other sites for internship placement will probably require criminal checks, immunizations, or other reviews. Do those requirements then need to be included as admission requirements to the program? No. Students need to be appropriately informed that employers or external agencies may have additional requirements and students who have not met such requirements may have difficulty obtaining placements or employment. However, gathering personal information, beyond that required for the delivery of our academic programs, is an invasion of privacy. A thorough review and, when necessary, a revamping of admission criteria may be required.

BUILDING AN INSTITUTION-WIDE TEAM

In large organizations, it can be particularly difficult to ensure admissions excellence across the institution. Some or all admission processes may be diversified. Application processing and overall responsibility may rest centrally, but those activities may intersect with admission committees based in faculties or programs. These committees are often comprised of faculty members and, occasionally, public citizens. The committee membership can change annually. Unlike admissions professionals in a central office, these individuals typically have careers focused in teaching or research, and often come into admission decision-making positions with little training in best practices in admissions. It's easy for minor 'tweaking' in processes or requirements to occur that over time may result in a disconnection of the institution's strategic objectives and admissions practices.

Watch for clues that things aren't going well. Are there a higher number of complaints or admission appeals in one area? Are Web sites describing processes and requirements that differ from those that are approved through the institutional governance process? Are units building IT databases outside the student information system to manage admissions?

KEEPING AN EYE ON QUALITY

It is important for the Director of Admissions or other senior admissions specialists to train faculty and department-based admissions teams. Clear expectations with respect to privacy and scope need to be set, and regular process reviews with an eye to incorporating best practices is critical. Institutions should build a network of admissions staff across the institution and meet regularly to share issues and ideas, ensure the centralized student information system is meeting the needs of the diverse units within the institution, and ensure that the applicants to every program are being well informed and well supported. SEM practices should be disseminated and well understood. In the absence of strong guidance from "the centre," it's easy for individual staff or committees to slip into questionable admission practices.

Accreditation reviews of academic programs will usually include admission processes and principles as a focus, so be ready. Review the accreditation bodies' expectations of the academic programs and graduates' competencies. What are the retention and completion rates of students in the program? Can each admission decision be defended against the regulations? Which admission requirements are required and how will those contribute to ensuring that the applicants have the appropriate background to succeed when they enter the program and to have a high likelihood of professional success upon completion?

GETTING THE DATA TO INFORM GOOD DECISIONS

Tracking the behavior of applicants is a great way to take admission data and put it to good SEM use. As institutions move into a data rich environment with better analytics tools, we can use modeling to evaluate and predict yield and retention rates. Depending on what is captured at the admission stage, we can over time build a great deal of intelligence about which applicants are most likely to enroll and thrive at our institutions, and even which applicants will remain engaged alumni.

The numbers only tell us part of the story. Surveying applicants is a great way to get the 'straight goods' on what parts of the process you're doing well in and where you're falling short, thereby quickly identifying your highest priority in admissions service improvement. Applicants can tell us which aspects of the process most influenced their relationship with our institutions and tell us how we scored. Applicants will also often share who helped them in their decision-making both outside and within the institution, what their primary reasons were for choosing your institution, and when in the recruitment and application process they became serious about the prospect of joining you. The view from the outside looking in is a valuable one. You may believe that the offer package you send to students needs serious improvement, only to discover it achieves just want you want it to, but your phone hours need to change.

FINAL THOUGHTS

The role of admissions in Canadian post-secondary education has shifted over the past decades. Adoption of SEM principles has caused admission professionals to revisit traditional approaches. Changing how we evaluate candidates, how we personalize the services, or even how the paper (and increasingly electronic) files move through the process plays a pivotal role in achieving our SEM goals. Capturing data, building relationships and ongoing review of business processes are paramount.

Although the process and approaches have changed and will continue to change in the future, the main goal of the admissions office will always remain to enrol students who will be academically successful and engaged in student life and beyond.

Peter Dueck

7

FINANCIAL AID
BALANCING ACCESS AND EXCELLENCE

/ **Chapter 7** /

The role of financial aid in Canadian post-secondary institutions is in transition, steadily shifting from that of an essential student support service to that of a key strategic enrolment management activity. This is driven by at least three factors: rising tuition fees at most universities and colleges, increasing competition for students as the number of prospective students declines in many of Canada's regions, and an increasing awareness shown by students themselves of their choices in the higher education 'marketplace'.

AWARDS, SCHOLARSHIPS AND FINANCIAL NEED

Not long ago, institutional awards programs in Canada were largely donor driven and only incidentally related to the institution's enrolment projections and goals. Institutional bursary and loan programs were designed to meet the financial needs of applicants and, though relatively small amounts were spent on entrance scholarships designed even then as registration incentives, most institutional awards were not built to influence the behavior of either prospective or in-course students.

The changes have come slowly but are now gathering momentum. Simple prizes, offered as rewards for outstanding academic achievement and requiring no subsequent registration, have been giving way to more scholarships, usually larger in value and sometimes at least partially based on non-academic factors, that require students to make registration commitments to specific programs. Similarly, while merit-based awards are changing, so are need-based awards like bursaries or grants—offered now by some Canadian institutions on a timeline that allows even these awards to influence the choices students make.

Some would trace the changing purpose of awards to the emergence of 'leadership' awards in the late eighties and early nineties—entrance scholarships that looked beyond academic achievement in an effort to attract a specific cohort of good academic students who also sported records of community service and voluntarism as well as 'potential' leadership. Others would suggest that the change began at about the same time, by fiscal restraint within provincial governments that forced institutions to make ends meet with significant increases in tuition. This resulted, in Ontario at least, in the emergence of 'tuition set-asides', which attempted to shore up accessibility by funding more generous need-based awards programs. For the same reason, and at the same time, provincial governments across the country were converting student aid programs based on relatively generous grants into all-loan programs, while most governments in Canada, both federal and provincial, were holding the line on maximum award limits. This left more and more students with increasing amounts of 'unmet need' while in school and significantly higher debt after graduation.

A DIVERSE NATION: GOVERNMENT STUDENT AID IN CANADA

Against such a backdrop, it quickly becomes clear how important it is for strategic enrolment management practitioners in Canadian post-secondary institutions to understand at least the basics of how government-sponsored student aid works in their jurisdiction before they attempt to bend their institutional financial aid programs toward the goal of supporting their enrolment management objectives. This is complicated by the fact that there are 14 different student aid programs in the country—one for each province and territory and another that is federal—all of which can and do change frequently, making the task of keeping up almost impossible, especially since students at any one institution can be receiving aid from any number of these Canadian jurisdictions. Another complication is that virtually all of the literature on the use of financial aid in SEM is based in the United States. While the American financial aid systems bear a strong resemblance to Canadian programs, the differences are significant enough to short-circuit any blind attempt to adopt U.S. practices in this area.

Little attempt will be made herein to compare Canadian and American student aid programs; rather, an effort will be made to paint the Canadian context in very broad strokes, to identify a number of the important issues to consider, and to suggest a number of possible approaches in the Canadian student aid programs. In addition, as tempting as the topic might be, no attempt will be made to analyze the SEM-like efforts of a number of Canadian governments to 'shape the class' of Canadian post-secondary education. For example, the conservative government of Brian Mulroney tried to boost enrolment (of women primarily) in the physical and applied sciences. Similarly, the liberal government under Jean Chretien attempted to identify and support (and encourage to stay in Canada) the most promising of Canada's young leaders and scholars with the establishment of the excellence awards of the Canada Millennium Scholarship Foundation.

Notwithstanding these two noteworthy ventures by Canada's federal government into the area of 'merit-based' awards, most of the government-sponsored aid in Canada since the inception of the Canada Student Loan Program (CSLP) in 1964 has been designed as 'need-based' aid, with the goal of encouraging and supporting comparatively needy students who could otherwise not afford post-secondary education.

It's also important to note, from a SEM perspective, that the very existence of government-sponsored student aid divides the world of prospective students into at least three broadly distinct groups: first, almost 50 percent of all undergraduates, according to the Canadian University Survey Consortium (CUSC), never have to rely on this form of financial support; second, just over 50 percent apply for and receive some government aid at some point in their first undergraduate program; and, third, an unknown number of otherwise capable prospective students chooses not to continue studies beyond grade 12, possibly because of fears that student aid will be inadequate, too costly to repay, or both.

The old joke among Canadian financial aid officers was that the federal government met 60 percent of a student's financial need, the provincial government met 40 percent of the need, and then the institution, with its various need-based programs, met the remaining 10 percent. This was only grimly funny, of course, to those who understood that an aid package valued at 110 percent of the government assessed need might still be insufficient to get a student through the year. But, it also clearly underscored the understanding that post-secondary educational (PSE) institutions were usually only able to tinker with a student's aid package after the government had quit the field.

STUDENT AID NEED ASSESSMENTS

In general, the way student aid works is easy to understand. Each application is subjected to a 'need assessment', where 'assessed need' is the difference between 'allowable expenses' and 'expected resources'. Assessed need rises as governments permit increases in a student's allowable expenses, alongside hikes in tuition and the cost of books and living costs; assessed need falls as governments expect more by way of a student's personal resources, when higher contributions are expected, for example, from parents or from summer earnings. An 'aid package' is then identified consisting of federal and provincial loans and grants (in amounts that vary by jurisdiction) up to either the level of 'assessed need' or the maximum aid package available, whichever comes first. It sounds simple, but of course the devil, as always, is in the details.

Why is it so important for institutional SEM practitioners and their partners in awards offices to understand the government-sponsored student aid context in their jurisdictions? One example may help to clarify this. Suppose a student is single and living 'away from his parents', and suppose his 'assessed needs' are met and his 'expected resources' (*i.e.*, his parental contribution and his pre-study period earnings) are in place. How much is he allowed to spend each month on living costs? Using Manitoba as an example, the answer for the year 2009–10 was exactly $929. But, because of exemptions set by the program, this number can change. The basic monthly allowance of $929 can increase to $1141 if the student earns the full earnings exemption of $1700 (or more) during that year's eight month study period. Or, even if he earns nothing but instead wins awards totaling the full awards exemption of $1800 (or more), he could now spend $1154 per month. And, finally, if he earns $1700 *and* receives $1800 in awards, taking advantage of exemptions applied in both categories, he could now spend $1366 per month, an increase of almost 50 percent over the basic allowance.

WHEN A STUDENT'S REALITY DOES NOT MATCH EXPECTATIONS

Let's consider another case that would almost certainly cause a student to consider dropping out of school. Suppose this student's 'expected resources' from a parental contribution falls short by $4000. In the first instance, her living allowance would fall precipitously by $500 per month (*i.e.*, by $4000/8 months), or from $929 to

$429, an amount too low to support her in any reasonable way. Now, suppose the institution she was attending decided to help her financially by replacing this short-fall with a bursary of $4000, exactly filling the gap. Would the student again be able to spend the basic monthly living allowance of $929?

No. Because the award exemption for the eight-month study period is only $1800, the student's monthly living allowance would increase by only $225 (*i.e.*, by $1800/8 months) to $654. Knowing this, the institutional awards officer would be more careful in order to maximize the available exemptions, offering the student a bursary of $1800 and a work-study position or other employment promising income of $1700, leaving the student with a more generous monthly living allowance of $866.50.

Aside from going underground or taking unreported gifts in kind, there really is no better option for the student in this example—or the institution. More generous solutions can actually be counterproductive. Any additional award money or in-course income is either clawed back by the student aid program in the second term disbursement or declared an 'over-award' and clawed back at the start of the next academic year. (To be fair, the provincial authority may be persuaded to waive the parental contribution if it is made aware of something like a serious rift in the family, so the awards officer would first have negotiated on behalf of the student for a more satisfactory resolution of the circumstances.)

Whatever feelings might be about the efforts government-sponsored aid programs make to level the playing field for all applicants, the need assessments themselves are unlikely to change overnight. The optimal solutions to these kinds of problems cannot be simple and will require the input of awards officers familiar with student aid program structures.

GOVERNMENT AID FROM A STUDENT PERSPECTIVE

Among the characteristics of government student aid in Canada, there are a number of factors that are likely to play some role in the decisions prospective students make when determining whether a post-secondary education is accessible to them. Students are advised to consider the following variables and ask themselves:

- *Reliability of anticipated funding sources*: Will the need assessment reflect my actual financial circumstances? Do I actually have the resources expected of me, and will my parents or spouse really make the contribution expected of them?

- *Unmet need*: Will the aid available to me be adequate? And, if not, how can I make up the difference?
- *Debt load*: Will I be able to afford to repay the loan portion? Do I have enough good information to make a reasonable decision about this?
- *Financial security, transparency and predictability*: Is the system fair and reasonable? Will I be able to understand how it works? Will I make it through my program before I lose eligibility?
- *Contingencies*: What about a safety net? What happens if there is a financial emergency?
- *Timing*: When will I know what my total aid package will be? (How much risk is associated with a very late promise of an aid package?)

SUPPLEMENTING GOVERNMENT AID WITH INSTITUTIONAL BURSARY SUPPORT

In Canada, student aid packages are put together by provincial and territorial governments. Consequently, most financial aid officers argue that post-secondary educational (PSE) institutions can only respond reasonably to accessibility concerns for financially needy students after need assessments and aid packages are determined by provincial and territorial jurisdictions—often only shortly before the start of classes. The timing of these provincial decisions explains why need-based (*i.e.*, bursary) programs at PSE institutions often have application deadlines about one month after classes begin and selection decisions shortly before the end of the first term. In SEM terms, these institutional need-based awards are designed not to recruit students but to help retain those who might otherwise withdraw from courses when funds dry up at the end of first term– a marked difference from the experience in the U.S.

Nevertheless, some universities in Canada are timing their institutional bursary programs to more closely resemble what happens at American institutions. McGill University is one such institution, which is not surprising since McGill attracts a large number of American students. McGill starts awarding need-based aid to newly accepted students in February and completes this process in June, using College Board financial need assessments for American and other international students. While no direct link is made by McGill between this relatively early offer of need-based aid and the university's SEM initiatives, the point is that the timing of the bursary program allows prospective students to make decisions about where to go to school with much better information about how much need-based aid will be available to them at this institution, and this is the kind of tactic that supports the accessibility initiatives in a SEM plan.

The fact that government-sponsored student aid applications become available in late April or early May—and sometimes as late as June—presents a significant challenge to SEM practitioners in Canada, particularly for institutions that cannot rely solely on the local catchment area for enough new students. Other institutions besides McGill, like the University of Toronto and the University of Waterloo, also offer some need-based awards as early as spring and early summer. SEM-focused recruitment 'yield' activities require such timing but are challenged by the late need assessment at the government level. At the University of Windsor, for example, deans frequently ask to identify ways to build and offer comprehensive award packages not only for American prospects, but also for Canadians. The challenge arises not only from the timing of the government-based aid, but also from the very fact that institutional aid and government aid are packaged independently.

The problem can be largely overcome by institutions that trust their own need assessments (or, for their American students, the need assessments provided by an authorized third party like the College Board). While there may be no direct way to synchronize the institutional need-based aid package with the one provided by government, it should at least be possible for the government need assessment to incorporate institutional aid as a partially exempted resource. Because of fairly high exemption levels for institutional awards in the government need assessment, the government aid package for most students would not even be affected by these 'early offer' institutional bursaries, except occasionally in a positive way. Even when institutional bursary amounts exceed government exemptions, the affected students would simply be getting lower loan amounts, which is usually a desirable result from the student perspective; significantly more non-repayable institutional aid plus slightly less repayable government aid adds up to more aid for the year and less debt overall. (Complications arise in those relatively few instances when the institutional bursary replaces provincial non-repayable assistance; few institutions are happy to provide bursary support that is then clawed back, dollar for dollar, by government.)

OTHER APPROACHES TO INSTITUTIONAL BURSARY SUPPORT

The University of Winnipeg, with its campus located in that city's core area, is building a so-called 'Opportunity Fund' to allow it to create post-secondary educational options for youth from inner-city neighbourhoods, Aboriginal students, and young people from war-affected nations and refugee populations. The program is comprehensive in its approach, including: a "tap on the shoulder" for students who show academic promise in the form of tuition credits earned as early as Grade 4; fast-track bursaries for tuition fees, emergency childcare, food, and shelter; and on-campus learning spaces and service supports. The Opportunity Fund program includes a transition year experience for entry-level students and a hands-on educational experience for younger children, with a focus on science, the environment, and traditional indigenous knowledge.

From a SEM perspective, what makes the Fund program compelling is the fact that its construction so deliberately supports the institutional mission of making the university as accessible for students as possible, and "a community which appreciates, fosters and promotes values of human dignity, equality, nondiscrimination and appreciation of diversity" (University of Winnipeg 2010).

Programs like this demonstrate that Canadian institutions are taking the call for more comprehensive approaches to the issues of under-represented and at-risk populations to heart. York University offers another example of this type of approach. Its transition year program is for at-risk students or former students in the local community who have experienced significant personal and financial challenges and who are receiving financial support. Students in this program take 30 credits in total, partly for credit and partly as academic bridging. Meanwhile, the university provides students with full financial support in the pilot year with awards covering tuition and living expenses.

A recent study by the Social Research and Development Corporation (SRDC) provides evidence that the timing of an offer of aid may have a significant impact on the kinds of choices made by prospective PSE students who are concerned about finances. An aspect of the study called *Learning Accounts* promised lower-income

New Brunswick students entering Grade 10 an $8,000 bursary for PSE. Among first generation students, *Learning Accounts*:

- Increased from 40 to 52 percent the proportion [in Francophone schools] strongly recognizing that they needed to keep studying after high school to achieve what they want in life...
- Increased from 87 to 96 percent the proportion [in Anglophone schools] with aspirations to achieve a post-secondary credential... (SRDC 2009a)

And, in another demonstration that a comprehensive approach works better, the study also offered enhanced career education workshops, called *Explore Your Horizons*, in the last three years of high school, finding that among lower-income, lower-education families, this program also resulted in similar changed attitudes in students about PSE attendance (SRDC 2009a).

Furthermore, a 2006 study on the impact of bursaries on student persistence showed the importance of this non-repayable aid, finding that:

> *Students who receive a grant as well as or in addition to a loan complete more required credits than those who do not; they are also more likely to have earned their degree during the five-year tracking period ... [and] grant-and-loan recipients with the highest levels of financial need were almost five times as likely to earn a degree as those who got only loans* (McElroy 2006, p. 2).

This conclusion has been supported elsewhere in studies initiated by the Millennium Foundation. One of these, *Foundations for Success*, was a pilot project run at three Ontario community colleges set up in three groups:

- A 'services' group that was supplied with case managers to refer students with questions and concerns to services that could help.
- A 'services plus' group that included students who received the same benefit but were also eligible to receive a bursary valued at $750 (*i.e.*, about half the value of one term's tuition) if they participated in support programming.
- A control group that received neither of these benefits.

Interim results from the project "show that financial incentives can be effective at influencing the behaviour of at-risk students...[and] participation in the support services leads to better academic performance and persistence" (Parkin and Baldwin 2009a, 80–81). Two lessons are suggested. First, non-repayable awards of even fairly modest amounts can influence the behaviour of students, and, second, at-risk students who avail themselves of the support services set up to help them tend to be more successful.

Most PSE institutions in Canada have designed need-based supports to help students 'in-course' and to help prevent them from withdrawing for financial reasons. These retention supports commonly include emergency loans and bursaries, work-study, and even food banks for students with the most extreme need. They also include tuition deferrals, which serve in place of short-term emergency loans to ensure that aid recipients can, at best, avoid late payment penalties and, at worst, avoid having to drop out of school when their student aid disbursements do not arrive before tuition payment deadlines.

In this context, it is important for SEM administrators to take care when attempting to divert resources from in-course awards designed to support retention or student persistence to fund entrance awards for recruitment purposes. A careful balance between recruitment and retention initiatives must be struck when resources to fund awards in both categories are limited. After all, while financial distress is only one barrier to student persistence, the effect of insufficient in-course support, especially when combined with other factors, can be significant.

SUPPORTING SEM GOALS

Post-secondary institutions that have adopted SEM initiatives are interested in 'shaping their classes' while enrolling the optimum number of students for their various programs. Besides overall target enrolment numbers, many institutions set targets for specific groups of students, such as international students and Aboriginal students. Some SEM programs also set special student population targets for other identifiable cohorts, like visible minorities, students with disabilities, and so on. Some institutions run differentiated scholarship programs in an effort to focus on undersubscribed academic programs, offering different scholarship amounts to prospective students for different programs.

In 2008, Don Hossler and David Kalsbeek, two leading American SEM theorists, identified six primary SEM goals (here conflated to five):

- Improving market position and market demand.
- Enhancing academic profile.
- Opening opportunity and improving diversity (economic, geographic, first generation, racial/ethnic, under-represented, international).
- Improving persistence and graduation rates.
- Increasing net revenue.

These goals, of course, would have to flow from the institutional mission and vision. Put another way, if SEM is about 'shaping the class,' the institution should first be clear about what an appropriate class would look like. Choosing which of the primary SEM goals to emphasize and which aspects of each to highlight helps to shape and define SEM tactics—including student financial aid strategies.

Most Canadian universities have been focused for a long time on 'enhancing the academic profile' of their student body and 'opening opportunity' to students with insufficient financial resources—the long-standing pursuits of excellence on the one hand and accessibility on the other. As such, Canadian universities have been practicing a rudimentary form of SEM for at least three decades, and probably much longer than that. Entrance scholarships meant to attract the most capable students and bursaries (or need-based awards) meant to support financially needy students have been in existence in many cases almost as long as the institutions themselves. That said, the increasing competition for students, especially students with particular characteristics, and the growing use of both merit-based and need-based awards to gain advantages in that competition are more recent phenomena. (Meanwhile, Canada's colleges, typically with less selective admission policies and significantly less by way of scholarship and bursary money than Canadian universities, are more recent converts to the notion of using financial aid to support enrolment goals.)

A CAUTIONARY NOTE

Because SEM is by definition so intentional and because it usually relies at least in part on the use of awards funded by operating budget dollars to achieve its goals, it seems particularly prudent for institutional administrators, especially those at public institutions, to enter the SEM arena with clear eyes and a balanced approach. Hossler and Kalsbeek point to critics of SEM who "have equated enrollment management with a range of specific strategies designed to deliberately shape enrollment outcomes such as increasing selectivity, optimizing net revenue, and improving student academic profile—all in ways that work against broad educational values and the social good" (Hossler and Kalsbeek 2008, p. 4). They go on to note that "enrollment management strategies can and do bring a calculated, empirical perspective on and market orientation toward the real costs and the consequences of espoused values such as increasing diversity and access" (p. 4).

True enough. In the Canadian context, the criticism serves as an important reminder to administrators, especially those at public institutions, that the institutional mission and vision should accord with the educational and social values of their regions and that SEM strategies and tactics, particularly those that include student financial support, should always be practiced with these values in mind.

SHAPING THE CLASS: INSTITUTIONAL MERIT-BASED AWARDS

The most common use of financial aid to help 'shape the class' is with entrance awards, also known as tuition discounts when funded from operating budgets. Most Canadian universities attempt to attract high-achieving entering students with these tuition discounts, and these are often renewable (especially for the best students) for each year of the academic program as long as academic and sometimes other performance thresholds are met.

These entrance scholarships are usually awarded either strictly on the basis of high school averages, though most universities now offer entrance scholarships based in part on leadership and community service as well. The focus on attracting student leaders is seductive since these kinds of students are likely to raise the school's profile and also because it seems likely that other students, the friends and classmates of these leaders, might follow them to the school.

Some institutions have begun to offer 'value-added' awards, where traditional scholarship dollars are supplemented with other 'perks', ranging in value from passes to sporting events (worth less than $100) to guaranteed graduate fellowships (worth tens of thousands of dollars). The University of Manitoba has such a program for its President's Scholars, open to all entering students with high school averages of 95 percent and higher. Academic mentorships, highly prized by many top scholars, are another way to add value to traditional recruitment awards. The

University of Windsor is one example of an institution that offers a generous and well-organized program of this sort, even providing employment income to undergraduate researchers in this program.

Brock University has chosen to focus on entering students who combine high academic achievement and personal leadership abilities. As previously noted, Brock is hardly alone in offering awards that recognize leadership and voluntarism alongside academic achievement, but Brock has extended the idea, building the Brock Leaders Citizenship Society. High-achieving student leaders in the Society organize the activities of members and are required to contribute about 40 hours of volunteer time to their communities in order to qualify for award renewal. Opportunities also exist for Society members to take advantage of a laddered multi-year leadership training program.

How effective are entrance scholarship programs, particularly guaranteed programs that offer progressively larger scholarships to entering students with better high school averages, in attracting more academically gifted students? A recent study of Ontario universities by researchers at McMaster University suggests that "with one exception [*i.e.*, for Engineering programs], merit scholarships have at most a small effect on the ability of a university to increase its share of academically strong students," adding that, because "...a higher net cost is associated with an increase in the proportion of students from high income areas relative to the proportion from low-income areas...merit aid influences not so much the number as the type of academically strong students that a university can attract." The suggestion is that this "form of 'sticker price' competition...may have stronger appeal to students from less affluent families." (Dooley, Payne, and Robb 2010, p. 24)

The authors note that only two of the 19 universities in the study offered guaranteed entrance scholarships to students with averages of 80 and better in 1994, but that this number rose to 13 by 2005. This observation supports a wide-spread belief that there is something of an 'arms race' underway in Canada in our efforts to attract top students with these types of awards; most universities do not want to be out of the competition, and, as a result, no real competitive advantage may be gained. Since a non-proliferation treaty is probably not in the cards, there is at least an implicit suggestion that institutions would do well to find the most balanced approach possible under the circumstances while continuing in their attempts to develop and assert other forms of differentiation specific to their particular higher education context.

One response to the 'arms race' is to try something completely different and to test the effectiveness of the new approach. The University of British Columbia is exploring ways to repurpose current entrance award funding to be used for high impact experiences for students. UBC's Strategic Plan, *Place and Promise,* talks about providing all students with at least two enriched educational opportunities during their course of studies. (University of British Columbia 2009) In an effort to deliver on the promise, UBC piloted a "Place and Promise Award" with the Faculty of Forestry in September 2010, with a portion of entrance award funding used to support the program. Each direct-entry undergraduate Forestry student receives the promise of up to $2,000 to engage in an activity of their own choosing, such as 'Go Global', undergraduate research with a faculty member, a volunteer experience, community service learning, field trips, and so on. The experience cannot be a requirement of their program and may be completely outside their Faculty. The funding may be applied to an experience any time after completion of their first year, and the money will go directly to the coordinator of the experience to help the student defray costs. Most significantly, a review of the pilot program could lead to an expanded program for all entering students.

In fact, the intention currently is to roll the program out to all undergraduate students entering UBC in 2011. Although the administrative details have not yet all been worked out, the money will likely flow directly to the student who has been accepted for one of these extracurricular experiences. The disbursement is not to be seen as employment income, but rather as an offset to the unique costs associated with the experience, including lost earnings elsewhere (*e.g.*, if a student is accepted to do some undergraduate research that may preclude full-time summer employment). Clearly, UBC wants to make a statement about the fact that these types of high-impact experiences are valued as a unique component of an education there, while encouraging broader participation among middle-income and lower-income groups in sometimes quite expensive activities like exchanges and community service learning projects.

But, suppose the goal is not to enhance the university's academic profile, but to improve opportunity and diversity. How would one use the institutional awards program to make real gains in this area? The answer to this is not simple, and begins with other questions: Opportunity for whom? What kind of diversity? If the goal is to provide more opportunity for financially needy students, it would seem prudent to tailor non-repayable need-based aid awards (usually called bursaries in Canada) to complement the government-sponsored aid programs of the provincial authority. In addition, bursary programs should be set inside a more comprehensive program to assist needy students, along with work-study, food banks, and emergency aid programs, and alongside supports that focus on non-financial needs, be those academic, social, cultural, or personal. Targeted student recruitment campaigns, engaging high school counselors in selected schools and parents or community organizations in selected communities or neighbourhoods and focusing on the total aid packages available to capable students, should front the effort.

ADEQUATE AID: AN INSTITUTIONAL PROMISE

What if an institution is already active in all or many of these ways? Perhaps what is needed then is a simple and concrete message on affordability, backed by a plan that reduces financial risk. Since no institution is likely to have the resources to go it alone in this area, it makes more sense to work in partnership with the provincial or territorial student aid authority. One example is the effort currently underway in Manitoba to provide 'unmet need' grants or bursaries to 'high need' students in most programs (not including certain professional programs like Medicine and Dentistry). The province has committed to providing the first non-repayable award of up to $5,000 and the institutions have committed to do what they can, again up to $5,000 per student. Awards of this size, communicated early enough to prospective students who have already demonstrated a strong desire to attend a PSE institution, might not have a great influence in recruitment but should have a much stronger effect on student persistence.

An even bolder approach was taken by the University of Toronto beginning in 1998, when its governing council approved a policy on student financial support making it unique among Canadian universities in providing assurance of financial support and in promising that students will have access to financial counselling. The statement of principle said that "no student offered admission to a program at the University of Toronto should be unable to enter or complete the program due to lack of financial means" (University of Toronto 1998). Students are expected to rely on support from the Ontario Student Assistance Program (OSAP), up to the level of the maximum OSAP loan; assessed need which remains unmet above the OSAP maximum will be met primarily through grants for students in first-entry undergraduate programs and through a mix of grants and institutionally negotiated loans for students in second-entry professional programs (both undergraduate and graduate), with the appropriate mix of grants and loans varying across these programs. Of course, a promise like this assumes a sufficient level of resources within the institution to allow it to follow through on the promise, and it also depends on the provincial government to maintain or shrink the unmet need levels of its student aid recipients so the promise remains affordable (a point noted in the policy itself).

This idea was picked up by the government of Ontario in 2006 and mandated for all of the province's colleges and universities as the Student Access Guarantee. Through this guarantee, the Government of Ontario requires that every public college and university in Ontario provides enough financial aid to cover the assessed needs of their students for tuition, books, and mandatory fees if these are not fully met by OSAP. Students in a first-entry program are automatically considered for the guarantee based on their OSAP application, whether or not they also apply to their post-secondary institution for financial aid. The aid is provided through a combination of bursaries, scholarships, work-study programs and summer employment programs. Presumably, much of the funding to support the guarantee comes from tuition set-aside revenue, potentially creating a significant burden on institutions that enrol larger numbers of students from low socio-economic backgrounds. While the real impact of this program is still unknown, it does warrant the careful attention of SEM administrators. Large-scale external initiatives like this change the way awards programs are structured and managed, especially in light of the need to ensure the availability of adequate resources to fund them.

SUPPORT FOR INTERNATIONAL STUDENTS

Targeting awards for international students, a group of particular interest at many institutions because of the higher tuitions paid by these students (besides the obvious benefits to classroom diversity), brings its own set of complications. International students are required by Canadian immigration authorities to demonstrate sufficient resources before they are eligible for study permits. Need-based awards would therefore have to fully round out the 'expected resources' of each award recipient; at the extreme, students with no visible means of support would require awards of $20,000 per year or more, depending on tuition rates. Performing realistic 'need assessments' for these students is notoriously and understandably vexing, though institutions like McGill University, as mentioned earlier, are using the College Board need assessment instrument to help standardize the calculation.

Building suitable and equitable selection criteria for merit-based international student awards is also a challenge, though more possible if scholarships are allocated on a country-by-country basis. Some institutions have been criticized for widely marketing international student scholarships, even though only one or two awards of relatively little value are available for students from any one country or, even worse, for all international students at that institution. There are critics in the PSE community who argue that such efforts raise false hope; however, as long as these programs are clear and transparent in the available benefits, they are not, strictly speaking, unethical. Put more positively, every consideration should be given to building awards programs that are authentic and realistic in what they offer. Meanwhile, given the in-country local media coverage that awards to international students can often generate, not to mention the elevation of visibility and status that the Canadian institution can enjoy, a carefully developed international student awards program is likely to boost recruitment success.

These are real issues for nearly all institutions, since both universities and colleges are quickly ramping up efforts to become competitive in the international student marketplace. While participating institutions could be competitive without scholarship offerings a few years ago; a carefully considered award program for these students is now essential. More thought needs to be given to how SEM principles are used to examine international student support in the coming years.

FUNDING SEM FINANCIAL AID INITIATIVES

As we know, institutional awards are generally funded in one of three ways: from the interest earnings on endowed capital (usually received from individual or multiple private donors); from pledged annual donations (often received from corporations or associations); or from the institution's own operating budget. Twenty-five years ago, members of the Canadian Association of Financial Aid Administrators reported relatively minor contributions from the third category, and most awards were funded from endowment income or from pledges. This has changed dramatically over the years and awards officers at many institutions now report that at least the bulk of their entrance scholarship programs are funded from operating budgets.

Both endowment funds and amounts pledged to support annual awards have risen sharply over the same period, especially as universities, and more recently colleges, have built significant and sophisticated fund-raising offices and programs. Assisted in some cases by government-sponsored matching donation programs—those in Alberta, Ontario, and Manitoba come to mind—an increasing number of donors are eager to help fund student support initiatives with either merit-based or need-based aid usually as directed by the donor.

USING DATA IN FINANCIAL AID PLANNING

Rather than relying solely on donor directives to shape these programs, it might be advisable from a SEM perspective to undertake intentional fundraising initiatives that are designed to build support for comprehensive and targeted awards programs. Institutions should at least examine their current awards, faculty by faculty and level by level, and then consider what a more optimal program would look like, always with an eye to achieving specific student recruitment and retention targets. Such an approach is likely to require considerable cooperation among leaders in the academic units, the fundraising office, and the awards office. Kick-starting an effort like this might fall to the director of the awards office, since this is where the profile of the awards program in each academic unit is most easily drawn up. Given the increasing numbers of alumni who live abroad, this area is also likely to require more energy and attention in the fundraising office.

Data are required to understand the current situation, identify gaps and barriers, and suggest a future path. The specific data needs of an individual institution will depend on its SEM recruitment and retention goals, but some basic questions will be common to most institutions. Consideration should be given first to the awards profile report, listing awards by academic unit against both the total amounts disbursed by award type (*i.e.*, bursaries, loans, work-study, scholarships that require subsequent registration and prizes that have no such requirement, and so on) and the total number of award recipients (perhaps also by type, depending on what subpopulations are of interest). How do these numbers vary by academic unit and how do they compare to the institutional 'norm' or average? Are other external benchmarks available?

A good analysis of a need-based award program depends on knowing the unit-based profile of those students who have identified themselves as financially needy, namely the student aid and bursary applicants. It also depends on knowing the government-sponsored student aid context, particularly that of the local provincial jurisdiction. For example, how do student aid recipients, on the one hand, and how do institutional aid recipients, on the other, compare with all other students when looking at voluntary withdrawal rates (full-time to part-time and complete drop-outs); when looking at year-to-year continuation rates, graduation rates, academic achievement (as measured by GPA at predetermined points in time)? How do Aboriginal students or international students (or other identifiable sub-populations) compare with all other students when looking at those same characteristics?

Tracking institutional efforts to recruit and retain under-represented students, while essential to the process, can be difficult. A recent study by the Social Research and Demonstration Corporation (SRDC) points to the importance of collecting meaningful data on under-represented groups, while cautioning institutional practitioners on the challenges inherent in trying to achieve useful results. The study points to common data gaps that result from challenges in a number of specific areas, as follows:

- A lack of consistent definitions for under-represented groups, resulting in incomparability over time and across institutions and jurisdictions.
- Difficulties identifying the target groups, including the potential reluctance to self-identify especially at sensitive points in the student cycle.
- The inability to access or link datasets due to a lack of common identifiers and limitations imposed by the regulatory environment.
- A lack of outcome measures and longitudinal data.
- A lack of adequate resources to collect and analyze data.

(Currie and Leonard 2009)

It makes sense to keep these challenges in mind as persistent efforts are made to collect more meaningful and helpful data in this area.

Then, if the provincial student aid context is so important, what is the local 'living allowance rate' (per month, say, for a single student living 'away from parents')? What are the federal and provincial exemptions for in-course income and awards? How many students in each academic unit have identifiable 'unmet need'? And, what is the total and average amount of that 'unmet need'? What is the debt-load of the institution's graduating students? What is the student loan default rate of the institution's former student aid recipients?—an important number since institutional eligibility for government aid designation now depends on it. And, how much of this information can be broken down by academic unit?

BUILDING SEM-BASED AWARDS PROGRAMS

As architects of institutional student award programs that support the enrolment goals of the academic unit, deans working alongside fundraising and awards administrators might do well to sketch out the gaps between their current award programs and more optimal future programs and seek to engage prospective donors in efforts to build stronger and more comprehensive award offerings. This turns what is now often a relatively passive effort to raise award dollars into a much more purposeful and intentional SEM-oriented initiative.

Baldwin and Parker (2007) and the College Board (2008) outlined a number of principles to guide the reform of government student aid; the slightly modified list offered here could guide the construction of effective new aid programs as a part of an institutional SEM initiative.

Institutional student award programs should be:

- Student-focused; targeted to the right students at the right time and in the right amounts.
- Supportive of both access and success, with an appropriate mix of bursaries, scholarships, and other aid.
- Constructed to fit within the context of government student aid programs and other institutional recruitment and retention/success efforts.
- Clear, predictable, and well communicated.
- Adequately funded and administratively efficient.
- Monitored continually for effectiveness in meeting stated goals.
- Ethically sensitive.

HUMAN RIGHTS LEGISLATION AND TARGETED AID

The last point noted above may seem particularly obvious in this politically correct age; after all, no institution today would consider accepting a donation to support an award for a white Protestant Canadian male student entering Medicine, for example, no matter how much money the donor is offering. But, ethical violations need not be nearly this blatant to run afoul of Canada's numerous variations of provincial human rights legislation, not to mention plain common sense. Whether overtly adopted as institutional policy or not, most institutions would not "administer a new [award] that discriminates on the bases of the 'applicable characteristics' enumerated in the [provincial] Human Rights Code" (The University of Manitoba 2009), except where it can be demonstrated that students with those characteristics are significantly under-represented in the student population. And, when those applicable characteristics include ancestry (including colour and perceived race); nationality or national origin; ethnic background or origin; religion or creed; age; sex; gender-determined characteristics; sexual orientation; marital or family status; source of income; political belief, association, or activity; a physical or mental disability (all of which are outlined, for example, in the Manitoba Human Rights Code), targeted awards deserve close scrutiny to ensure that affirmative action can clearly be demonstrated in light of current legal and ethical realities. Furthermore, if affirmative action in specific cases should no longer be warranted or legally defensible, sunset clauses and fall-back criteria should be contemplated within the terms of reference of these targeted awards.

At the University of Manitoba, for example, exceptions to the policy outlined above "are occasionally warranted when it can be demonstrated that systemic discrimination may exist that results in the under-representation of identified sub-populations in the province and/or when the proposed award has as its objective the amelioration of conditions of disadvantaged individuals or groups..." As a result, awards that identify any of the 'applicable characteristics' listed in the Code "shall be made only with the consent of the unit concerned, the Senate Committee on Awards, and the Senate." Because of this policy, awards at the University of Manitoba for women in the physical sciences, for example, can generally only exist if female students number less than 40 percent of the students in these programs on a three-year running average.

All of this suggests that institutional SEM practitioners have their work cut out for them as they bend their award programs to the purpose of improving their student recruitment and retention efforts. Nevertheless, there appears to be significant room for new and creative solutions in this complex field. Begin initiatives in this area by learning as much as possible about the needs and wants of our students themselves, as well as the obstacles or perceptions of obstacles that stand in the way of so many capable high school graduates who choose not to participate in the post-secondary educational experience.

EVALUATING OUR WORK AND THE WAY FORWARD

The final word in this discussion of the role of financial aid in Canadian SEM should remind us to remain vigilant in evaluating the various strategies and tactics we adopt to help us achieve our enrolment management goals. Is the PSE sector ready to handle this issue with more rigour than has been evident in the past? The previously mentioned article on institutional data-readiness undertaken by the SRDC and published by the Canada Millennium Scholarship Foundation serves to underscore the importance of this evaluative function for improving our efforts with any student subpopulation:

> *In addition to developing and implementing innovative support programs and strategies, improving the access and retention of under-represented students in Canadian PSE also requires a commitment to evaluating and measuring the impacts of these investments. Institutions themselves can demonstrate such commitment by ensuring that their vision and objectives for access and retention are clearly articulated and broadly communicated, thus enabling program delivery staff to design their evaluation questions and data collection instruments so that [the data generated] 'feeds' naturally into the institution's access and retention objectives* (Currie and Leonard 2009, p. 19).

Part of what makes this evaluative function so difficult is that we already know that a single intervention, with impacts that can be easily measured, is likely to be less effective. Because of this, we are more likely to build initiatives with multiple interventions, some financial and others not. While this might complicate the evaluation process, we should stay the course.

In broad terms, the work ahead is not hard to understand. When Andrew Parkin, research director at the Canada Millennium Scholarship Foundation, mused on a decade of ambitious research undertakings at the Foundation's close, he concluded that

> *...an effective access policy must have three pillars:*
> * *Better outreach to and preparation of students well before they reach post-secondary education;*
> * *More effective student financial assistance programs;*
> * *Improved support programs for students once they have enrolled in post-secondary education.*

(Parkin 2009, pp. 210–211)

Adding the institutional SEM perspective, a fourth pillar is needed:
- More focussed institutional student financial assistance and related programs that support the institution's mission and its clearly articulated SEM objectives.

Years ago, the Canadian Institute for Nonprofit Organizations published a fundraising guide for nonprofit groups entitled, somewhat ironically, *Money Isn't Everything* (Fisher 1977). Though the context is different, the title is instructive, even when we understand that money in the form of scholarships and bursaries can be significant enough for students who are weighing their various study options and critically important for students who believe that the resources available to them are either insufficient or too debt-heavy in the long run to allow them a reasonable opportunity to study at the post-secondary level. Money for students *is* important, of course, but it isn't everything. A well-designed and well-executed SEM plan will include more comprehensive and holistic approaches that address other obstacles believed by prospective and current students to stand in their path as they consider which institution to attend or, more fundamentally, as they consider whether a post-secondary education in Canada is within their reach.

Stefanie Ivan and Gail Forsyth

8

STUDENT AFFAIRS

/ **Chapter 8** /

Student affairs organizations in Canada's post-secondary institutions continue to evolve to meet the complex student and enrolment needs of their institutions. In recent years, there has been an increased recognition of the contributions of student affairs on strategic enrolment management (SEM) practices in Canada. In some institutions, student affairs leaders are being invited to take part in strategic planning and curriculum development to optimize enrolment and university goals. In other institutions, it is the student affairs professionals who are leading SEM initiatives and inviting academic leaders and senior administrators to discuss SEM practices designed to improve the student experience. This is a significant paradigm shift and forms the foundation of the future of student affairs and SEM in Canada.

HISTORY AND CULTURE OF STUDENT AFFAIRS AND THE ACADEMIC COMMUNITY

To more fully understand why this shift is important, one needs to understand the foundations of the student affairs profession. Historically, the philosophical focus has been on the individual student and what is best for that student. The literature that guides the overarching mandate, mission and operational philosophy of student affairs is, for the most part, defined by student development theory. Student affairs professionals tend to conceptualize their roles in terms of fostering individual student growth and development and embracing the concept of "*in loco parentis*." Arthur Chickering (1993), Richard Keeling (2008) and George Kuh (2005a) have argued that paradigm shifts are necessary, and maintain that learning occurs everywhere on campus. They believe that more can be achieved when an institution considers all aspects of the student learning experience, especially if it is done in an intentional and integrated manner.

Due to the particular services that student affairs areas provide to students, individuals or units, many student affairs practitioners tend to focus on specialized areas of strength and provide personalized support services to individuals or groups of students with similar needs. Their areas of focus tend to be in academic, employment and career advising, services to international students, health services, counseling support, sports and recreation, co-operative education, residential life, volunteer experiences, campus clubs and other out-of-class services. Individuals who are hired to work in student affairs are often attracted to the profession and recruited because of their specialization and interest in working with students and supporting individual and personal development. This specialized service approach and structure has sometimes meant that student affairs professionals are insulated from one another, resulting in mini-silos within the field. It has also limited the ability of student affairs professionals to understand their role within the institutional context. This has often posed interesting internal operational and organizational challenges.

ORGANIZATIONAL STRUCTURES

When one looks at organizational structures of student affairs in Canada, many models exist. Often student affairs departments have been organized as separate units with very different reporting structures, leading to varying opportunities to engage with the academic community.

At some institutions, the student affairs division reports directly to the president. Although one would assume that this would be an ideal model offering many opportunities for collaboration, too often this has not been the reality. That is, the traditional silos have been maintained with student affairs professionals continuing to focus on the "out-of-class" experience in isolation from academic affairs, which oversees academic and curriculum development. Even at colleges and universities where the registrar's office—traditionally viewed as an academic support service— has been placed organizationally within the student affairs portfolio, the silos have been maintained.

Over the past five to ten years many institutions have created senior student affairs positions (some at the vice presidential level) that have attempted to break down the "two solitudes" of academic and student affairs. The presence of the senior student affairs professional at this level generates new opportunities for collaboration and reciprocal learning and creates a wider lens of organizational understanding. Both academic and student affairs acquire a heightened awareness of the institution's complexities, and there is a greater opportunity to benefit from existing synergies and to address the systemic issues that have been problematic. This new forum has led to the development of a new range of initiatives designed to enhance the learning experience of students in a more holistic manner. It is an exciting new era for both student affairs and academic affairs professionals—and provides an opportunity to overcome differing philosophical views for the overall betterment of the institution. It also results in benefits to students because they are given a more integrated learning experience.

Case Study: Wilfrid Laurier University, Waterloo

Wilfrid Laurier University is a mid-sized, multi-campus university. It is known for its campus vitality, sense of community and passionate school spirit. During the university's envisioning process in 2008, it became clear that student affairs contributed significantly to the student experience and the institution's reputation. In 2009, an organizational realignment was undertaken and in 2010, Wilfrid Laurier University appointed its first Vice-President of Student Affairs. This appointment is important as it illustrates the recognition of the impact of Student Affairs on the total academic and student experience. In June 2010, the Vice-President of Student Affairs invited and secured the support of the Vice-President of Academic and Vice-President and Principal of Brantford Campus to co-lead a team of senior officials at the AAC&U Greater Expectations Institute focusing on "Leadership to Make Excellence Inclusive," in Nashville, Tennessee. The team's formation is an important step for the institution and student affairs because it demonstrates to the University community that collaboration is needed to create the best possible learning experience for students. In fall 2010, the team of leaders jointly presented an integrated plan to the campus community on how to advance university education at Laurier.

A COLLISION OF PHILOSOPHICAL VIEWS

When student affairs professionals have engaged in dialogue with their academic colleagues, there has often been a collision of philosophical views. The long-standing perception of academic affairs as the "rule maker" and student affairs as the "rule breaker" (or the perception of academic affairs as the guardian of academic quality and student affairs as the advocate of the student—at any cost) has often prevailed. Historically, this philosophical divide is further amplified by the very way institutions are funded and evaluated. For the most part, universities, governments and external agencies reward teaching and research. Thus when financial resources are limited, student affairs services are often considered "non-essential" and are often the first areas targeted for budget reductions.

The introduction of national surveys such as the Canadian University Survey Consortium (CUSC) and the National Survey of Student Engagement (NSSE) is changing this landscape. As institutions face increased pressures of volatile and diverse enrolments, space limitations, funding cuts, increasing student expectations, accountability agreements and the wider dissemination of data, there is a more profound need to partner informally and formally to address identified areas of weakness and to improve. Many institutions are now emphasizing ways to enhance student satisfaction, student experience, student retention and success. There is a growing recognition that all areas within our colleges and universities must explore new opportunities to work with student affairs to influence student survey and evaluation results and—most importantly—to foster the ultimate success of our students. The silos are beginning to crumble, and the philosophical views within both academic and student affairs are beginning to change.

Case Study: MacEwan International, Edmonton

MacEwan International is a centre that formally reports to the Associate Vice President Academic and Research (AVPAR) and is led by a director. While the director reports to the AVPAR, staff working in MacEwan International has different reporting relationships because this unit operates according to a matrix model. While the department has existed since the 1990s, the new organizational structure was created in 2002 when student recruitment (which had been faculty-based) and admissions (formerly housed within the Office of the Registrar) were moved into the new centre to support the institutional goal of increasing international student enrolment and retention. International counselors are also available, although they operate out of a separate location due to confidentiality and space issues. There are several units within the centre, each with a distinct role, but all support the overall mandate of the centre.

The organizational realignment has had great benefits for MacEwan's international learners and has increased the understanding and interconnectivity of those who work with and provide support to the learners. The new organizational structure allows for immediate dialogue on matters relating to international applicants and students in one location and has expedited the admissions and enrolment process and removed many barriers. Between 2002 and 2010, MacEwan experienced an increase in international applications of 188 percent, which translated to a 32 percent jump in international full load equivalents. In addition to the increase in international enrolment, the service to international learners has improved. Erisa Seggumba (2010), a former international student from Africa who studied at MacEwan, believes that:

> *The International Centre at MacEwan is a great integral part of the university which helps international students adjust, get comfortable and integrate successfully into the university life as they pursue their educational studies. It's the backbone hub for international students to help them address their education, social and cultural needs, as well as act as a support centre to equip them to handle their changing needs. From my experience, I was so blessed to be supported by the International Centre, in the many ways it did. It was a one-stop centre which directed and guided me to all the help I needed to successfully pursue and graduate with my education ambitions. The Admissions, Registrar's Office and International Counselors personnel were simply great. Their unwavering support and desire to help students succeed, especially me, made a real difference in my life at MacEwan.*

CHANGES OF THE LEARNER DEMOGRAPHIC PROFILE

Student affairs organizations have been challenged to respond to the changing demographic profile of post-secondary learners, the increased numbers of learners, and the changing expectations of the learners and those who provide them with services. During the second half of the 20th century, enrolment at Canada's universities, particularly the urban universities, increased by 19 percent, mainly in full-time studies (Statistics Canada 2007). During the same period in the Canadian college sector, the increase in learners was 24 percent (Statistics Canada 2010b). This increase had a significant impact on the provision of student support services. Student affairs professionals who had met with students one-on-one (for example, in counseling and accessibility support programs) were challenged to find service strategies to accommodate the growing number of learners without having a proportionate increase in the number of staff. This was exacerbated by cutbacks to provincial funding of post-secondary education.[16] In the period between 1992–2000, for example, Alberta experienced a decrease in provincial funding of almost 28 percent (Hauserman and Stick 2005). These decreases meant that registrarial and student affairs units generally had fewer human, financial and other resources to deal with the increasingly diversified enrolments at their institutions.

DIVERSITY

Canadian post-secondary institutions have experienced increasing diversity in the composition of the student body over the past two decades as well. Examples include students with disabilities; international students; First Nations, Metis and Inuit learners; first-generation learners; lesbian, gay, bi-sexual and transgendered students; and students with different spiritual and faith backgrounds. In addition, there has been a general increase in the mobility of students transferring between colleges and universities.

Student affairs practitioners have worked with others in their institutions to develop and expand support services for these learners in order to enhance access and retention. Centres for students with disabilities, international students and Aboriginal students have emerged, and new types of programming to support student learning have been put in place. Workshops for faculty and staff hosted by student affairs professionals in tutoring and learning support services help to educate the campus community on learning styles and learning support strategies for the diverse student population. Library learning commons and learning communities are

---

[16] From the period of the early 1990s to 2000, provincial operating grants to Canadian universities decreased by as much as 25 percent in Alberta, Saskatchewan, Ontario, Nova Scotia and Prince Edward Island (Hauserman and Stick 2005).

also examples of partnerships between student and academic affairs that serve the needs of the increasingly varied range of learners.

Case Study: Residence at the University of Western Ontario, London

The University of Western Ontario presents an excellent example of structures designed to address integrated matters of student diversity, community living, and faculty involvement and engagement in learning communities. Through direct inspiration from a George Kuh visit to campus in 1992 and more indirect inspiration from active involvement in housing associations and conferences and research by Astin (1977) on student educational outcomes, creative staff worked together to address many areas to assist students with their integrated development as learners, residents and whole human beings. As early as 1993, UWO started the introduction of faculty floors, and this concept gradually expanded to include focused interest floors in 2001 and learning communities in 2007. The offerings in residence include floors such as the following: global village, health/lifestyle, creative arts, quieter floor, volunteer and service learning, scholar's elective, leadership development, and faculty learning communities (arts & humanities, engineering, health sciences, information & media studies, kinesiology, music, scholar's elective program, science, social science and social science Bachelor of Management and Organizational Studies). The programming to manage this model involves not only staff from Student Affairs and Residence, but also Academic Affairs (faculty, Deans and Associate Deans), Librarians, Student Success Centre and Learning Skills staff, Faculty Student Councils, Residents' Council and more. This model demonstrates both the integration of student affairs into strategic enrolment management initiatives on our campuses in Canada and how the diverse needs of students are being addressed through innovative and integrated models of service delivery.

On some campuses, student affairs practitioners have assisted by educating others about the spiritual and faith-based needs of learners. Examples of this include working with facilities to secure spaces for students to accommodate spiritual practice (for example, Muslim prayer rooms), dialogue and socialization, and partnerships with academic affairs to ensure religious accommodations within classrooms. Gay, lesbian, bisexual and transgendered students have also added to the diversity of our institutions. Student affairs staff now provides such students with meeting spaces and support services, educates their campus communities, advocates for changes in institutional policies, and promotes student, faculty and staff population activities, policies and professional development opportunities designed to support them in a welcoming ("positive space") environment.

For students with disabilities, proactive work has been done by those in student affairs to ensure that facilities are accessible, that classrooms and other learning spaces are equipped with appropriate technology, that there is faculty support for alternate format material preparation and that there is support for note taking, exam accommodations, interpreter services, and tutoring. The diversity of the learners and the different needs that they present has forced everyone to respond—both inside and outside of the classroom.

Student governance bodies have been very active in promoting the needs of learners on our campuses. The number of formal clubs or social groups supported through student associations or student unions in institutions throughout Canada has increased. Student leaders have advanced the cause of specific groups of learners through participation on institutional policy and governance committees. In some cases, student leaders establish their own business entity, collect fees, advocate for students and collaborate with institutional services to enhance services.

EMERGING COLLABORATIVE INITIATIVES

Student relationship management issues such as discipline and judicial affairs are examples of increased collaboration on our campuses. They are complex and often necessitate a cross-departmental approach and shared responsibilities—that is, student (mis)conduct has been the purview of not just student affairs, but increasingly includes input from academics and others on campus. Significant benefits are realized when a collective effort is employed to address difficult and complex issues.

Is a new organizational structure required or will enhancing collaborative partnerships suffice? SEM is instigating discussions across other institutional silos and influencing the organizational structure on our campuses. For example, some institutions have re-organized student service units. Questions are being asked whether recruitment and financial aid advising—units normally found in either academic or student affairs—should be separate units or whether they should be more carefully organized to support strategic enrolment goals.

Other new initiatives are integrating the student and academic affairs silos. Examples include the creation of one-stop shops, library/learning commons, community service-learning centres, triage teams and orientation.

ONE-STOP SHOPS

One-stop shops, where students can complete all of their transactional services, illustrate how institutions are shifting from a silo mentality to a collaborative approach. The physical set-up of one-stop shops creates a visual landscape to bring organizational units together to work on common transactional activities that better serve their constituents (in most cases, students). Longer-term benefits have also emerged for administrators, faculty and organizations. IT synergies are identified, activities streamlined, and new best practices emerge as one-stop shops also move into the virtual realm.

EXPECTATIONS OF STUDENTS AND THE INFLUENCE OF TECHNOLOGY

The expectations of students, and how they wish to receive services, have also impacted student affairs. Students have come to expect "instant" or "just-in-time" services at institutions, and they are now turning to Web sites and student portals for transactional and interactive services. The delivery model of services students need and expect has changed: from face-to-face to online, that is, to a one-to-one student/service delivery model. Student counselors and academic advisors are now exploring the ethical and legal intricacies of assisting students online as well as through traditional in-person, face-to-face sessions.

The combination of changing expectations of students and the impact of technology and the Internet is also having a profound impact on collaboration. The demand of students that services be streamlined and offered online is forcing organizational units to address contentious issues that blur the lines of ownership and the historical modes of delivery. Prior to the development of one-stop web-based portals, for example, students commonly had access to numerous online services and learning communities, each requiring its own login and password; the advent of these new portals forced institutional service providers, including faculty, student affairs and others, to create unified service pathways with one login and password. In the eyes of the students, all the service providers represent one institution; technology has led to student expectation that we present ourselves as such even though services are met by multiple providers on campus.

In addition, staff and faculty are recognizing the importance of technology to assist them as they provide services to students: online "early alert" or "at risk" intervention systems are examples of initiatives that allow collaboration through virtual portals. Institutions like Kwantlen Polytechnic University, John Abbott College and Wilfrid Laurier University have adopted online referral programs that allow staff, faculty or even the students themselves to identify students as potentially "at risk" of academic failure. From there, a system of referrals and interventions designed by the institution are put into place to support the learner. The systems include a wide variety of campus support from academic advising, financial aid, and study skills to personal counseling services.

LEARNING COMMONS

In addition to one-stop collaborations for services, many institutions have fundamentally changed the spaces where students learn outside the classroom. Scott Bennett, Yale University Librarian Emeritus, has argued that, "The most important contribution that library space might make to the educational mission of colleges and universities would flow from a better understanding of how students learn and how faculty teach, and form designs consciously meant to support those activities" (Bennett 2003). He maintains that institutions should develop a "learning commons" that provides a space for collaborative learning. He further notes that the re-conceptualized library-learning space needs to be owned by learners, rather than by librarians and teachers. "A learning commons must accommodate frequently changing learning tasks that students define for themselves, not information-management tasks defined and taught by library or academic computing staff" (Bennett 2003). This model, once considered groundbreaking, has been adopted by a number of Canadian colleges and universities.

Library redevelopment is being driven by many factors, including the need to create space for growing library collections, electronic and flexible classrooms, and additional study areas. Also critical, however, is that the exponential increase in online resources has forced a transformation in the traditional role of the library. To respond to this shift, libraries have become "re-branded" as learning commons. New partnerships are being forged with academic skills professionals and information technologists, and new space designs (incorporating food courts and cafés) are being built to entice students into the library. These new partnerships and the clustering of formerly disparate units bring new opportunities to enhance the total learning experience for students.

The Learning Commons at the University of Guelph, co-directed by Library Services and Student Affairs, was one of the first Canadian Learning Commons and was considered a novel and unique partnership for its time. This formal partnership created a forum for professional academic support staff, faculty and librarians to work collectively and collaboratively to develop programs and services designed to best support the learning needs and experiences of their students. Students can now receive specialized support in one location. The physical infrastructure was redesigned for students and the departmental units that guide the programs (Student Support Services and Teaching Centre) were relocated to the Learning Commons, further enhancing an environment that encourages collaboration. Other exemplary Learning Commons models include the University of Victoria, University of Toronto Mississauga Campus, and Seneca College.

COMMUNITY SERVICE-LEARNING

The significant expansion of Community Service-Learning programs is another example of collaboration by academic and student affairs to enhance the learning experiences of students. Most post-secondary institutions have a long history of community involvement—valuing the contributions of community partners and fostering environments that engage community partners in research and scholarly projects. Similarly, many student affairs portfolios have included programs that encourage students to volunteer with the community. Community service-learning programs have professionalized and formalized the student learning experience. Faculty members work collaboratively with student affairs professionals to expand and enhance the in-class experience for students by integrating course work and using reflective journals and e-portfolios that capitalize on the out-of-class learning experience. Not only does the cross-pollination of course and out-of-class work experience benefit the faculty and the students, it provides a formal bridge to the external community. The University of Ottawa, for example, has an Experiential Learning Service that includes a community service learning program and a formalized co-curricular record. The program activities allow for students to engage with community partners within and beyond the classroom.

TRIAGE TEAMS

A triage team model to deal with students in crisis—often involving teams of experts who gather together to review complex psychological, physiological, medical and emotional student situations and provide appropriate advice and expert resources in a holistic manner—is another example of a shift occurring. The triage approach requires individuals from different service areas to focus on the student as a whole to ensure that the student and others in the community are safe and supported. In some cases, faculty, counselors, learning support services, financial services and others are included in the discussions to better assess and serve the needs of the student in a holistic manner while maintaining necessary confidentiality by restricting information to a well-trained group that is familiar with provincial and federal privacy legislation.

This inter-unit and inter-disciplinary model provides opportunities for student affairs practitioners, who have traditionally worked independently from other areas, to work with academic affairs and other service providers and have a positive influence on disruptive student behavior within the institution. These teams also allow the institution to respond quickly to imminent or emerging risks or safety issues that may cross over traditional silos, streamlining administrative efforts and resulting in increased collaboration and efficiencies. For example, at the University of Windsor they have developed a Behavioural Intervention Plan that guides their Assessment and Care Team (ACT). It was created in accordance with the University and University Assessment Care Team (CUACT) model that was introduced by the National Center for Higher Education Risk Management and is consistent with the Council of Ontario Universities Violence Prevention and Emergency Management best practices, and other relevant guidelines and recommendations in Canada. The overall goal of the ACT team is to promote a safe environment for all students and staff focused on student learning and student development.

ORIENTATION WEEK CONTINUES TO EVOLVE

Another example of teamwork in institutions is orientation week, a program that in the past has been led by student affairs and/or their student associations/unions. Although students enjoyed orientation events, traditional orientation activities did little to prepare students for the academic expectations of post-secondary learning and the experience ahead of them in the classroom. Many faculty members complained of the students' lack of preparedness. The focus of these events was to "have fun" as the institution aimed to socialize and acclimatize students to their new learning community and, in cases where student residences are on campus, living environments. Academic Affairs focused on educational expectations of students in the classroom.

At many institutions orientation week has undergone a major transformation. At some institutions, the changes are so profound that their orientation now bears little resemblance to what students experienced in the past. For example, Mount Royal University in Calgary, Alberta, now holds a two-day integrated university-wide academic orientation program that includes a "welcome convocation," parent orientation, an overview of academic expectations and start-of-term service activities (registration, campus card, parking, tuition payment, etc.). Thus academic affairs, student affairs and other on-campus service departments are now all active participants in planning orientation, which extends through the first year and enables the institution to meet the needs of students as they transition into post-secondary studies.

FIRST-YEAR EXPERIENCE AND LEARNING COMMUNITIES

First-year experience programs and learning communities are interesting initiatives that continue to evolve in an effort to respond to the complex student and enrolment needs of institutions. Generally speaking, these are unique partnerships that are jointly supported by the academic community and student affairs and are designed to improve student success. They are centred on a common theme of research, a set of courses, or an area of general interest. Students enrolled in a first-year experience curriculum or learning community receive intentional support that focuses on the emotional, social and academic skills necessary for a successful transition to post-secondary studies.

Models range from learning course clusters to themed learning communities to residential learning communities. The role of the academic community varies from significant involvement with oversight of course content and delivery to minimal interaction, often involving academic advisement or mentorship. The role of student affairs varies dramatically from primary deliverer and/or coordinator of the program to minimal involvement providing a small number of social and skills development workshops. The credit weighting of these learning communities varies from non-credit to optional to mandatory course credit. As these communities mature and evolve, two interesting trends are emerging. First, student affairs is increasingly being invited to participate in the curriculum development of these learning experiences/communities, and second, course credit is being included in the total course evaluation. The inclusion of course credit is particularly noteworthy because it affirms the contributions of student affairs to the development and success of the student.

An excellent example of this concept is being piloted at Saint Mary's University in Halifax, Nova Scotia. Saint Mary's University has launched a two-year pilot program that intentionally addresses first-year transition issues by incorporating academic skills development (writing, study) into discipline-specific courses. The program, called LEAP (Learning, Engagement, Achievement, Peer Mentors) or LEAP to Success, is a multi-disciplinary team-taught program that involves three courses and a partnership with student affairs. Faculty have agreed to allot 10 percent of the course content and evaluation to student affairs, who are responsible for delivering academic skill development workshops and overseeing peer mentoring and training.

St. Mary's launched the program with six sections in September 2010 and will continue to expand the program over the next two years. The school has incorporated learning outcomes in its course design and will be using tools to measure and assess effectiveness. This is a significant shift in practice. The former and previously common University 101 skills development courses are maturing into courses with academic- and discipline-based curriculum and are increasingly viewed as essential for student development and learning.

CONCLUSION

Over the past two to three decades student affairs professionals have become instrumental in the strategic enrolment management of our institutions. New models of partnerships that increase the engagement of students throughout the entire student lifecycle have enabled student affairs practitioners in Canada to redefine the way our institutions develop and implement programming to engage and retain learners. The institutions and those working within them must continue to be nimble to stay on top of emerging trends and issues within their own institutions—provincially, nationally and abroad—and to sustain the energy needed to continually educate and re-educate those with whom they work to continue to positively impact the engagement, retention and success of learners.

The "whole student" experience has challenged those in student affairs to support enrolment efforts on campuses in non-traditional ways. Some of the approaches have also blended services for students, faculty and staff together to meet the needs of everyone in the larger institution. These models have proven particularly effective, not only in meeting the initial needs of those involved, but in establishing relationships in the context of larger learning organizations.

Joy Mighty and Alan Wright

9

STUDENT ENGAGEMENT

/ **Chapter 9** /

This chapter expounds the central importance of student engagement in the strategic enrolment management process within the Canadian context. We discuss in particular the role of enhanced pedagogy and effective teaching practices in engaging the student in the learning process, as well as the vital role of leadership that supports such practices. We also address how SEM is improved when campus leadership provides opportunities to contribute to the holistic development of the student throughout the entire educational process.

After discussing the concept of student engagement, we identify some of the major issues that make it particularly relevant to strategic enrolment management. A case study is described that both represents innovative pedagogical practices that many Canadian institutions are using to engage students and illustrates how such practices are advancing the strategic enrolment management mission. Finally, we recommend a range of other professional practices that institutions might consider if they wish to leverage student engagement to achieve SEM goals. Let us begin with an overview of higher education in the Canadian context.

OVERVIEW OF HIGHER EDUCATION IN CANADA

In Canada, education at all levels, including higher education, falls under provincial and territorial, rather than federal, jurisdiction. This means that there is no single, comprehensive national strategy for education. Instead, priorities and decisions about educational initiatives are determined by provincial governments working collaboratively with school boards at the primary and secondary levels or, at the post-secondary level, with individual institutions as well as provincial and regional networks such as the Council of Ontario Universities (COU), the Conseil des Recteurs et Principaux des Universités du Québec (CREPUQ), and the Association of Atlantic Universities (AAU). There are over 260 post-secondary institutions located in the ten provinces as well as in two of the three territories. Of these institutions, 94 are universities offering degree programs, most at the bachelor's and master's levels, and some at the doctoral level. There are also 175 community colleges which offer diplomas for vocationally-oriented educational programs. In addition to universities and colleges, several provinces have university-colleges, polytechnics, and institutes that can grant degrees, many of which provide vocationally-oriented training. The province of Quebec has an extensive and unique College of General and Vocational Education network, commonly referred to as the CÉGEP system, which offers general and technical education between high school and university.

The landscape of higher education in Canada has been undergoing change for over a decade. The distinctions between different types of post-secondary institutions are becoming somewhat blurred and in some cases have been eliminated altogether. Some colleges, institutes, and polytechnics have become degree-granting institutions with many changing their name to include the word "university." In some parts of the country, university-colleges have increased rapidly. These changes mean that competition for students is very high, with many institutions adopting unique strategies to increase enrolment, targeting particularly those demographic groups with traditionally low participation in post-secondary studies. Such groups include students from low-income families, students with no history of higher education in their family (called first-generation students), Aboriginal students, and some groups of new immigrants (Wright *et al.* 2008). Despite special financial assistance programs offered by governments as well as institutions, these demographic groups still lag behind the general population in their PSE participation rates (Statistics Canada 2008a). For example, among young adults (aged 25 to 34) there is a 25-percentage-point gap between Aboriginal and non-Aboriginal post-secondary attainment (Statistics Canada 2006). Several intervention programs have sought to increase access for all of these groups, but an increase in access has not necessarily resulted in a corresponding increase in success (Wright *et al.* 2008). In light of these findings, strategic enrolment management initiatives must of necessity include ways to help students learn and to motivate them to persist in their studies. In this context, student engagement has become a vitally important strategy for increasing student success.

THE CONCEPT OF STUDENT ENGAGEMENT

Student engagement refers to students' sustained involvement in learning activities. Early studies of student engagement focused on time-on-task behaviours and on student willingness to participate in routine activities, such as attending classes, submitting required work, and following teachers' directions in class. Negative indicators of engagement included unexcused absences from classes and cheating on tests. But student engagement was also inferred from more subtle cognitive, behavioral, and affective indicators as in this explanation offered by Skinner and Belmont (1993):

> [Students] who are engaged show sustained behavioral involvement in learning activities accompanied by a positive emotional tone. They select tasks at the border of their competencies, initiate action when given the opportunity, and exert intense effort and concentration in the implementation of learning tasks; they show generally positive emotions during ongoing action, including enthusiasm, optimism, curiosity, and interest.
>
> The opposite of engagement is disaffection. Disaffected students are passive, do not try hard, and give up easily in the face of challenges; they can be bored, depressed, anxious, or even angry about their presence in the classroom; they can be withdrawn from learning opportunities or even rebellious towards teachers and classmates (p. 572).

From a different perspective, Pintrich and De Groot (1990) associated engagement levels with students' use of cognitive, meta-cognitive and self-regulatory strategies to monitor and guide their learning processes. In this view, student engagement is motivated behaviour apparent from students' willingness to persist with difficult tasks by regulating their own learning behaviour and from the kinds of cognitive strategies they choose to use—such as deep processing strategies as opposed to surface processing strategies, concepts to which we will return later.

In essence, the evidence from decades of studies indicates that the level of challenge and students' time on task are positively related to persistence and subsequent success in post-secondary institutions and that the degree to which students are engaged in their studies impacts directly on the quality of their learning and their overall educational experience. As such, characteristics of student engagement can serve as proxies for quality or, as the National Survey on Student Engagement (NSSE) terms it, "effective educational practice" (Indiana University 2010).

NSSE refers to a survey of good practices in undergraduate education that was developed in the USA and formally launched in 2000. To date 1,452 institutions have participated (Indiana University 2010). In Canada, it was used for the first time in 2004 by the then G10 (now U15) universities, a group of leading research-intensive universities that engage in joint research and data-exchange programs. Since 2006, all universities in Ontario are required to use it and almost all provinces now have universities that participate regularly in the NSSE. The survey is designed to obtain, on an annual basis, information from colleges and universities across North America about student participation in programs and activities that institutions provide for their learning and personal development. In order to paint a fair picture of the overall university experience, the survey is administered to samples of students at two points in their academic careers. It is administered to first-year and senior-level students who have attended the institution for at least two terms. The results provide an estimate of how undergraduates spend their time and what they gain from attending post-secondary institutions.

For NSSE, student engagement refers not only to the time and effort students devote to their studies and related activities but also to how institutions organize learning opportunities and provide services to induce students to take part in and benefit from such activities. In general, the questions on the survey fall into three broad categories: institutional actions and requirements; student behaviours; and student reaction to the institution. Institutional actions and requirements include specific items about how students have experienced the curriculum and faculty behaviour. "Student behaviours" include survey questions asked to determine how students spend their time inside and outside of the classroom, while "student reactions" to the institution include questions that elucidate student perceptions about the quality of their experiences. This last category also includes questions about self-reported gains in skills that students feel they have developed as a result of attending the institution. Forty-two key questions ask about both student behaviours and institutional features that are among the more powerful contributors to learning and personal development. Results from these items are grouped into five categories known as the NSSE benchmarks, which are:

■ *Level of academic challenge*: This refers to challenging intellectual and creative work and high expectations for student performance. It is evidenced by such behaviours as preparing for class, reading and writing, and emphasizing academic work.

■ *Active and collaborative learning*: Research evidence indicates that students learn more when they are more intensely involved in their own education and that collaborating with others prepares students to handle practical, real-world problems. Examples include behaviours such as working with other students and making presentations.

■ *Student interactions with faculty members*: This benchmark examines whether students learn first-hand how to think about and solve practical problems and if teachers become role models and mentors for learning. Examples include working with a professor on a research project and discussing assignments or career plans with a professor.

■ *Enriching educational experiences*: Questions in this category ask students whether their institution provides learning opportunities that complement the goals of the academic program, and opportunities to integrate and apply knowledge. Such opportunities ("high impact experiences") may include internships and study abroad programs, using technology, experiencing diversity, and culminating senior experiences via capstone courses.

■ *Supportive campus environment*: Students perform better and are more satisfied at institutions committed to their success and supportive of positive working and social relationships between students and different groups on campus.

MAJOR ISSUES

Responsibility for Student Engagement

It is clear from this overview of student engagement that it is the responsibility of both the student and the institution. Although a particular individual or unit may coordinate or monitor the impact of all the institutional initiatives to promote student success, ultimately student engagement is everybody's business. This explains why in the NSSE instrument, student engagement is a set of constructs that measure both the time and energy students devote to educationally purposeful activities, and how students perceive different aspects of the institutional environment that facilitate and support their learning. At the core of the institutional efforts to facilitate student learning is the faculty member whose pedagogical approaches can ultimately determine the level of student engagement.

Faculty Behaviours

Several pieces of literature can be brought together to help us understand how faculty behaviours can influence the level of student engagement. First, Chickering and Gamson in their classic 1987 article, "Seven Principles for Good Practice in Undergraduate Education," drew on over 50 years of research regarding the way teachers teach and students learn, how students work and play with one another, and how students and faculty relate to each other. Their well-known seven principles summarize the features of good practice. According to Chickering and Gamson (1987), good practice:

- Encourages student-faculty contact. Frequent student-faculty contact in and out of classes is the most important factor in student motivation and involvement.
- Develops reciprocity and cooperation among students. Working with others often increases involvement in learning, and sharing one's own ideas and responding to others' reactions sharpens thinking and deepens understanding.
- Encourages active learning. Students must talk about what they are learning, write about it, relate it to past experiences and apply it to their daily lives.
- Gives prompt feedback. Students need feedback to help them focus on learning. Feedback helps them to reflect on what they have learned, what they still need to know, and how to assess themselves.
- Emphasizes time on task. Students become engaged when they spend time on tasks, and this leads to increased learning.
- Communicates high expectations. Expecting students to perform well becomes a self-fulfilling prophecy.
- Respects diverse talents and ways of learning. There is no one best way of learning. Students need the opportunity to show their talents and learn in ways that work for them instead of being pushed to learn in new ways that do not come so easily.

When faculty engage in these pedagogically sound practices, they increase student engagement, which leads to persistence and ultimately facilitates student success.

A second classic that provides advice about what faculty can do to engage students is the famous 1995 Barr and Tagg article in *Change*. In their article "From Teaching to Learning: A New Paradigm for Undergraduate Education," Barr and Tagg challenged the professoriate in higher education to shift from the traditional, dominant "instruction" paradigm to a "learning" paradigm (Barr and Tagg 1995). They called for a transformation from a faculty- and teaching-centered model to a student- and learning-centered model; from a focus on providing instruction to a focus on producing learning. According to Barr and Tagg, the Instruction Paradigm rests on conceptions of teaching that are increasingly recognized as ineffective because they diverge from almost every principle of optimal settings for student learning, such as those identified a decade earlier by Chickering and Gamson. The Learning Paradigm, on the other hand, employs whatever approaches best promote learning in a particular context by particular students. In the Learning Paradigm, learning environments and activities are learner-centered and learner-controlled, with teachers facilitating learning by linking material to be learned to prior learning, directing students to resources, stimulating discussions and collaborations, encouraging peer instruction, and guiding and providing feedback.

Barriers to Student Engagement

Despite these well-known recommendations by Barr and Tagg and Chickering and Gamson, the Instruction Paradigm persists as the dominant approach to teaching and is one of the most pervasive barriers to success in post-secondary institutions. As many of the contributors to *Taking Stock: Research on Teaching and Learning in Higher Education* (Christensen Hughes and Mighty 2010) have pointed out, several studies have found that traditional didactic or transmission approaches to teaching influence students to use surface approaches to learning that rely on memorization and regurgitation (*see for example*, Entwistle 2010; Lindblom-Ylänne 2010; and Trigwell 2010). The effects of such approaches to teaching and learning are deficient outcomes, such as little retention and shallow understanding of material. In addition, students are often dissatisfied with their learning experiences and become disengaged and alienated. Many quit, particularly students among disadvantaged groups, because this academic dis-engagement is compounded by issues involving well-being, self-esteem, finances, support networks, and basic motivation (Wright *et al.* 2008). However, when faculty operate from the Learning Paradigm, students take ownership over the material, defining what is relevant to their needs and becoming deeply engaged in their learning. From the perspective of strategic enrolment management, teaching and learning approaches based on student engagement can promote student retention and, most importantly, student success.

PRACTICES THAT FOSTER STUDENT ENGAGEMENT: ACTIVE LEARNING STRATEGIES

How can the potential of student engagement for advancing the goals of strategic enrolment management be realized? A simple but effective way is for faculty to use active learning strategies. In its most basic form, active learning requires that students participate in the learning process and that they use content knowledge, not just acquire it. Some of the most common active learning pedagogies that promote student engagement include community service learning, inquiry-based learning, problem-based learning, and team-based learning. Other active learning experiences occur through interactions with peers in learning communities, first-year seminars, internships, senior capstone courses, experiences with diversity, and study abroad programs. Such activities have been called "high-impact" practices because of their significant benefits on student learning in particular and on student development in general (Kinzie 2010). Such activities have such enormous benefits that Kinzie strongly recommends them:

> *The strength of the benefits associated with high-impact practices suggests a prescription for institutions of higher education: to effectively raise students' level of learning, institutions should ensure that all students experience at least two high-impact practices during their undergraduate education* (Kinzie 2010, pp.147–148).

The wide range of activities included in Kinzie's recommendation emphasizes once more that student engagement is not the sole responsibility of faculty. On the contrary, it is an objective that is shared by all the units with some responsibility for strategic enrolment management. However, according to some researchers and practitioners, for the full benefits of student engagement to be realized, all of these individuals and units must work more collaboratively and intentionally at aligning the various factors that could influence student learning. For example, as Wright (2010) points out, departmental leaders and educational developers have significant roles to play in the process, as do the students themselves. Knapper (2010) describes an international study that further indicates that departmental leaders should create environments to facilitate faculty behaviours and promote student engagement.

In Canada, the Society for Teaching and Learning in Higher Education (STLHE) has been providing leadership in advancing student engagement for over three decades. The STLHE is a national organization that advocates for excellence in teaching and learning in higher education. It seeks to advance the scholarship of teaching and learning and to contribute to the professional development of its membership, consisting of approximately 800 faculty, administrators, educational developers, and students from post-secondary institutions across Canada and beyond. The STLHE also has approximately 65 institutional members. Although mandatory training for university teachers does not exist in Canada, the Society has actively promoted the professional development of teachers through the work of its Educational Developers Caucus (EDC). EDC members work collaboratively with many other units in their institutional settings to provide training and development opportunities for faculty in the application of the active learning strategies previously identified.

INNOVATIVE ENGAGING PRACTICE: A CANADIAN CASE STUDY

A major publication on the subject of accessing and persisting in post-secondary education in Canada appeared in 2008 (Finnie, *et al.*). While the collection of 14 essays tends to emphasize what Canadians can learn about financial issues impacting access and success to PSE in Canada, it reveals significant national data regarding other factors of importance to students. Over one-half of students who leave their PSE programs in Canadian institutions point to a lack of interest in their specific program or a lack of interest for higher education more broadly as their reasons for dropping out (Meuller 2008, p.48). These findings underline the importance of designing programs and adopting practices with a view to capturing the interest of the student, and of engaging the student in a rich and meaningful path of inquiry and discovery.

The very future of the university depends, in the views of some observers, on the institution's potential to "regenerate" its approach to, and understanding of, teaching and learning. According to Summerlee and Christensen Hughes, "Teaching and learning need to become more focused on the process of learning, and helping the learner understand exactly how learning occurs." For authentic learning to occur, students should be "motivated and empowered...building self-efficacy." Learning should present "problems that are relevant, or have intrigue or immediacy that makes investigating them and understanding them an absolute challenge" (p. 257).

What directions have Canadian institutions of higher learning taken with regards to the development of programs and courses designed to provide undergraduates with meaningful and engaging academic experiences? The so-called University 101 seminars, popularized in the United States in the 1980s, did not take flight in Canada. Anecdotally the authors can recall that there was some interest in the "University 101" solution to engaging first-year students in universities in the Atlantic provinces during this period. In fact, some of us asked colleagues who had introduced such courses for copies of syllabi with a view to presenting the concept to our own local deans. The deans rejected the idea of developing similar courses in our institutions as they felt their faculty members would find the courses weak on content and academic credibility. Other detractors suggested that rather than developing 'guerilla' courses on how to survive in the university while tolerating deficient practices across the curriculum, we should put our energies into re-inventing the mainstream course of studies in an integrated approach in order to provide students with a globally enhanced undergraduate experience.

Authors who have documented the Canadian approach to the first-year experience suggest that some institutions have, however, developed original initiatives to provide first-year students with experiences designed to engage them and to ease their transition to higher education. Ursula Trescases of Ryerson University cites an example of how a university librarian has made a significant contribution to the information literacy component of a broad-based and successful interdisciplinary first-year credit course at the University of Windsor in Windsor, Ontario (Trescases 2008). Trescases concludes that the information literacy objective of the course is better integrated in the Windsor model than elsewhere.

Trescases focused especially on the information literacy component of the course in question, but what are the other elements of the course that attract our attention in this context? Let us start with the official course description as listed in the University of Windsor undergraduate calendar:

Faculty of Arts and Social Sciences: General Courses
WAYS OF KNOWING

This course investigates a topic through the lens of a variety of perspectives representing the range of learning at the university. Students will see the way specific viewpoints, for example from the arts, sciences, or social sciences, provide very different insights into our world. This course combines classroom instruction with a workshop component in which students will develop the skills of inquiry to explore the world around them. They will have the opportunity to work with senior student mentors and a variety of community and university resources. The topic for each year will be announced in advance and might include: space, time and place; identity and voice; isolation and community; or creativity and invention.

A look at the standard course description of *Ways of Knowing* reveals many components of interest in the context of this chapter:

- The perspectives of several disciplines are introduced to the students.
- Links between theory and practice are emphasized.
- Inquiry-based learning is introduced.
- Trained mentors (senior students) work with the first-year students.
- The course takes into account the nature of the first-year experience.
- Active learning is basic to the course.
- Community outreach is an integral component of the course.

The *Ways of Knowing* course is meant to provide an exceptional, engaging experience for students new to the higher education environment. For example, significant in this Windsor model is the involvement of senior students in the first-year course as "trained mentors." The senior students are trained as mentors in a credit course at their level. The calendar description of the senior course is as follows:

MENTORSHIP AND LEARNING

This course is an intensive exploration of the theory and practice of learning and leadership by mentoring first-year students. Students will mentor first-year students taking the *Ways of Knowing* interdisciplinary course. They will meet regularly with a group of first-year students and help them complete assignments involving various activities to assist in developing their problem-solving skills. They will also study theories of learning and leadership and engage in seminar discussions. The course will run over two semesters.

A look at the standard course description of the *Mentorship and Learning* course reveals many components of interest to the themes of this chapter:

- Emphasizing the theory and practice of learning and leadership.
- Pursuing interdisciplinary study.
- Developing small group leadership skills.
- Stimulating the development of problem-solving skills.
- Developing seminar leadership skills.

The examples of original courses described above illustrate cases of interest in the Canadian higher education landscape insofar as they involve innovative, engaging approaches to student engagement. Of particular interest is the fact that the Faculty of Arts and Social Sciences has addressed the need for engagement at the introductory level as well as the need for a more sophisticated, pre-work life, leadership experience at the senior level. The fact that the two courses are inextricably linked makes this model especially appealing in the current context.

How do faculty involved in the design and facilitation of the *Ways of Knowing* and *Mentorship and Learning* courses see the purposes of the courses? In a recent article, three academics involved state that, "The primary purpose of these two courses is to help students to develop the skills and abilities needed to help them regard learning as a lifelong endeavour" (Bolton, Pugliese, and Singleton-Jackson 2009, p. 21). The "secondary goal," according to the authors, is to "help students understand how the university functions and what their roles are, so that they may effectively navigate through their university careers." The so-called "secondary goal" relates closely to the traditional objectives of the "University 101" concept, and the close involvement of faculty from a number of disciplines as well as a faculty-librarian affords this pair of courses a high level of credibility.

Additional statements describing the purpose and benefits of the courses, according to the authors/teaching faculty follow:

- The courses "are opening the door to thinking about information literacy and curricular integration in very different ways."
- The courses were "originally designed to help with retention and transition issues"
- The courses were "founded on the concept of peer-led learning at the university level."
- The "students are able to organically connect with their peers."
- The "peer mentors (act) as conduits in the transfer of information literacy skills."
- "The library can accomplish far more..."

The two complementary courses, then, are seen as contributing to retention and providing exceptional learning experiences to mentors and mentees. The library faculty members see particular gains in terms of transition, retention, and important literacy skills:

- "While universities struggle to deal with transition and retention issues, they also continue to cope with serious concerns regarding the information literacy skills of students entering and graduating from their institutions."
- The *Ways of Knowing* course is shown, in fact, to have a positive impact on the retention rates at the University of Windsor; retention rates are higher than for non-participants.

The above example describes how one Canadian university has grappled with the need to provide undergraduates with significant, memorable learning experiences. As stated above, Kinzie claims that engagement is the most robust indicator of success known to us in higher education at this time. The students in *Ways of Knowing* and *Mentorship and Learning* are living this engagement experience.

This chapter concentrates on the academic perspective of student engagement and perseverance in higher education, providing a detailed look at an example of innovative curriculum change, course design, and pedagogy to illustrate the potential benefits of specific "high impact" experiences on student engagement. While this chapter does not delve into the many other factors influencing student engagement and perseverance, the authors would like to recognize their central importance.

After studying the literature and scouring the Canadian higher education land-scape for institutional practices promoting access and success, particularly for student populations traditionally under-represented in colleges and universities, researchers found that a number of factors contributed to student decisions to pursue studies or to drop out. These factors, it is not surprising to note, went beyond academic preparation and strength to include self-image, self-confidence and well-ness, financial situation, family and social network, community support, campus student service support, institutional administrative structures and readiness to accommodate and serve the student population. (Wright *et al.* 2008). The researchers concluded that, at many levels, a "holistic" or "ensemble" approach involving a multitude of campus employees and services, academic and non-academic, would be the ideal way to support student perseverance (Wright and Monette 2010). Although examples of such comprehensive approaches go beyond the scope of this chapter, the authors wish to emphasize the need for collaborative, cross-cutting solutions to the challenge of student engagement in Canada and beyond.

SUMMARY AND CONCLUSION

In this chapter, we have emphasized the importance of student engagement for Canadian institutions, academic administration, educational developers, and faculty as well as for the students themselves. Student engagement, as described in decades of academic literature and as studied through the NSSE surveys, is closely linked to student decision-making with regard to the pursuit of studies. Student retention remains a major issue for those professionals involved in strategic enrolment management both in Canada and at the international level. The authors venture to list some of the main understandings arising from empirical and theoretical influences regarding the matter of student engagement in our universities and colleges.

Since higher education in Canada is governed by provincial structures rather than federal regulation, it is likely that conditions to improve student engagement are best understood by examining developments at the institutional and provincial levels. The availability of national, longitudinal data on access and persistence in post-secondary studies in Canada has improved greatly in recent years. Many authors have delved deeply into various aspects influencing student access and success.[17]

Some Canadian populations such as Aboriginals, first generation, and the economically disadvantaged are under-represented in higher education and challenges of access and success are greater for members of these groups. Engaging academic programs and innovative pedagogies is one way of increasing levels of persistence among students from these and other groups of students.

The issue of student engagement, academic and extra-curricular, is high on the agendas of Canadian colleges and universities because many academic administrators and faculty are now convinced of the importance of the concept in promoting student persistence. Engagement is recognized by Canadian institutions as a proxy for academic persistence and success. It is understood that adopting more sophisticated retention strategies that emphasize high-impact academic as well as non-academic components form an essential component of a comprehensive strategic enrolment management plan. Due to increasing internationalization of academic writing and scholarly journals as well as close economic, cultural and linguistic ties, colleges and universities in Canada often turn to the experiences of institutions in the U.S. and internationally, especially those of other members of the British Commonwealth. For example, Canadian colleges and universities are committed to participating in and learning from the National Survey on Student Engagement (NSSE), as are their counterparts in the U.S. and in the United Kingdom.

Although Canadian institutions have been influenced by what might be termed the "first-year experience movement" as it developed over the last decades in the United States, the take-up of first-year seminars or "University 101" courses as a favoured solution to help students adapt to university academic requirements has been relatively limited. Many Canadian colleges and universities have, however, adopted original programs to increase student engagement and persistence. Some of these innovative programs have been designed to help students to see connections from one discipline to the next and to provide sense and coherence to their studies. This in turn is intended to foster motivation and persistence.

---

[17] See especially the ground-breaking discussion in "Who Goes? Who Stays? What Matters?" (Finnie *et al.* 2008).

Leading professional groups such as the Society for Teaching and Learning in Higher Education (STLHE) and the Educational Developers Caucus are examples of Canadian initiatives dedicated to the improvement of pedagogy and teaching and learning conditions in Canada. These groups run conferences and events, publish newsletters and academic journals, sponsor national teaching awards and develop educational position papers and policies to promote enhanced teaching and learning in Canadian higher education. It is worth noting that the Society has ties with the U.S.-based Professional and Organizational Development Network (POD) and that both belong to the International Consortium for Educational Development (ICED). Teaching and learning centers in Canadian institutions have developed over the past two decades and have contributed to strategies to introduce effective teaching and to recognize the importance of student engagement. Once again, it is useful to understand the Canadian perspective on student engagement and enrolment management as it relates to international issues and trends. While the STLHE and the teaching centres have produced a considerable amount of original work, the organization as well as the employees of institutions frequently looks beyond Canadian borders to adopt and adapt findings from theoretical models as well as empirical and institutional research.

In 2008 the Higher Education Quality Council of Ontario sponsored a research symposium to "take stock" of what we know about teaching and learning in higher education. The ambitious symposium, organized by former presidents of the STLHE Joy Mighty and Julia Christensen Hughes, brought together a team of leading international researchers in higher education to pool current knowledge in the field. The resulting book, in part a proceedings, called for educators "to challenge practices of convenience, to commit to providing learning environments that encourage deep learning and transform students" (Christensen Hughes and Mighty 2010, p. 275). This multi-facetted challenge includes, as a key component, a major renewal of curricular, pedagogical, and assessment practices.

Strategic enrolment management has many dimensions. In Canada, academics and leading educational developers advocate attention to the issue of student engagement, both academic and extra-curricular, as a key to promoting student persistence and eventual success through graduation. This important element of sound enrolment management suggests that pedagogical issues and curriculum dynamics must be given prominence by those concerned with the perseverance and success of students.

Lynn Smith and Dave Morphy

10

THE ROLE OF
RETENTION

/ **Chapter 10** /

Strategic enrolment management (SEM) has become a significant methodology used by universities and colleges to address enrolment trends and concerns about the student experience. Historically, the focus of SEM was on student recruitment and on optimal enrolment in our universities and colleges, both by academic program and by course. However, within SEM and more recently in the Canadian SEM context, the focus has shifted to a concern about student retention and the complex challenges for institutions as they look beyond the traditional pipeline of recruitment. The SEM focus now also encompasses a holistic model of engaging potential students and providing a student experience that both retains students and fosters student success.

SEM approaches in Canada have often mirrored the trends evident in American institutions, including the development of retention strategies. Many Canadian universities and colleges now recognize that more attention must be paid to the 'student experience,' which our American and international counterparts have already realized. While many colleges and smaller universities in Canada are successfully providing environments and programs that support student success, the large, public institutions continue to face the greatest challenges.

ASSESSING RETENTION BY STUDENT DEMOGRAPHICS

It is important to establish the context for both universities and colleges and to comment on how it relates to first-year students as well as students in general arts and science and undergraduate professional programs. It is also important to consider special populations—including Aboriginal students, international students, first-generation students, transfer students and other groups of under-represented students that would be relevant in establishing the context for a full understanding of retention and success. Of the above special populations, many Canadian institutions are purposefully focused on Aboriginal students, international students and first-generation students. Some information about these special populations is included in a section of this chapter on key retention issues. Full consideration of these topics is presented in Chapters 11–15 of this book.

It is also necessary to consider the moral and social obligations of post-secondary education institutions to retain the students they recruit and to ensure and enhance student success. Finally, every consideration must be given to the financial and emotional investment being made by students in pursuing a post-secondary education, as well as the investment being made by the institution, to understand the importance of retention and the subsequent impact on student success and satisfaction. Many institutions "recruit to retain" their students. It is critical to focus on which prospective students can succeed at our institution and explore what is required so students have every opportunity to achieve success.

DEFINING RETENTION

Retention is usually defined from an institution's perspective and is measured by the number of students who continue from one point in time to the next. The first six weeks are critical for students to become connected to an institution; retention measurements sometimes feature metrics about the dropout rate at this time. Traditionally, retention from first to second year has also been an important retention index. In the 2010 ranking issue, *Macleans* magazine reported that the percentage of full-time, first-year students enrolled in fall 2008 who returned to university the following year ranged from 70.3 percent to 95 percent in 45 Canadian universities, with 34 of those universities reporting retention at 80 percent or above (p. 158).

Retention throughout a program of study and completion of a program or matriculation have also been commonly used as a measure of retention. *Macleans* also reported that the proportion of students who graduated within seven years of entering the first year of their program ranged from 72.4 percent to 89.8 percent.

Studies compiled by provincial education departments, for example in Manitoba and Saskatchewan, measure and analyze 'early leavers' from post-secondary institutions. Individual institutions may also conduct research, such as exit interviews, to determine why students leave. While there are factors impacting retention that may by beyond the institution's sphere of influence, there is great value to institutions in knowing why students leave. Attention to retention data can identify the areas institutions can improve upon to provide a quality student experience, and how they might improve student success.

The paths of attrition are becoming more complex as more students sample different providers of post-secondary education. The term 'swirlers', coined to indicate this trend, has infiltrated SEM in Canada. The patterns of highly mobile students—transfers, visitors, drop-outs, stop-outs, and samplers of distance education—make it difficult for institutions to get a true picture of retention. It follows that institutions must devise ways to assess retention patterns across the institution and identify the points in time when students are most likely to leave and for what reasons. This data and analysis is critical to the development of retention strategies.

From the student's perspective, continuing in an academic program is likely not connected to our use of the term 'retention' or that of 'persistence.' For students, there are hosts of factors—academic, social and personal—that underpin their ability and desire to continue with their studies. As noted above, that continuance can take many forms. There are even some instances where a student's decision to withdraw from an academic program may actually be measured as success.

The implementation of retention strategies illustrates the extent of the institution's focus on student success. Strategies and programs should not be confined simply to increasing numbers, for example, of students continuing from year 1 to year 2, but should assist students to achieve their educational objectives. Any definition of retention needs to be linked to the life cycle of the student and to student success itself. It is clearly important for success to be defined in terms of a student's educational and career goals, but it is equally important for student success to be defined in a manner that reflects the growth and development of the student on any number of dimensions and skill sets. The basic elements of success are defined both within the classroom and outside the classroom. The success continuum covers the student's university/college career from recruitment to career attainment, from the traditional enrolment perspective and from the SEM perspective.

As universities and colleges consider how they will define retention within their specific institutional environments, they must take into consideration all aspects of retention including persistence, engagement and involvement, as well as student life on campus and all else that an institution can do to ensure an outstanding student experience. Many institutions increasingly use both engagement and satisfaction indices as proxies in the assessment of retention.

THE IMPORTANCE OF DATA

Data must drive any discussion on retention and the development of any retention strategy, including the development of policies and programs that embrace and support student success. National data is available in Canada through the Canadian University Survey Consortium (CUSC), which focuses on student satisfaction; as well as the National Survey on Student Engagement (NSSE), which has gathered data across Canada at the university level, focusing on five categories of engagement:

- The level of academic challenge
- Active and collaborative learning
- Student-faculty interaction
- Enriching the educational experience
- The supportive campus environment

The Community College Survey of Student Engagement (CCSSE) is NSSE's counterpart for colleges and recently the Higher Education Quality Council of Ontario (HEQCO 2010) endorsed the use of CCSSE as an effective assessor of student engagement in Ontario colleges. However, CCSSE had been used infrequently in Canada with only three colleges participating since CCSSE's launch in 2001.

The CUSC surveys, fielded annually since 1994, are particularly critical in enabling universities to gather information on retention. The data provides universities with satisfaction data at their own institution as well as the ability to compare themselves with other institutions across the country. The data on university students is gathered on incoming students in one year, graduating students in the second year and all students in the third year and the cycle then repeats itself. In addition to standard questions being asked in each survey, each institution has the option of adding questions specific to their situation. A customization of the CUSC survey for colleges would be worthy of serious consideration.

The CUSC survey gathers student satisfaction data across many dimensions. The implication is that satisfaction levels affect retention rates, particularly with first-year students. The premise is that the more institutions become informed about what elements satisfy students and what elements do not, the more they will be able to react and respond appropriately. Retention strategies at Canadian institutions can thus be specifically developed from this data. The challenge that follows is to measure the impact on retention related to the programs or strategies that were implemented to increase student satisfaction.

Many universities in Canada have used the NSSE survey and have access to data about the level of engagement that students report. Data about the five NSSE indicators can assist institutions in identifying which category or categories of student engagement might warrant immediate attention and what type of retention strategy/ intervention would be most likely to lead to increased engagement based on student responses.

What is missing in institutions in Canada, and internationally as well, is data that connects the student experience outside the classroom with retention rates. NSSE's "supportive campus environment" and "enriching educational environment" embark on the frontiers of learning beyond the classroom—but this area needs more extensive exploration and programming.

Most programming related to retention tends to focus on 'academic' and learning skills and not on the quality of the experience itself. Most institutions in Canada promise in one form or another to deliver an outstanding student experience. This is not well defined and therefore difficult to measure. Again, linking academic support programming to retention may be more doable than linking programming outside the classroom to retention.

KEY RETENTION ISSUES

Retention is a shared responsibility between faculties and academic departments, instructional staff, support staff in administrative units and student affairs units—including the registrar's office, enrolment services, student services and residences. There are a number of issues that impact retention that need to be identified and considered. Although these issues are not necessarily different in Canada than in the United States, they must be addressed specifically by Canadian universities and colleges.

Institutional Plans: Strategic, SEM, Financial and Retention Planning

A university or college's strategic plan should identify SEM as one of the institution's highest priorities. Retention, a key component of SEM, will then be incorporated, along with recruitment, as a priority for the institution. Resources to address these priorities must necessarily follow. The entire institution needs to marshall its resources to support the institutional retention plan: "it takes a whole college or university to retain a student."

In addition to focusing on campus climate, friendly staff and well-trained faculty, Canadian institutions are now paying added attention to enhancing orientation, academic advising, early warning systems (through which first-year students in academic or non-academic difficulty can be identified and action taken to support them), integrated learning, and the creation of vibrant student life programs. These vital initiatives require a commitment from all levels of the institution.

A second issue is the impact of retention on institutional budgets. There is a positive impact on revenue for those universities and colleges that are successful in retaining students through to graduation. Institutional data is extremely helpful to identify the revenue-generation potential for retaining students from year one to matriculation.

Being fiscally accountable in a challenging economic environment is another overriding concern in post-secondary education. It is important to complete a cost-analysis of retention programs and activities. This type of analysis may provide another powerful argument for institutions, in addition to the argument related to student success, to direct funding toward retention efforts. Because much of the retention effort will flow from student affairs units, this is a critical argument. Institutions that can track retention data to specific faculty-based initiatives might consider allowing the increased revenue resulting from higher enrolments in second year and beyond to flow back to the faculties. Faculties would then see direct value from the institution's retention efforts and they would be more likely to support retention initiatives.

Retention and a Renewed Focus on Learning

The relationship between retention and student learning is another issue that needs to be addressed by Canadian institutions. Firstly, what are the priorities of academic staff and the balance of their roles between teaching and instruction in the classroom (and in other instructional venues), and focusing on the research enterprise and the acquisition of grants and patents? This is a critical issue to universities in particular but it is important for colleges to consider as well.

Secondly, universities and colleges must address the reality that today's students learn very differently than previous cohorts of students. The traditional approaches to instruction, and particularly the lecture method, are no longer the most effective way for teachers to teach or learners to learn. How students learn and how institutions respond to changing ways that students learn will impact the retention of students.

In a high-technology world, the application of technology in the classroom is critical for student retention and student success. Students are familiar with the latest technological advances and expect similar modes in the delivery of course information—for example, podcasts, on-line course notes and powerpoint presentations, interactive tutorials, and electronic bulletin boards. The introduction of technology within the classroom and lecture hall, such as the use of clickers, has also changed the way students can participate in large class sessions. Finally, students are also demonstrating their affinity towards online education and hybrid or blended courses.

The ways new pedagogical approaches impact retention must be assessed. Integrated learning is a relatively new focus in higher education that must be considered. Wilfrid Laurier University has moved in this direction in order to gain significant insight into the impact of new learning approaches on both student success and student retention.

Special Student Populations

An issue that is of paramount importance in Canada is the retention of Aboriginal students. Gathering data on the numbers of Aboriginal students in our institutions is a particular challenge, given that Aboriginal students are only required to self-report their status. If we do not know how many students have registered in programs, it is impossible to calculate retention rates. In many jurisdictions, a stronger focus on improving Aboriginal students' basic academic skills and learning strategies is necessary to ensure that they can succeed. It is therefore important for those who work in both admissions and Aboriginal student services to encourage Aboriginal students to self-declare so that appropriate retention strategies can be developed.

Universities and colleges must be proactive to ensure Aboriginal students are academically prepared for post-secondary education. Providing advising and career counseling at an early age is critical. We must connect with and advise Aboriginal prospects and work with junior high school, if not younger, Aboriginal students to identify those with the interest and ability to be successful in post-secondary education.

The retention of international students must also be addressed more intentionally by Canadian institutions. Competition for international students is high in Canada and different recruitment strategies have been adopted. The acquisition of language skills is key for the success of international students, and most institutions in Canada do a good job in ensuring that language skills are sufficient for the students to be successful. Many institutions have also invested in English as a Second Language (ESL) programs that students have to successfully complete before being admitted formally to the institution.

It is not clear if the retention rates of international students who are admitted directly through an ESL program or who are admitted through a transfer route differ from each other. This data is particularly critical to collect so that institutions can target their retention strategies appropriately to enhance the success of international students who are admitted. The recruitment of international students is expensive so institutions need accurate retention data to make appropriate recruitment and admission decisions.

RETENTION STRATEGIES

Strategies that are reported to improve student retention are numerous but to be effective, an initiative must fit the context of a particular university or college and the needs of the students attending it. Retention is not simply a synonym for persistence or lack of attrition. There is, in the use of the word 'retention', the implication that we are not simply holding on to students but rather that students are compelled to stay at an institution because they feel a good sense of fit. This fit or belonging to the higher education community relies largely upon the components the institution provides for engagement, making connections, academic development, student life, student experiences and ultimately academic success. Ideally, the student is actively engaged in his or her own education, becomes a participating member of the university community, and is satisfied overall with the educational and social experience. An additional outcome of a successful, engaged, and enlightened student is that he or she may be more likely to become a supportive alumnus.

Students should become connected to the institution at a deeper level than being a mere consumer of higher education. The institution should engage the student in positive, educational and social ways so that retaining that student is a natural outcome.

In a further extension of the ideal, the student becomes an 'educated' person, one whose life will have purpose. It is becoming more commonplace for institutions to look beyond the program credential or degree as the only measure of an education and to aspire to provide 'something' more. Often that extra element is tied to what the institution values and what is currently a way to distinguish or brand an institution's unique offerings. Accordingly, some different retention strategies in practice include the development of a set of competencies that define an educated student; the use of a strategic plan as a springboard to delineate 'promises' to students; and the introduction of capstone courses or service learning activities that often aim to provide experiences that mirror a student's expectations (*e.g.*, to become a global citizen).

This latter point suggests another lens with which to view retention strategies. That is, improving the learning experience appears to be gaining support as institutions are broadening the definition of what learning is, where it takes place and how the institution teaches students (Christenson Hughes and Mighty 2010).

To date, the focus of retention strategies in Canada has related primarily to providing support systems for students who are struggling, or are projected to struggle, academically. The resources being used in most Canadian institutions are found in student affairs/services programs, enrolment services and the registrar's office. These types of programs/services include but are not limited to orientation, college success courses/workshops, learning skills centres, academic support centres, early warning systems, student mentoring and tutorial services and the establishment of learning communities or special interest groups (FIGS). Examples of such activities can be found throughout the Web sites of most Canadian universities and colleges.

Beyond the supports and services provided to students, there remains room for institutions to strategize about specific retention initiatives. When considering the creation and implementation of a specific retention initiative, the institution must develop or adapt a strategy that is custom-designed to meet a specific institutional challenge. There is considerable evidence to suggest that we should front-load retention strategies within the first year of students' studies so that it can become a high-impact program geared to connect first-year students to the institution or to the communities within the institution. Programs and activities should be devised that intentionally foster student connections with other students and staff. Finally, our retention strategies should provide for different locales of learning that create an integrated learning environment through informal out-of-class experiences and co-curricular learning opportunities.

BEST PRACTICES

Although Canadian institutions may have been late in focusing on SEM as a priority in comparison to our U.S. colleagues, great strides have been made in the past number of years.

Retention Embedded in SEM Plans

SEM plans are becoming increasingly more common in Canadian institutions and retention strategies are an outgrowth of the plans that are in place. The University of Manitoba's SEM plan is being developed by a SEM committee populated by members representing various university constituents. The identification of the need for such an institutional plan is embedded in the strategic planning process which is under the direction of the Office of the Vice-President (Academic) and Provost (SEM Summit 2010). The initial phase deals with developing a framework for the plan. This has been a shared responsibility between Student Affairs and the Faculties. The plan features four fundamental promises to students:

- *Excellent education*: A commitment to students' academic success.
- *Research experience:* A commitment to providing an opportunity for students to receive a research, scholarly or creative experience at the undergraduate level, if desired.

- *Community:* A commitment to providing an opportunity for students to become engaged in rich and diverse opportunities on and off campus, nationally and/or internationally.
- *Career enhancement:* A commitment to providing students with an education that will enhance their career opportunities and advancement.

Most institutions today emphasize the importance of the student experience to student success. The commitment to the delivery of an outstanding student experience drives the University of Manitoba's SEM plan. How the institution defines the student experience, planning the programming that will be put in place to enhance student success and development, and ensuring that assessment data is collected and analyzed will be the next areas of focus. This is a total community effort that involves faculty, staff and students. Academic policies are being reviewed and simplified; a welcoming environment is being created with a renewed approach to orientation and an enhancement of physical facilities and study space; teaching and learning is gaining a renewed focus; and students are being encouraged to be more engaged and involved in student life, service learning and student activities.

SEM sub-committees have been established to develop specific strategies for the SEM plan. As SEM is an evolving and dynamic process, the retention strategies developed and implemented at the University of Manitoba will also evolve and be integrated into the overall strategic planning of the institution as a whole.

The SEM plan at the University of Saskatchewan is a second example of an effective approach to SEM planning. Some notable features of the University of Saskatchewan approach to SEM and to retention have been: the adoption of the phrase 'an engaged university'; the creation of a new position, Vice-Provost of Teaching and Learning, designed to provide leadership in the area of improving the student experience; and the adoption of six commitments to provide direction for this priority area. Responsibilities for the commitments have been allocated and there is evidence of moving the 'promises' from paper to reality. As well as accountability, assessment plays an important part of the plan. The University of Saskatchewan Achievement Record (September 2009) includes key performance measures such as completion rates, student retention and student satisfaction.

A final example is provided by recent changes at Wilfrid Laurier University. Senior administrators at that institution have embarked upon a deliberate plan to integrate learning and development by changing the organizational structure and reporting relationships. For some positions, including a new Associate Vice-President of Teaching and Learning, there are dual reporting relationships to the Vice President (Academic) and the Vice President (Students). This is intended to support the collaborations between teaching and learning and learning beyond the classroom. Laurier's new institutional brand, reflecting their positioning and commitment, is "Inspiring Lives of Leadership and Purpose." Renewed attention to revising and enhancing the curriculum is given to reflect the promise that opportunities for purposeful study and life will be provided to students.

Retention Strategies

The SEM plan should provide direction as to what retention initiatives should be considered. In determining what strategy or program might work best for an institution, there are a multitude of best practices that have been described in the literature, with regular updates and new approaches described in sources such as *Academica*, a Canadian-based daily electronic newsletter about developments in higher education.

UPGRADED TEACHING METHODS

Financial resources must be invested in the teaching and learning enterprise. Develop teaching methodologies to be more interactive and less didactic or lecture-oriented in style. There is also a need for additional resources for upgrading classrooms and lab facilities, implementing more co-op programs and field placements, and integrating research into the undergraduate curriculum. The curriculum should also feature alternate learning experiences such as student exchanges and study abroad, service learning programs and student leadership development programs.

EXTENDED ORIENTATION

Many institutions have realized that students have varying 'readiness' and attention levels when presented with information at orientation. One way to support students is to have different points in the semester or year at which information is made available in different formats and at times in the academic cycle where students may be most receptive. For example, a year-long orientation program based out of the University of Calgary's Office of Student Experience consists of parent orientations, a spring registration orientation, and an e-magazine for students. These additional orientation initiatives were designed to complement the University of Calgary's extended fall orientation program.

Extending orientation can also mean having transition programs overlap with recruitment initiatives and the recruitment process. For example, NorQuest College's Enrolment Management Project (SEMP) included the launch of a new prospective student office, as well as the implementation of a student admission and retention information system, designed to empower prospective students to make informed decisions. Such pre-enrolment advising is not always possible for many institutions due both to limited resources and a belief in some jurisdictions that this is the responsibility of high school counseling offices.

INTERNATIONAL EXPERIENCES

The University of British Columbia has developed a retention strategy that delivers on the promise to students of a commitment to community and international engagement. The foundation for this strategy is the UBC Strategic Plan, entitled *Place and Promise: The UBC Plan.* The plan addresses nine commitments: Student Learning, Research Excellence, Community Engagement, Aboriginal Engagement, Alumni Engagement, International Understanding, International Engagement, Outstanding Work Engagement and Sustainability. The intent of this strategic initiative is to provide each UBC student who wishes to engage in an international experience with financial support of $2,000, financed by a reallocation of scholarship funds. Although in the initial stages of project implementation, the UBC example provides insight into the development of a unique retention strategy and the creativity required to deliver on a promise to students—a promise that, if successful, will enhance the engagement of students at UBC and meet the expressed goal of increased student participation in learning and service abroad.

BRIDGE PROGRAMS

Student success programs and bridge programs have been introduced at many universities and colleges in Canada. At the University of Manitoba, several partner units host a three-week, three-credit course in August for incoming Aboriginal students. The course is taught by a Native Studies professor and features guest speakers from campus who assist in orienting students. Although data is not available with respect to the success of this initiative, self-reports indicate that the program has contributed to Aboriginal students making a successful transition to university work. The University 1 program, also at the University of Manitoba, is an example of a common first-year program for all incoming UM students (with the exception of Engineering, Fine Arts and Music). An in-depth orientation program, front-loaded academic advising, and intrusive interventions for students who are academically at-risk have helped University 1 students transition to post-secondary studies.

SECOND CHANCE PROGRAMS

The University of Toronto's Engineering ReFresh Program is another good example of a bridge program, albeit one that has been designed for students who were initially unsuccessful in their Engineering program. This program is designed to give first-year students who failed Engineering in their fall semester the chance to re-develop their understanding of the core engineering curriculum as well as learn vital life skills to determine whether they can return to engineering or whether another program or institution would be more suitable to them.

The University of Alberta's Fresh Start Program is another example of a "second chance" program for students who have been unsuccessful in a university program. This program gives students who were required to withdraw from their academic program an alternate way to re-establish satisfactory academic standing so that they can continue to study at the institution. The Fresh Start Program helps students find effective cognitive strategies and gives them academic credit for successful completion of the program. This is a retention strategy that keeps students at the University, shows that the institution cares about the student's experience, and endeavors to provide another opportunity for the student to be successful in the initial program of choice or an alternative program based on the student's needs, interests and skill sets.

Seneca College was awarded the Education Policy Institute's (EPI) 2009 Outstanding Retention Award. In 2005, the SUCCESS@Seneca project was initiated with four main initiatives aimed at high-risk students. These initiatives offered the students an orientation; an interactive and informative online 'success' portal; 'success' workshops and social networking opportunities and "The College Coach Approach." This last tactic connected students to a 'college coach'. The 'coach' was a Seneca employee who helped the student succeed by providing a contact, information and advice about college and the choices faced by students.

EARLY WARNING SYSTEMS

Implementation of an early warning system is relevant to any discussion on retention strategies. There are several points along the student life cycle where alerts or indicators to the institution afford an opportunity for intervention. Such systems should be tied closely to the provision of advising, counseling and learning services. There are products on the market that begin identifying 'at-risk' students during the admissions and registration process. Further along the continuum are those systems that focus on identifying vulnerable first-year students by alerting the student and a 'triage' team to an instructor's concerns about behaviour and performance in the academic setting.

Kwantlen Polytechnic University has implemented an early warning system that links faculty, Student Affairs and the student who is encountering academic problems. The Early Alert Referral System (EARS) allows the faculty member to assess the level and type of difficulty the student is having, whether academic or personal, and this information is then made available to Student Affairs staff. Different intervention strategies are then employed to contact the student and link the student to the appropriate forms of assistance. EARS is a proactive system of intervention designed to provide students with opportunities to deal with the issues at hand and positively impact student success. The EARS system also attempts to draw attention to students who are unsuccessful academically due to personal issues, which is an added value of this particular early warning system.

SERVICE LEARNING

Service learning is programming that is directed at volunteering and contributing to the community, typically beyond the institution. Students are provided opportunities to participate in activities that are located in a local, national or international community. Many institutions have created programs that take students to a developing country where the students' contributions range from helping to build a road or a school to teach skills. Through these efforts, students learn about other people and cultures. They are also encouraged to reflect on how their experiential learning relates to their academic program and their own personal development. That is, service learning requires the student to not only become an engaged volunteer but provides for and requires substantive reflection on the experience. This is an area that bears watching as universities and colleges strive to provide learning opportunities that extend beyond the traditional classroom and feature more experiential and integrated learning opportunities.

Somewhat related to service learning are other programs such as student exchanges, institutes and internships that provide students with enhanced learning and development opportunities. Although these types of initiatives may be 'for credit' and do not contain a 'volunteer' component, they may attract students to select, and persist at, an institution.

STUDENT LEADERSHIP AND CO-CURRICULAR RECORDS

Students are increasingly interested in having a formal record of their campus activities. The Co-Curricular Record (CCR) enables students to have their involvement in various out-of-class activities recognized along with their academic transcripts. The CCR has been developed at many institutions including Wilfrid Laurier University, the University of Calgary, McMaster University, the University of Waterloo, University of Windsor, Seneca College and Trent University. The programs and activities recognized on the CCR include governance, leadership, service learning, awards/achievements and participation/volunteerism. To the student, this reflects the value-added component of their university experience. It contributes to student development and career enhancement and has a direct impact on the marketability of students as future employees. The development of the CCR also has significant potential for student engagement, student retention and the enhancement of the student experience.

Student leadership development has been a focus on many Canadian campuses and the Leadership Centre at Wilfrid Laurier University was one of the initial leadership centres established in Canada. The Centre supports all aspects of student leadership development, student involvement and student leadership experiences.

The Centre is the focal point for Laurier's Co-Curricular Record, provides leadership workshops and hosts leadership conferences.

SUMMARY AND CONCLUSIONS

As more Canadian institutions have become aware of SEM and the importance of retention to SEM planning, there is a growing resource of plans, strategies and initiatives that are uniquely Canadian. Colleagues at universities are learning from their counterparts in colleges and vice versa. Similarly, programs at small institutions serve as exemplars for similar initiatives at large comprehensive institutions. There is a thirst for retention strategies and ways to improve the quality of the student experience in Canadian universities and colleges. Retention is directly impacted by providing an improved student experience. Many Canadian institutions have sought information from students through both CUSC and NSSE instruments and it is that data that contributes to an evidence-based model of SEM planning. Retaining students is a mark of being accountable to all constituents—the students, the general public, provincial governments and society in general. It appears that the spotlight is on retention in this current phase of SEM and as many institutions grapple with understanding retention patterns and assisting students to be successful in their academic programs there are some emerging issues that will require further exploration.

- In an attempt to be data-driven, institutions may be challenged by having too much data and/or not the right kind of data. It is recommended that a SEM Data Sub-committee coordinate the data needs and reports of the SEM planning committees.
- In the attempt to be informed by our students, there is a glut of surveys causing survey 'fatigue'. Surveying students and creating reports has become a complex commercial enterprise that is, in Canada, further complicated by publications of rankings and coverage in national media. These rankings are not clear indicators of how institutions and students are faring. Institutions must be judicious about what surveys and tools are used to assess retention and what data forms the base of a SEM retention plan.
- There are new tools, typically new software programs, that can assist institutions in finding out what students would like to tell us about their experiences and

how they are faring. In addition to early alert systems there are other programs that use analytics to identify and assist universities and colleges in helping high-risk students.

- The tracking of students would be assisted greatly by giving each student a provincial student number. This number would follow a student from entry to school in the primary years through to post-secondary education. A provincial student number would permit institutions to more accurately track students and their mobility through the post-secondary system and would be instrumental in making retention a wider priority.

- As more emphasis is placed on the student experience, a tension may develop between the direct service providers in student affairs and those who coordinate student life programming. This tension may develop if there is an uneven resourcing of these two critical areas of student support.

- There are indications that funds for leadership and 'extra' curricular programs can be gained successfully through sponsorship and corporate partnerships. While this is beneficial to both parties for a number of reasons, institutions should evaluate and fully consider the risks involved with such partnerships.

- Assessment and evaluation of retention strategies and activities including student life programming continues to be challenging; however student affairs professionals must become more expert in creating programs with outcomes and devising methods to assess those outcomes.

- All programming that extends beyond the classroom has the potential to support integrated learning. One example is service learning and this type of experiential learning will likely become a growing area as it becomes more fully integrated in the curriculum. A service learning experience that ties to, builds upon and influences the course material enhances the student experience and creates integration between student affairs and faculties.

- The potential for student engagement in the community, and particularly the non-profit sector, can serve to enhance the reputation of post-secondary institutions. Linking student power and civic engagement has great potential for the student, the community and the college/university.

In conclusion, the notion of retention is being extended from the early contact with potential recruits to the provision of programs and activities that take the student far from the classroom but ultimately reinforce learning. Retention is becoming the common thread of the SEM plan rather than simply an add-on or follow-up to recruitment. With this new, major role to play, those involved with retention are encouraged to help shape the future approaches to retention at Canadian institutions. While much has been accomplished, there is considerable work to do at the individual institutional level as we strive to provide exemplary post-secondary educational experiences to engaged and successful students.

Larry Gauthier

11

INCREASING
ABORIGINAL
STUDENT SUCCESS

/ **Chapter 11** /

Student retention is perhaps the most significant issue facing post-secondary institutions in Canada, particularly for Aboriginal students.[18] The lack of Aboriginal student success in post-secondary institutions is well documented (Grant 1995, Deloria and Wildcat 2001). These studies indicate that retention rates for Aboriginal students are generally fifty percent lower than that of non-Aboriginal students. More recent studies (Timmons 2009, Preston 2008a, Mendelson 2006) identify the many barriers that prevent Aboriginal students from being successful. Not surprisingly, these barriers include a wide array of historical, educational, social, economic, geographical, cultural, pedagogical and financial funding issues (Preston 2008a). Timmons (2009), while recognizing these barriers, suggests that perhaps more importantly, Aboriginal students come 'ill-prepared' for university education. Mendelson (2006) points out the urgency of Aboriginal education in Canada stating that "the future social well being and economic prosperity, particularly in Western and Northern Canada, rests at least partly on better results for Aboriginal Canadians in the post-secondary education system" (p. 1). While many institutions have developed and designed support services specifically for Aboriginal students, they have done so without a theoretical framework and generally do not take a strategic approach to the issue. This chapter will offer some insight into Aboriginal student success and suggest a new approach for increasing Aboriginal student success.

---

[18] Note: While the Canada Act 1982, Section 35.2 identifies Canada's Aboriginal people as Indian, Métis and Inuit, for the remainder of this paper I refer specifically to Indian and use the term First Nations and Indian interchangeably. The term Aboriginal is used to denote all groups.

BACKGROUND

Many First Nations students are taught the concept that "education is our buffalo". That is, in the past buffalo provided all the means for subsistence, food, shelter, clothing, implements, and fuel for Indian people. Today education is seen as the means of providing for life's necessities — not only for themselves but also for their families, communities and nations. Thus there is considerable pressure applied on First Nations students by their own communities to be successful. In this respect, for Aboriginal students the purpose of education is not seen as an individual undertaking. While it is accepted that education will enhance the quality of life for the individual, the expectation is that the student will return to assist and provide leadership in developing or at least improving the socio-economic conditions of the community.

Aboriginal post-secondary student demographics are fairly consistent across Canada. In 2007 the University of Winnipeg hosted a roundtable discussion on Aboriginal post-secondary education for western universities (Mendelson and Usher 2007). At this gathering each institution noted that approximately 70 percent of Aboriginal students were admitted via mature, open or unclassified admissions. That is, they did not have the high school prerequisites for direct admission to their program of interest. Interestingly, Aboriginal student retention rates varied from as low as 30 percent to a high of 75 percent.

The Urban Aboriginal Peoples Study, conducted by the Environics Institute (2010), identified four reasons why Aboriginal students decide to attend university: to get a job/career, to acquire the financial benefits that will ensure a better quality of life, for personal enrichment, and (for a small number of individuals) the drive to give back to their community. The UAPS survey also found that family is critical to the success of urban Aboriginal peoples attending university. UAPS noted that 60 percent of current university students were influenced by their parents/guardians to attend university.

Aboriginal students have the lowest completion rates of all ethnic groups enrolled in university programs. Obviously there are problems with the retention of Aboriginal students. The study also points out that 65 percent of current Aboriginal students identified emotional, motivational and financial support as the three main factors making a difference in terms of persistence.

Many support programs for Aboriginal students are delivered to the Aboriginal student population as a whole. That is, in most cases post-secondary institutions develop support programs without recognizing the diversity within the Aboriginal student population. Although many Aboriginal groups share common geographical environments and some have similar traits, they remain distinct in their cultural identity and beliefs. For example the Blackfoot of Alberta have a distinct culture compared to the Cree in Alberta. At Mount Royal University approximately one third of self-declared Aboriginal students are Blackfoot, one-third are Cree and one-third Métis (or non-status), with a small number identifying as Inuit. All these groups are served by the Iniskim Centre yet each of these groups has their own unique needs. As Aboriginal student service providers it is incumbent upon us to recognize these needs and develop specific support programs appropriately.

OBSERVATIONS OF THE FIRST NATION STUDENT EXPERIENCE

Data

While much research has been conducted on the access and persistence of Aboriginal students in post-secondary education, many universities fail to collect and maintain statistical data (Mendelson and Usher 2007). Only in the last few years have institutions made a concerted effort to track Aboriginal students. Universities and colleges need to develop information systems that track Aboriginal student data including information relating to admissions, grade point averages, persistence and graduation rates, and reasons for early departure. The dilemma with data, of course, is that the information extracted is only as good as the data input into the system. Identifying an Aboriginal student requires self-declaration. Many Aboriginal students are wary of self-identification and many do not do so. It is clear that not all Aboriginal students are captured in institutional data.

Finances

The federal government's Department of Indian and Northern Affairs funds First Nations post-secondary education through the Post-Secondary Student Support Program (PSSSP). These post-secondary funds are distributed to Indian governments (Band/Tribal Council) based on a historical funding formula rather than student financial need. First Nations prospective students must be accepted by a recognized post-secondary institution and then submit an application for sponsorship to their post-secondary program. In 1988 Indian Affairs placed a two percent funding cap on annual budget expenditures. This has placed significant pressure on the post-secondary program's ability to adequately meet the post-secondary needs of First Nations students. Preston (2008b) points out that an estimated 8,000 Indian students did not receive post-secondary funding for the 2000/01 academic year. The Assembly of First Nations estimates that since 1996 over 10,000 prospective students were denied sponsorship as a result of inadequate PSSSP funding. As a result many First Nations have introduced stricter measures for students to receive post-secondary financial aid. For example, most First Nations post-secondary programs will only fund students who are registered as full-time students. In most cases, this is defined as four classes per semester. Thus inadequate funding from the Post-Secondary Student Support Program continues to be a challenge for First Nations students. [19] Additionally, the funding cap has resulted in a substantial decrease in the number of students funded and attending post-secondary institutions.

For those students who do receive funding from the government or their communities, money management is often a bigger issue than lack of adequate funding. For these students, stating that they withdrew from their studies because they could no longer afford to go to school is not necessarily a truth but a means of saving 'face' in the community.

Scholarships and bursaries awarded in one-time payments do not have a significant impact on the retention and success of First Nations university students. Many universities attempt to solicit scholarship and bursary donations to address the financial need of Aboriginal students and support their retention and success. Yet sadly, some Aboriginal scholarships and bursaries are not awarded. First Nations students are reluctant to apply for scholarships and bursaries. They see writing an essay highlighting their accomplishments, achievements and service to community as "bragging" and are reluctant to do so.

There are certainly legitimate financial situations that arise which may influence a student's decision to withdraw prematurely. Institutions would better serve their

---

[19] Note that the Canada Student Loan program considers full-time students to be those students who are enrolled in a minimum of three courses—a much more liberal definition of "full-time."

students and increase Aboriginal student retention and success rates, if the financial aid funds were provided in the form of emergency loans and bursaries rather than scholarships.

Historic Factors

Residential schools have had a profound effect on First Nations peoples. Cultural conflict, alienation, and poor self-concept are just some of the intergenerational issues that result from the residential school experience. That is, not only are those who attended these schools affected but so are their children and grandchildren.

The socioeconomic effects of poverty also raise issues for First Nations students. These issues have been well documented perhaps nowhere as succinctly as in the report of the Royal Commission on Aboriginal Peoples, Volume 3 (1995). Almost 70 percent of First Nations students are female. Many First Nations women who attend university are not supported by their spouses—indeed in most cases the spouse becomes a dependent. Many of the women who attend university are faced with personal issues that may affect their ability to commit to their studies. Counsellors deal with a wide range of issues that affect and result in early departure. Many Aboriginal students identify families and daycare (as well as appropriate housing) as a major barrier for First Nations students. Universities could increase success rates by providing more daycare options for First Nations students.

Academic Preparedness

Almost 50 percent of Aboriginal youth (ages 15–24) have not completed secondary school (Mendelson 2006). As Timmons (2007) points out "Many Aboriginal students arrive at university ill-prepared to succeed, lacking proper academic preparation or knowledge of how to excel at university" (p. 8). Preston (2008a; 2008b) further notes that First Nations elementary and secondary schools do not adequately prepare students for post-secondary education. Across Western Canada, approximately 70 percent of Aboriginal students are admitted into universities without high school matriculation (Mendelson and Usher 2007). Yet these students are expected to conform to the academic rigors and standards expected of all students and to produce quality academic work.

Many Aboriginal students considered at risk are traditional-oriented students with critical reading and writing skills identified as problem areas. Many of these students come to their studies with English (or French) as a second language or with very little mastery of the language of instruction. In addition to the lack of academic preparedness, academic integration is a major challenge. Most traditional-oriented Aboriginal students do not understand the world of academia and see their studies as a process of developing critical skills. In fact, some traditional-oriented students argue that it is not their place to question. It is thus helpful to show these students that traditional Aboriginal societies had highly developed critical skills and that knowledge can be found with a questioning frame of mind.

Academic Engagement

Most universities and colleges in Canada have established Aboriginal Student Centres to provide culturally appropriate support services. These centres also work to sensitize faculty and staff on issues affecting Aboriginal students and communities. In addition, most colleges and universities, in collaboration with student unions/associations, provide Aboriginal Student Association/Councils with physical 'space'. This allows for additional space for Aboriginal students to gather socially and organize various social activities. Aboriginal centres have been successful in providing 'learning communities' or a sense of belonging and have contributed to increasing the success of Aboriginal students. On the other hand, some Aboriginal students gather in Indian/Indigenous/Native Studies and access programs and are reluctant to 'engage' with their institutions. It is important that Aboriginal students feel comfortable within the entire institution and not just the Aboriginal student centre.

Class attendance is a significant problem for Aboriginal students, particularly notable among first-year students. Many students often do not understand why they failed a class or have done poorly, even after it has been pointed out that they have missed more than half the class. Due to funding implications (where funding may be withdrawn if the student withdraws from a course), First Nations students tend to remain registered in a class even when the instructor has indicated the student does not have a reasonable chance of obtaining a passing grade.

Culture

Due to the nature of programming within Aboriginal student centres and faced with limited resources, Aboriginal service providers rely too heavily on the support and participation of individual Elders. Some Elders may have knowledge of the stars, others tribal history or medicine, and others are spiritual leaders. Yet we call upon the 'resident' Elder to speak to all aspects of cosmology, epistemology, history, culture, values, beliefs and practises assuming they have expertise in all of these areas. Elders are indeed repositories of knowledge, but in specific areas; it is incumbent upon those working in post-secondary institutions to learn which Elders hold what expertise and to utilize that knowledge accordingly. It is true that Elders serve a critical role in Aboriginal/Native/Indigenous studies academic programs. However, as noted in the UAPS, urban First Nations people seek spiritual and cultural knowledge from their home communities (p. 63). Moreover, only 34 percent of Metis surveyed indicated Aboriginal spirituality as an important factor.

Cultural factors impact Aboriginal student retention and success. For example, there is considerable prestige for First Nations students who enrol in post-secondary studies. Communities hold university students in high regard. Consequently, relatives will often call upon students to assist in ceremonies in the community. The relative fails to realise that by, for example, asking the student to assist in keeping the fire during a traditional funeral ceremony, they are asking the student to miss a week of classes. The student is obligated to accept the request particularly if protocols were followed.

THEORETICAL CONSIDERATIONS

As indicated above, there are many contributing factors that lead Aboriginal, and in particular First Nations, students to withdraw or simply 'drop out' of post-secondary (and especially university) programs. Perhaps the most significant factor is the 'sense of belonging'. Many First Nations students do not feel welcome or part of the educational process. This is due largely to the historical relationship between First Nations peoples and European settlers. When Europeans began colonizing North America, they believed First Nations peoples were without culture, religion, and law and lived in societies where life was as Thomas Hobbes theorized, 'nasty, brutish and short'. Europeans took it upon themselves to educate the First Nations populations hoping that in the process they would be transformed into the image of themselves. In effect, they sought to eradicate First Nations peoples of their value and belief systems. Over the past 500 years, there has been much success in this policy. Today, there is a dichotomy within First Nations communities and particularly within the youth population that is most often expressed as the 'traditionalists' pitted against the 'assimilationists'. For traditionalists who have maintained and practise their values and belief systems, exposure to post-secondary education becomes a traumatic experience. On the other hand, the 'assimilationists' have integrated into western institutions successfully. The reality of this diversity is that both groups of First Nations students do not share the same university success rates.

Bill Hansen (1995) provides an excellent description of this stratification in First Nations communities by examining what he refers to as the 'industrial/change oriented' and the 'subsistence/traditional oriented' realities. Currently, anywhere from 45 to 65 percent of First Nations people have relocated to urban centres. Moreover, many First Nations members living in urban centres, while having maintained connections to their reserve, have never lived on the reserve. Hansen argues that members of this group have developed characteristics, motivation and capabilities to be successful within the complex modern industrial (mainstream) society. In addition they have accepted the individualistic pursuit of material wealth, the work ethic, the religious flexibility "and have modified and internalized the social behaviour acceptable to others" (p. 24) within the industrial society. In many cases this acculturation process is so effective that their function as a 'role model' is limited or non-effective except to those in this same group. It is interesting to note that Hansen also suggests that others see these 'industrial oriented' people as "accepting and often promoting, the life-style which is the cause of many of their problems" (p. 24). Because of their industrial/change-oriented background, these individuals understand and are more effective in the industrial society's institutions, including its universities.

In contrast, Hansen contends that because of choice or circumstances, traditional-oriented individuals have remained bonded to a historical way of life. However, alienation from the traditional land base has required these individuals to make major adjustments to their social, cultural and economic lives. As well the educational system teaches that western knowledge is correct and that indigenous knowledge is not or is, at the very least, questionable. As two prominent scholars note: "One of the most painful experiences for American Indian students is to come into conflict with the teaching of science that purports to explain phenomena already explained by tribal knowledge and traditions" (Deloria and Wildcat 2001, p. 4). To the traditional-oriented, "welfare, and other forms of transfer payments, are often seen a token compensation for the loss of the physical and spiritual relationships with the homelands" (Hansen 1995, p. 26). These individuals are faced with continued alienation from their former holistic environment and the disintegration of their institutions (traditional) which in the past gave meaning to their lives. Consequently,

...the traditional group of Aboriginal people, often identified by their sense of detachment from most others, are a socio-cultural minority within their racial community. Because their remoteness is often social, cultural, psychological, economic and geographical, it cannot be assumed that their needs can be effectively addressed by the imposition of programs and services created to serve the change oriented (p. 86).

Tinto (1987, 1993) advances an interaction student persistence theory/model based on the student's social and academic integration that is very connected to the Aboriginal student experience. He contends that students enter post-secondary institutions with pre-existing characteristics that are associated with family background, varying degrees of skills, abilities and high school preparedness. Tinto's theory fits well within the context of Aboriginal post-secondary retention issues. The more the student feels a fit or 'congruence' with the institution, the more likely he or she is to persist. In this respect Tinto is addressing the mismatch between the student's interests and the needs of the institution as well as a lack of interaction between the student and other members of the institution. In effect, the student is unable to become integrated because they are unable to establish personal bonds with other members of the institution. Tinto contends that students are insufficiently prepared for the scale of academic and social change required of them. He suggests that lack of adjustment is especially common among disadvantaged students. This he attributes in part to a lack of academic preparedness and an "inability of individuals to separate themselves from past forms of association." In contrast, student engagement is the degree of connectedness between students and their institution, especially with their educational programs (Kuh *et al.* 2005b). Engaged students are very connected. They are more likely to persist in their studies and be successful. This process of engagement is what Tinto refers to in his description of academic integration.

It is interesting to note that in Tinto's discussion of individual goals, he states that many students change goals while attending college/university and that some have difficulty in determining what goals they wish to pursue. Hansen indicates that the industrial/change-oriented individual is concerned with long-term goals such as completing a university education while the traditional/subsistence-oriented individual is more concerned with day-to-day survival. These factors present some unique perspectives to which Aboriginal student services providers must consider and respond.

HeavyRunner and DeCelles (2002) developed a successful retention strategy for Indian students based on the predication that family is central to their way of life. Without a doubt, poverty and family concerns increase the burdens and stress shouldered by Indian students. The authors point out common issues with both Native American and First Nations students where a student may drop out because a car breaks down and there is no money for repairs. Another may leave because no one is available to take care of the children and daycare is unavailable. Other students come to post-secondary studies with more profound needs. Counsellors report that alcoholism, drug abuse, and domestic violence are prevalent among students and their family members. Other challenges, including high morbidity rates and the breakdown of the nuclear family, weigh heavily on the minds of First Nations students. For example, the suicide rate for Indian people is more than double that of other racial or ethnic minority groups, the number of alcohol-related deaths is extremely high, and the already large number of single-parent households continues to increase. Often First Nations students are called upon by relatives to assist in addressing these issues taking them away from their studies.

HeavyRunner and DeCelles postulate that "the successful completion of one's educational goals is more likely when the student has a supportive family and participates in community events." They suggest that: "First, the colleges need to help students and their families to meet pressing personal and family needs. Second, the colleges must seek to enlist, to develop and to structure the ability of family members to support students. Third, the colleges must engage family members in the life of the college by enlisting them as partners and involving them in supportive activities." Students and their families must be invited to participate and join in institutional activities, especially those aimed at social integration. For example, seminars can be provided to assist in dealing with issues and problems students and families face including communication skills, anger management, substance abuse and mental health.

A NEW APPROACH TO ABORIGINAL RETENTION

Aboriginal support services are best situated to respond to the retention issues raised in this chapter. In 2005/06 a new model of support services was piloted at the First Nations University by Student Success Services, which resulted in first-year retention rates that increased from 53 to 76 percent (Gauthier 2007). It is suggested that this approach can be adapted by other institutions.

A new model to enhance Aboriginal student success should place emphasis on the process of academic and social integration. It should begin with grounding students in higher learning traditions, academic expectations, student responsibilities, rights and so on. Aboriginal student service providers should work with students in building competencies in these areas. Elders should be called upon to help students learn who they are and where they come from. The students' families should be invited to the campus and be provided with an orientation to educate the family as to what the student's educational journey involves and on how to support the student. Together with their families, students need to develop clearly defined short- and long-term educational goals. In addition, students need to be taught the historical and cultural process of colonization and its impacts on First Nations communities and peoples today. This will help them begin to develop 'self-autonomy', validating the students' identity as Aboriginal peoples.

Throughout the process outlined above, students' critical reading, writing and thinking skills need to be developed through academic assignments. These assignments should be designed to enhance academic skills (such as study skills, note taking, and so on). Assignments should be spaced throughout the program/class (and not just mid-point or at the end) ensuring that students learn a deeper understanding of the topic/issue being considered. Ideally, this process would be presented as an "introduction to university (or college)" credit course delivered by the Aboriginal student support centres.

CONCLUSION

If Canadian post-secondary institutions are committed to increasing Aboriginal student success, they must not only depart from Eurocentric thinking, but also allocate financial resources to restructure their Aboriginal retention programs. Timmons (2009) contends that while western universities have implemented a number of strategies, approaches and solutions aimed at increasing Aboriginal student success, they have had little success. She concludes that they have failed to develop a successful Aboriginal student retention model. From a First Nations perspective, Verna Kirkness (1999) argues that in order to free oneself from the shackles of colonialization, one must take a realistic view and be prepared to make the sacrifices needed to be successful. What Kirkness is suggesting is that in order to be successful, First Nations students must take responsibility for their own educational experience. Certainly the observations above point out that a) Aboriginal students are failing to take this responsibility, and b) post-secondary institutions—and especially universities—can do a much better job at helping their Aboriginal students succeed. It is imperative, however, that institutions share in this responsibility and re-think retention strategies. The model presented above provides a foundation on which universities and colleges can begin to develop their own Aboriginal retention strategy.

Barry Townshend and Laurie Schnarr

12

FIRST-GENERATION

GENERATION

STUDENTS

/ **Chapter 12** /

ENGAGING FIRST-GENERATION STUDENTS TO OFFSET DECLINE IN STUDENT POPULATION

Despite recent increases in post-secondary enrolment in Canada, it is projected that a demographic shift in the Canadian population will result in roughly nine percent fewer university- and college-aged Canadians by 2021 (Berger *et al.* 2007). The only way to counteract such a significant decline is to create an off-set by increasing participation rates. Even if this is accomplished, some models suggest it may not be possible to fully ameliorate this effect, with the impact being felt differently across the provinces (Hango and Broucker 2005). In order for our post-secondary institutions to continue contributing sufficient graduates to the workforce—and the global knowledge economy in particular—we must rethink our approaches to ensure that higher education is accessible to a broader swath of potential learners.

Recruiting young adults who have been traditionally under-represented in post-secondary education is one strategy that is gaining resonance (Berger 2009). In Canada, approximately one-third of youth attends college and another quarter attends university (Drolet 2005). Indeed, the overall participation rate in post-secondary education is estimated at almost 80 percent for the adult Canadian population (Butlin 1999; Shaienks and Gluszynski 2007). However, there continues to be a significant and persistent gap in participation rates across a variety of socioeconomic groups, and the two most important predictive factors are parental education and income (Finnie *et al.* 2010a). Those whose parents have the highest educational attainment are nearly three times more likely to attend university, and those from the highest income strata participate at roughly twice the rate of those from the lowest (Drolet 2005; *see also* Corak, Lipps and Zhao 2003). Although less dramatic, the same pattern holds true at the college level. Of special interest, therefore, is a sub-population referred to as "first-generation students" which encompasses many of the key characteristics shared with other notable groups such as low-income Canadians and Aboriginal peoples (Berger 2009, Rae 2005, The Association of Universities and Colleges of Canada 2007, Finnie, Childs and Wismer 2010c, Lasselle *et al.* 2009).

Familial Challenges of First-Generation Students

"First-generation" is a term that researchers and policy makers typically use to refer to those students whose parents have not attended *any* post-secondary institution (either college or university) (Malatest and Associates 2009). However, there is considerable variation in how this concept is applied and there are some notable arguments as to why it should be defined more broadly. For example, in some instances the parents of students deemed to be "non-first generation" were enrolled in college or university at one time but left before completing their academic programs. Similarly, parents' experiences at college may not result in a sufficient understanding of the university context, or post-secondary education in another country can lead to markedly different expectations than are appropriate in Canada.

There have also been questions as to whether a sibling's post-secondary experience may help to mitigate a student's adjustment difficulties (Auclair *et al.* 2008). Regardless, in each instance transition challenges are exacerbated by how different first-generation students' experiences are in comparison to those of their parents.[20]

Irrespective of whether a parent did or did not attend university or college, there is an observed correlation between parents' level of education and that of their offspring (Grayson 1997; de Brouker 1998; Knighton 2002; Drolet 2005; Martinez *et al.* 2009). Furthermore, a significant number of studies have found that first-generation students tend to have lower grade point averages (GPA), take longer to complete their program of study and are more likely to withdraw without completing their academic program (Kamanzi 2010; Chen and Carroll 2005). It is important to note, however, that these findings are not universal. For example, Finnie and colleagues (2010c) found that first-generation students in their study were not

---

[20] For a useful review of this theoretical construct, including its origins in the United States and application in a Canadian context, *see* Auclair *et al.* (2008).

at greater risk for leaving post-secondary education without graduating (though this may have been attributable to the population they were studying—low-income students who were recipients of the Canada Millennium Scholarship Foundation Access Bursaries.) Likewise, Innman and Mayes (1999) found that there might be as little as a three percent difference in retention rates for first-generation students as compared with other students.

A study of students at Toronto's York University in the mid-1990s revealed that having at least one parent who attended university had a small but noteworthy impact on GPA, particularly among those with the highest admission averages (Grayson 1997). Overall, it was suggested that first-generation university students did not have significantly different grades than their peers, which was attributed to two countervailing effects: these students tended to spend fewer hours on campus per week and had less cultural involvement on campus (both of which can contribute to a higher GPA), but they were also less likely to be involved in campus activities and clubs that were shown to negatively impact GPA. Classroom involvement was also noted to be lower for first-generation students. A key finding of this study was that not all first-generation students face equal risks, but that generational status in concert with other important factors such as admission average, results in a qualitatively different campus experience. As a result, one cannot understate the implications of lower levels of engagement among first-generation students when designing and implementing intervention programs for this population.

Our Analysis: First-Generation Student Characteristics and Applying SEM Principles to Promote Their Success

Once a first-generation student embarks upon post-secondary education, we argue that generational status interacts with other identities to create a qualitatively different experience for some individuals. For example, the adjustment process for Aboriginal first-generation students is markedly different from that of Aboriginal persons with university- or college-educated families (Mendelson 2006). At the University of Western Ontario, it was similarly noted that social class may significantly interact with generational status such that students from working-class backgrounds who are first-generation might have very different experiences from those who share one but not both of these identities (Lehmann 2007, 2009a, 2009b).

In this chapter we will provide an overview of some of the defining characteristics of first-generation students. We will examine the confluence of identities, their lived experiences and, finally, the effects of the institution at the individual level. As we will see, the identities and perspectives of first-generation students are often shaped by dramatic personal struggles. One's identity as a first-generation student rarely (if ever) is a source of affinity. These students often feel alone and misunderstood, and are frequently discouraged from their academic pursuits (Orbe 2004; Priebe *et al.* 2008). Understanding them and the nature of their experiences aids us in identifying important implications for colleges and universities within a strategic enrolment management (SEM) context. Likewise, it is clear that a number of characteristics about the institution play into shaping the person-environment fit (Tinto 1995; Orbe 2004; Lehmann 2007). Given the evidence of systemic differences in students' academic achievement, we propose that colleges and universities have a duty to carefully examine those differences and to take steps to create greater equity.

Where the first half of this chapter focuses on insights gleaned from the literature about the experiences of first-generation students, the second half draws on strategic enrolment management principles to guide us through a more applied view of how institutions can respond. In particular, we will draw upon a number of examples from our own institution, the University of Guelph, to highlight various approaches that have been shown to be successful in a Canadian context.

Complex Obstacles Faced By First-Generation Students

First-generation students are nearly two-and-a-half times less likely to pursue post-secondary education and, in many cases, have lower aspirations (Drolet 2005; Lasselle *et al.* 2009). Some researchers have identified a "web of barriers"—academic, financial, informational and motivational—that impede participation for this group (Berger and Motte 2007). The challenge for colleges and universities, therefore, is to examine how administrative processes can be adapted to address the unique needs of these learners. A student-focused approach that places individual experiences in context increases our capacity to facilitate seamless transitions to, through and beyond post-secondary education.

Another area of particular consideration is the way in which we orient students to the academic environment; a process that must be inviting, informative, responsive and acknowledge that first-generation students often misunderstand higher education, its practices, expectations and opportunities. Adapting marketing strategies to ensure that first-generation students and their families better understand the realities of these transition experiences is also important for an action plan that is responsive to students' needs. Finally, through strategic approaches to market conditions, colleges and universities can align the experiences and unique characteristics of first-generation students with the broader demands of society and leverage their competitive advantage.

Characteristics of First-Generation Students

Since 2007, the Government of Ontario has made a dedicated envelope of funds available for pilot programs that support first-generation students. Interest in first-generation students as a construct first emerged, however, in 1978 in the United States, and gained momentum in Canada during the 1990s when issues of access due to rising tuition rates became a concern (Auclair *et al.* 2008). Given this growing interest in first-generation students, it is somewhat surprising that there is a paucity of literature produced by Canadian scholars on this topic. Even more surprising is how many studies have been published by government agencies, particularly Statistics Canada (*e.g.* Butlin 1999; Knighton 2002; Rahman, Situ and Jimmo 2005). As would be expected, this literature focuses primarily on access and participation rates and has contributed greatly to our growing understanding of first-generation students and the factors that impede or promote their success. The Canadian post-secondary educational system would benefit, however, from an expansion of centres for scholarship that focus specifically on the student experience, and on sub-populations of students such as first-generation in particular.

Canadian research has provided some noteworthy insights concerning a variety of factors that have a significant impact on participation rates, including parental education, family structure, family income and gender (Butlin 1999; Rahman *et al.* 2005). Regional differences across the country have also emerged, with participation rates being highest in Ontario and Newfoundland and Labrador, and lowest in Alberta (Shaienks and Gluszynski 2007). Drawing conclusions about these trends is challenging, however, because of inherent differences in educational systems across the country. For example, Québec's CÉGEP program and British Columbia's university college system have garnered much higher college participation rates because students often begin their pathway to a university degree by attending college first in those provinces (Rahman *et al.* 2005).

A growing body of Canadian literature examining the holistic student experience and systemic barriers experienced by some segments of the population would undoubtedly lay a strong foundation for improved post-secondary outcomes. For example, although in 2005 Canada was ranked first in the world by the Organization for Economic Cooperation and Development (OECD) for participation in post-secondary education, we were sixth when it comes to the proportion of adults with university degrees and we continue to lag behind other countries on a number of measures of innovation, a critical dimension of a successful knowledge economy (Statistics Canada 2006; OECD 2009).

Nonetheless, when the existing Canadian literature is combined with that from the United States, a body of work emerging from the United Kingdom and some other countries around the world, a useful theoretical understanding emerges.

THE IMPACT OF STUDENT DIVERSITY

In 1996, results of an important longitudinal study of 4,000 students in colleges and universities at 23 institutions across the United States were published. It found that the most notable demographic characteristics that distinguished first-generation students from their non-first-generation peers was that they tended to have lower family incomes, were more likely to be Hispanic and more likely to be women (Terenzini, *et al.* 1996). The first characteristic, low family income, is one of the most salient features in the literature in that the connection between first-generation status and having a working-class background has been documented many times, including in the Canadian context (*e.g.* Berger and Motte 2007; Inman and Mayes 1999; Lehmann 2009a; Priebe *et al.* 2008; Martinez *et al.* 2009; Bui 2002). Those who have experienced classism were found to also be more likely to feel that they do not belong at their post-secondary institution (Langhout *et al.* 2009). Other research has also suggested that first-generation students are more likely to be members of a racialized group and to have English as a second language (Bui 2002). Taken in concert then, the research in this area shows that first-generation students often belong to *several* of the identity groups that have historically experienced disadvantages in our society.

In as much as first-generation students tend to share a lot of characteristics with other groups who experience discrimination, they also tend to disproportionately turn up in non-traditional learning environments. A recent study by Priebe and colleagues (2008) found that almost three quarters of students who enroll in distance education programs at Alberta's Athabasca University are first-generation. In addition, this group was found to commonly have been out of high school for at least two years and in many cases for a decade or more. The vast majority in this study also had children and identified childcare responsibilities among the factors that led to choosing a distance format. First-generation students, particularly distance education learners, are among those who frequently are referred to as "non-traditional"—they're older, have more life experience, and frequently face significant time and financial constraints because of family commitments.

Priebe and colleagues (2008) also found that many of the first-generation students in their study felt they had to conform to traditional gender roles, staying at home with the children and feeling discouraged from pursuing higher education by their spouse and parents. For these students, enrolling in university seemed to be an act of empowerment and possibly even resistance, while at the same time, maintaining commitments to parenthood and financial responsibility indicate that they also held onto the values instilled by their social contexts. Based on these findings, *first-generation students often spend their lives straddling two distinctly different worlds—their families and their educational institutions.*

Another example of this duality is illustrated through a case study of six first-generation Iranian women who had immigrated to Canada (Sadeshi 2008). This study suggests that cultural values and assumptions help to shape and define an individual's experiences, and often create a framework within which the meanings of these experiences take form. In other words, *family context helps students make sense of educational experiences, much as the values and ideas internalized from higher education can begin to shift how we understand our family lives.* In this study the status of the women as immigrants was intertwined with the marginal experiences of living and learning in a new country. In the face of traditional cultural images of women as housewives, negotiating new identities as educated women meant that they frequently found themselves on the periphery of their families while questioning and resisting men's domination.

Not all family systems of first-generation students are thoroughly disrupted by immersion in post-secondary education. As a point of comparison in a broader global context, a study of first-generation students in Israel (Gofen 2009) found that the values of family solidarity, respect and ambition often emerged as themes in the narratives of these students' lives, where parents had often put their children first in the family's priorities and also had high expectations of success. In some cases, therefore, the family of first-generation students is an important motivating factor and source of support (see also London 1989 and Shields 2002).

First-generation working-class students are often not consciously linked to a shared group experience and they do not generally express any class consciousness (Lehmann 2009a). When *they are able to identify any advantages from their working-class backgrounds, first-generation students see such benefits as attributes emerging from individualized experiences and family practices, not as group attributes.* Such benefits include familiarity with hard work and understanding value for money (Priebe *et al.* 2008; Lehmann 2009b).

Lehmann (2009a) goes on to argue that on campus, working-class first-generation students are often immersed in a world that they don't fully understand, where norms and expectations are confusing and, more specifically, where social class can take on a new and unanticipated significance. Young people who participated in this study were keenly aware of deficits in economic, social and cultural capital that placed them at a disadvantage. Lack of knowledge about procedural issues (*e.g.* course selection and registration) as well as doubts about their own academic abilities made their experiences more difficult than those of their more advantaged peers.

It is important to make one additional point about the differences in participation rates for first-generation students at colleges and universities: *first-generation students are more likely to choose college over university, which is the opposite of other students* (London 1992; Drolet 2005). In 2005, it was shown that Canadian first-generation students had a university participation rate of only 18 percent, less than half the rate of those where both parents had attended a post-secondary institution (Rahman *et al.* 2005). Overall, the participation rate was not significantly different at the college level across generational status (see the matrix in Table 3, on page 225).

In Canada, the overall post-secondary education dropout rate is about 15 percent (Shaienks and Gluszynski 2007), with notable differences by gender, region and type of home community (rural vs. urban). Graduation and drop-out rates in this particular data did not differ significantly when comparing first-generation students with their peers. On the other hand, *parental attitude towards post-secondary education was found to be significant on both graduation and drop-out rates*, once again demonstrating that there are subtle but important variations within the first-generation population.

Research by London (1992) was published at a time when relatively little scholarly activity had been devoted to the needs, interests and concerns of first-generation students. It describes one of the central themes of much research that has since followed: being a first-generation student can take one further from her or his family, class, racial and ethnic milieu than is generally recognized prior to enrolling. This rite of passage can propel individuals into new social contexts characterized by unfamiliar cultures and norms and results in renegotiating relationships with family members, friends and, in many ways, with themselves. This process can be tumultuous and frequently calls into question allegiances and even the perception of loving bonds. Upward mobility, London therefore argues, can produce a discontinuity that generates feelings of loss, conflict and disloyalty.

TABLE 3. PARTICIPATION RATE BY GENERATIONAL STATUS AT THE COLLEGE AND UNIVERSITY LEVELS*

	First-Generation Students (%)	Both Parents Have PSE (%)
College	32	30
University	18	43

*Source: Rahman *et al.* 2005

LIVED EXPERIENCES: THE IMPACT ON POST-SECONDARY EXPERIENCE AND WITHDRAWAL RATES

It is hardly possible to talk about the diversity among first-generation students without also talking about their unique lived experiences. In fact, a grounded understanding of the lived experiences of first-generation students is the only way to appreciate such a broad range of intersections of identity. Building on the significance of colliding values that students sometimes experience between their families and educational institutions, consideration of the lived experience begins with a closer examination of the themes that emerge from first-generation family lives.

The second noteworthy aspect of the lived experience relates to a consideration of students who withdraw before completing their studies.

First-generation students sometimes describe conflicting messages from their parents: on the one hand being encouraged to stay at home, and on the other to achieve in the outside world (London 1989). The message seems to be that leaving represents a disloyalty to the various roles and functions they play within the family, whereas staying is disloyal to the role of "emissary." Some first-generation students have also emphasized that given their family responsibilities, registering as a full-time student in a traditional university learning environment would seem self-indulgent (Priebe *et al.* 2008). This research describes a preference for independent study, noting that they often feel it is vital to support themselves while being a student. Beyond the experiences of their families, many first-generation students do not see college or university as a natural progression of their life trajectory as is commonly expected by other students (Lehmann 2009b). That is to say, given the lack of experience with post-secondary education by their parents, it is not a foregone conclusion that they will attend college or university. For them, there is a process of coming to this conclusion.

While being caught between being pushed out into the world and drawn back into the family, London (1989) recounts how some first-generation students are successful in using individual achievement and mobility as a way of deflecting guilt and a sense of disloyalty to their home communities. For these students, leaving as an emissary became proof of love and respect for the family. Such a mission, however, became troublesome and sometimes even harmful when the student, regardless of age, became so weighed down by family expectations that parental needs and wishes trumped personal growth and autonomy.

As with all students, there is a significant transition when one embarks on college or university education. When it comes to first-generation working-class students, Luckett and Luckett (2009) argue that the transition to a middle-class university and professional context requires a shift in identity, the development of a sense of autonomy, and a pursuit of social mobility through hard work. In a study of 75 newly admitted first-generation students, narratives of social mobility and hopes to break free from class constraints were commonplace (Lehmann 2009a). Participants often expressed a realization that the lives and careers of their parents had been limited by a lack of formal education, and some described encouragement from their parents in pursuing a university education in order to achieve "a better life."

It has also been pointed out that the home atmosphere for many first-generation students is the antithesis of a good environment for studying (Padron 1992). In this research, many participants reported that they come from cultures that regard post-secondary education as frivolous; often having families who are not only un-supportive, but frequently obstructionist. Padron describes how many parents who are indifferent or antagonistic towards education were failed by the system when they were students. As a result, they do not ensure that their offspring enroll in an academic stream while in high school and thus many of their children end up ill prepared for post-secondary education and feel embarrassed by their poor perfor-mance when applying. The feelings of inadequacy that result from this can often make it even more difficult to support their learning.

In a study of first-generation students that used focus groups and interviews, Orbe (2004) asked participants how conscious they were of being the first in their family to attend college or university. Many responded by indicating that it was something they thought about every day and that it often helped to motivate them. However, they also reported that this status was sometimes a heavy weight.

Not all aspects of being a first-generation student are negative. In Lehmann's work (2009a), participants believed that they possessed a stronger work ethic; had higher levels of maturity, responsibility, and independence; and were better able to draw upon first-hand experience in the 'real world of work' than their peers. Other research conducted by Reay and colleagues (2010) suggests that the identities of first-generation students remain relatively fragile and lack in confidence. This was primarily attributed to managing the weighty and competing demands of employ-ment, family responsibilities and being a student, which left little time to become immersed in curricular and campus life.

Although social class is often implied in many interviews of these students, when talking about their differences in background, lifestyle and wealth, surprisingly few directly address money as a barrier or reason for withdrawing (Lehmann 2007). The question, therefore, is what are the experiences of first-generation students who withdraw? Scholars generally agree that a high proportion of students fail or withdraw because of difficulties in adjusting or as a result of environmental factors, rather than because of intellectual difficulties (Pascarella and Terenzini 2005; Pit-kethly and Prosser 2001). Tinto (1995) has also demonstrated that *students who lack clearly defined goals, who experience a mismatch with their field of study or institutional culture, and those who experience significant feelings of isolation face a greater risk of withdrawing.* While first-generation students are known to frequently have clearer goals than other students (Lehmann 2009b), difficulties with institutional misfit are commonplace (Pittman and Richmond 2008). Pitkethly and Prosser (2001) pick up on Tinto's work by advocating for careful analysis of the reasons why students withdraw, recognizing that there is great variation in this regard across identity groups and across institutions.

Literature examining the reasons for attrition among first-generation students suggests that when they leave, the majority do so voluntarily and for non-academic reasons, often citing that they have family support for their decision (Lehmann 2007). This same research reveals that students with university-educated parents, in contrast, were almost always required to withdraw because of problems with academic performance. Lehmann goes on to suggest that social background plays an important role in how students experience university by shaping their perceptions and self-concept, which thus affects their inclination to either persist or drop out.

In addition to family lives and attrition, some other aspects of the experiences of first-generation students are noteworthy. Some research has found that as compared to other students, those who are first-generation are much more concerned with time management issues and identified many more things that made the university experience harder for them, thus suggesting that they have to work harder at managing the university experience (Shields 2002). It has also been reported that while in high school they are all too frequently mocked for working hard, and it is only when they start post-secondary education that they begin to find acceptance (Reay *et al.* 2009).

Other notable characteristics that distinguish first-generation students were described by Bui (2002) and include feeling less prepared for post-secondary education and being more worried about finances (similar to what Inman and Mayes found in 1999). They were reported to fear academic failure more and tended to know less about the social environment on campus than other students. In addition, they frequently had to put more time into studying. On the other hand, they were similar to non-first-generation students with regards to making decisions on their own about school, knowing about academic programs available to them prior to enrolment and feeling accepted at university. Finally, *first-generation students tend to face significant constraints based on geographic location in relation to the campus, place more emphasis on the value of the reputation of the institution for good teaching, and the importance of having specific courses that fit with their long-term objectives* (Inman and Mayes 1999).

One final note about the lived experiences of first-generation students: not all first-generation students agree that being first-generation is central to their identity and Orbe (2004) points out that this tends to be highly dependent on institutional context. Those who said it was core to their identity tended to be enrolled in more elite institutions where the student population seemed to have a lot of money (see also Lehmann 2007, Reay *et al.* 2009). Less prestigious campuses tended to have students for whom their generational status was a less prominent feature of their identity. Reay and colleagues (2010) similarly found that the way working-class first-generation students see themselves (and are seen by others) with regards to class identity and as learners is influenced to a significant degree by the type of institution they attend.

EFFECTS OF INSTITUTIONAL CULTURE ON FIRST-GENERATION STUDENTS

The culture of an educational institution can have a powerful effect on the individual. As already noted in the discussion about diversity, first-generation students often have to contend with very different value systems in their families and communities as compared with other students on college and university campuses. The developmental changes that occur in the transitions associated with becoming a student, engaging in academic pursuits and ultimately being transformed by the learning that takes place in post-secondary education, are mirrored and intertwined with those of progressing from adolescence to adulthood (London 1989). Post-secondary education brings with it a plethora of experiences that serve to impact the personality of the emerging adult (Robins *et al.* 2001). This research also shows that these changes include increased openness to new ideas and opportunities, a decrease in authoritarianism and ethnocentrism, and increased tolerance of individual differences.

While it is laudable for post-secondary institutions to pursue such lofty goals, even while seeking to accommodate students with diverse value systems, sometimes the result can be disastrous. When further exploring the perspective of first-generation students who had withdrawn, Lehmann (2007) reports that those from working-class backgrounds "expressed a fundamental rejection of university: its values, what it stands for, the central role of its degrees for success, and its essential middle-class culture" (p. 100). Such a strong reaction to their experience is the result of what Lehmann calls "a profound misfit" and clearly speaks to the way in which a negative experience with the university environment can create a lasting and pervasive aversion to the very notion of a post-secondary education. In contrast, non-working-class first-generation students who had withdrawn continued to see a university degree as an essential symbol and prerequisite for social mobility.

When we shift focus to the institutional level, Lehmann (2009b) argues that creating an inclusive student body requires a strong commitment to diversity in academic forms of engagement, and he points out that tokenistic responses to diversity through fancy promotional materials is a much too simplistic approach. Similarly, Padron (1992) suggests creating an atmosphere that celebrates different cultural backgrounds and he holds up example programs such as Hispanic or Black Heritage Months, which not only cater to the needs of current students, but also strengthen the overall campus environment, making it more inviting for recruitment purposes.

Academic engagement is an important consideration when it comes to addressing diversity at an institutional level. Some research indicates there is significant variation among students' preferences for different types of faculty interaction along identity group lines such as students' gender, race, social class and, of course, first-generation status (Kim and Sax 2009). This research found that working-class and first-generation students were more often excluded from faculty interaction in both research-related and course-related contexts. More specifically, students whose parents had attended university were more likely than first-generation students to assist faculty with research for course credit, communicate with faculty both by email and in person, and interact with faculty during class. Although it was also found that the differences in student-faculty interaction were statistically significant, the differential outcomes for first-generation students were generally modest in nature. On the other hand, there may be an indirect significance in that faculty-student interactions were closely related to a variety of positive outcomes. Students' experiences of assisting faculty with research were correlated with higher GPAs, higher degree aspirations and larger gains in critical thinking and communication skills. This effect was equally strong for both non-first-generation students and first-generation students, even though the latter group tended to experience this kind of engagement much less frequently.

INTEGRATING DIMENSIONS OF THE STUDENT EXPERIENCE

Post-secondary education can be both empowering and alienating. First-generation students can experience a collision between the values of their families and those of the college or university they attend. Such conflicts can leave students on the margins of both the student experience and their families (Sadeshi 2008). While universities and colleges knowingly, and sometimes even deliberately, seek to promote "identity development" (Chickering and Reisser 1993), the values and assumptions underlying this endeavour can leave first-generation students whose identities intersect with other forms of oppression with a sense of loneliness, self-doubt and heartache (London 1989). There is a dynamic interplay between diverse identities, lived experiences and the ways in which institutions affect students.

Thomas and Quinn (2007, as cited by Reay *et al.* 2010) argue that ambivalence is often generated when different cultural narratives about what it is to be educated and working-class collide. Indeed, the literature already cited about first-generation working-class students is replete with examples of the difficult personal challenges experienced by these students. Participants in a number of qualitative studies have described how their family systems have been turned upside down and relationships have been "cleaved" apart as a result of their educational experiences (London 1989). As a final example of this, in the dominant discourse about student development on university and college campuses, we often espouse the virtue of separation from one's family and a growing sense of autonomy. At the same time, we wrestle with the notion of "helicopter parents" (Cline and Fay 1990) and students with families who are overly intrusive. It is important to recognize that these values are deeply culturally rooted. Some cultures with traditional values and extended local kinship systems see the entire notion of separation from family as alien, devalued and even stigmatizing (London 1989).

London (1989) describes how for some individuals, being introduced to a larger and more intellectual world helped to fuel the process of separation from their families. At the same time, fears emerged that they would no longer be loved as a result of being perceived as "too different" because of changes in views towards sexuality, ideology and self-presentation. In such a context, intellectualism can contribute to a sense of exclusion as well as pride. Some first-generation students in this study felt lonely as a result of a sense of differentness, not only feeling disconnected from their families but also from the campus community.

In summary, the experiences and identities of first-generation students are heterogeneous. In order to make sense of the challenges they encounter, a significant degree of granularity is required in the analysis. Nevertheless, there are great opportunities for building more flexible, responsive and inclusive post-secondary institutions when we draw on new understandings of this segment of the population. Strategic enrolment management provides a framework for responding to the educational goals of first-generation students in a systematic and holistic way, and for our colleges and universities to adapt to future demands and achieve their missions.

CASE STUDY: SEM INITIATIVES AT THE UNIVERSITY OF GUELPH

Strategic enrolment management serves as a coordinated institution-wide process for recruiting, retaining and graduating students. In the context of first-generation students, its emphasis on fostering meaningful student-institution relationships, sound assessment principles, cross-institutional collaboration, a learner-centered orientation and the education of the 'whole student' is particularly relevant. In the following section we will explore the four dimensions of strategic enrolment management (administrative, student-focused, academic success and market-centered) described by Kalsbeek (2006a) as they relate to first-generation students, and discuss the implications for practice in a college and university context. We have highlighted some of the programs and services on our own campus that specifically (but not exclusively) respond to the needs of this population of students.

The University of Guelph is a medium-sized institution located approximately one hour west of Toronto in Southern Ontario. In contrast with commuter institutions, Guelph is residentially intensive with roughly 90 percent of first-year students living in on-campus residences. It is often categorized as a "comprehensive university" because of its robust combination of undergraduate and graduate programs and a strong emphasis on research and vibrant professional programs. The current interest in taking a more intentional approach to supporting first-generation students has been invigorated by the aforementioned funding made available by Ontario's Ministry of Training, Colleges and Universities. In the first year of our first-generation project, Guelph focused on students who were identified as academically "at risk" due to low academic achievement in their first semester. Since then, our initiatives have been expanded to include a broad range of programs and services that focus on the transition to university, particularly for those who are more likely to experience difficulties, such as first-generation students.

Administrative Perspective: A Centre for New Students and an Aggressive Long-Term Plan

It has been argued that strategic enrolment management must necessarily take a systemic view and as such, its scope has widened in recent years, demanding far-reaching coordination of the processes, practices and policies that impinge upon enrolment (Bischoff 2007; Bontrager 2004b; Kalsbeek 2003). While such efforts are ambitious, they can bring about efficiencies and improve strategies to engage and support students. Pitkethly and Prosser (2001) have discussed how those institutions that have been successful at bringing about significant change to better respond to the needs of first-generation students tend to do so by adopting a model that allows for voluntary participation by operating units while implementing new strategies in an incremental fashion. These authors make a strong case for a coordinated, informed, and institution-wide response to the transition needs of first-generation students in order to improve the overall learning experience. Some examples of administration-level approaches to supporting first-generation students include systems to enable effective and coordinated data gathering and analysis, articulation agreements, financial assistance, bridging programs across educational contexts, creating satellite recruitment centres, ensuring advisors are sensitive to the diversity within the student population and using student development theory to drive the creation of interventions and related assessment processes.

BUILDING A CULTURE OF COLLABORATION: SEAMLESS SERVICE DELIVERY

One of the University of Guelph's strengths is its emphasis on collaborative approaches to program development and service delivery across functional units. As with all large organizations, operational teams can have different cultures and priorities that sometimes impede collaboration. To counterbalance this, in recent years the criteria for funding new initiatives through internal sources have been rooted in the fundamental principle of collaboration. Indeed, during periods of fiscal restraint operating budgets in many departments have been flat from year-to-year (or sometimes reduced) with the exception of those units that were successful in securing funds through these means. This has provided a positive incentive to seek out collaborative and innovative ways of responding to emerging needs. One such program offered through the office of the Provost is the Learning Enhancement Fund, which grants up to $50,000 per year to applicants who address areas of strategic institutional importance, including projects that address the retention and success of at-risk student populations.

Another important aspect of collaboration at the University of Guelph results from the integrated approach we take to service delivery. While we seek to avoid duplication of higher-level expertise and specialization, there are many transition supports for first-year students that overlap between departments. For example, teaching about wellness-related principles is integrated into the activities of many units such as Residence Life and the Centre for New Students, but is also championed by the Wellness Centre located in Student Health Services. Likewise, the Centre for New Students focuses on the transition needs of students in their first year, but work in this area is also decentralized such that virtually every unit that engages first-year students—whether academic counsellors, faculty advisors, personal counsellors or learning and writing staff—addresses transition needs.

In the context of first-generation students the Centre for New Students plays a critical role in responding to gaps in supports, raising awareness about emerging needs, facilitating referrals and promoting collaborative and seamless approaches to service delivery. For example, in recent years we have advocated for a better understanding of first-generation students and the challenges they experience with person-institution fit, how family dynamics affect academic engagement and the importance of constructing a safety net that is responsive to the worldview of these students. This has, in turn, given rise to programs and services that are more flexible for a broader range of students and interventions that are offered at an earlier stage of students' difficulties. The more purposeful approach that arises from this deeper understanding of first-generation students has been instrumental in strengthening our orientation programs and a number of frontline programs that focus on advising and mentoring.

Collaboration at Guelph is an important value that is imbedded within our institutional culture. It is apparent at the highest levels of decision-making, tied to the evolution of budgets and operating units, and grows out of an environment where regular communication and information-sharing helps to forge strong working relationships. First-generation students have benefited from this through the creation of mentoring programs such as 'Back on Track' and 'Bounce Back' that use relationship-building as a vehicle for fostering connections with a broad range of campus resources. Rather than reproducing the services offered by other units like the Learning Commons, the Stress Management Clinic or Academic Program Counsellors, mentors use a simplified case management model to identify the most appropriate resources for each individual student's needs, and use the helping relationship to follow the student's progress, revising strategies as needed. The success of this approach rests on the careful development of partnerships with service recipients and collaborative relationships across service delivery units.

Yet another example is found in the data used to track first-generation students throughout their university experience. Information about GPA, enrolment status, contact information, age, and identification as belonging to an Aboriginal group or as a first-generation student is maintained by the institution's Registrar. Service delivery units rely on this data for targeted strategies to recruit program participants, and for assessment and reporting purposes. This approach allows for systemic, institution-wide strategies and ensures that the best possible data is used to inform decision-making. It also relies on careful attention to privacy concerns. Leveraging existing resources, we aim to advance core SEM principles by achieving greater efficiencies, optimizing the wealth of expertise that is available and promoting a holistic approach when addressing student transition needs.

Beyond the University of Guelph example, Engle and Tinto (2008) advocate for a strategic long-term plan that enables first-generation students to make a seamless transition from college to university (or vice versa) through the use of articulation agreements and transfer credits. In Ontario, several universities and some colleges have such agreements in place, and offer a range of flexible options that promote a certain level of student mobility, including prior learning assessments. However, a growing number of applicants are seeking to have prior learning formally recognized, and universities and colleges must consider more individualized approaches in order to respond to this growing demand (Constantineau 2009). A shift such as this will have significant implications for first-generation students, particularly given that many in this group are inclined to follow non-traditional pathways through the post-secondary education system. The University of Guelph has some measures in place to address this issue and is now exploring ways to strengthen its approach.

Irrespective of whether a first-generation student enters university or college directly from high school or by some other route, the support of financial counsellors and financial aid, transfer scholarships and bridging programs helps to ensure that students who might not otherwise be eligible for university can participate. Guelph, as with a number of other Ontario institutions, receives funds from the province of Ontario that are specifically earmarked for the financial support of first-generation students in need. Terenzini and colleagues (1996) advocate for bridging programs built on collaboration between high schools, colleges and universities. This is important given that significant differences were found between first-generation and other students in some areas of pre-admission academic skills (*e.g.* Terenzini, *et al.* 1996) and their experiences of curricular, instructional and out-of-class activities. This research also infers that it may be beneficial to increase the amount of study time available to first-generation students through tailored initiatives such as study groups, designated quiet areas in residence halls and libraries, peer-tutoring and financial assistance that reduces the need to work off campus.

In addition to a cornucopia of initiatives that seek to address these needs on the Guelph campus, the university is presently piloting a collaborative program between Writing Services and faculty in the department of Marketing and Consumer Studies. This project aims to enrich the experiences of first-generation students in a second-year core business course by providing writing-focused instruction and individual mentoring. The course focuses on improving students' communication skills by integrating writing-intensive assignments into the curriculum, and through small-group presentations and discussions both in the classroom and online. Upon commencement of the course, students' writing skills are assessed and various strategies are utilized to help them strengthen their abilities and hone their business communication skills. To complement this learning, Writing Services also provides drop-in writing help, scheduled writing appointments and workshops on a variety of topics. In addition, Graduate Teaching Assistants offer consultations and workshops specifically designed for first-generation students, and senior undergraduate students provide peer-based support.

Another unique bridging program found in the literature involves six weeks of training and work experience for staff members at feeder high schools who work with higher risk student populations (Padron 1992). The initiative helps participants (high school administrators and counsellors) to become familiar with trends in higher education and the target groups. They work on campus for six weeks and then recruit students from their schools when they return.

Developing a recruitment centre can be an inviting environment for first-generation students, establishing a less formal ambiance and responding to the needs of prospective students from a wide variety of backgrounds. Padron (1992) describes such a centre, which was designed to be welcoming and inviting by ensuring there were no counters to act as barriers between community members and staff, and where applicants sat at tables with a staff member as they completed the required application form. This approach seeks to ensure that the admission process does not feel impersonal and makes use of a satellite venue in a specific target recruitment community. Padron suggests that where there is a predominant alternate language spoken, it is useful to have resources and staff members who are bilingual. It is argued that this is particularly important when individuals first enrol in order to improve their English language skills before moving on to other academic programs, and also for building supportive ally relationships with parents who have limited abilities to engage in English. The marketing strategy employed by Padron's centre is not simply to promote enrolment, but also to educate the community about the realities of work-force demands.

While the University of Guelph does not have a recruitment centre in the manner described by Padron, many of the same objectives and principles outlined in this best practice are shared with our recruitment strategy for students from Aboriginal backgrounds. The necessity for an Aboriginal-specific approach dovetails with the needs of first-generation prospective students generally—that is to say, we are particularly interested in increasing our Aboriginal student population and many parents of prospective Aboriginal students have not attended college or university. To that end, Guelph has established a position that specifically focuses on the recruitment of Aboriginal youth. The incumbent is a staff member of the Aboriginal Resource Centre who receives extensive training from Admission Services and participates on the provincial "Road Warrior" Aboriginal recruitment team.

In addition to traditional recruitment activities that focus on First Nations youth, a critical dimension of this institutional strategy involves building long-term relationships with the Band Councils of students' home communities. If problems arise concerning third-party funding, for example, the Aboriginal Resource Centre helps to facilitate the payment of student fees and serves as an important conduit between the institution, the student, and the Band Council, helping to navigate bureaucratic processes along the way. The relationship between the institution and students' home communities is often the key to successfully recruiting, retaining and graduating these students. The Centre provides a "home away from home" for Aboriginal students, engages in traditional teachings, offers services such as counselling in a culturally-appropriate manner, promotes academic success and acts as an advocate for Aboriginal issues on campus. Recruitment efforts are at the leading edge of a host of programs and services designed to support Aboriginal students throughout their Guelph experience. This is the pinnacle of identity intersection and illustrates many of the ideals of SEM.

Research in a related area found that first-generation students perceive that academic advisors enquire less about their academic and career aspirations than non-first-generation students (Buissinik-Smith *et al.* 2010). Advisors who share a similar background and who are in tune with the unique needs of first-generation students can help to upend this tendency. Buissinik and colleagues assert that educating first-generation students about the types of advice they can expect and the sorts of questions they should be asking may also be beneficial. Another approach might be to draw on an anti-oppression model in order to educate academic gatekeepers about subtle forms of bias that can inadvertently creep into advising practices. Resources such as the Aboriginal Resource Centre and the Centre for New Students help to achieve these goals.

Social Class Curriculum Content

Institutions can conduct a self-assessment to evaluate whether the curriculum includes content that adequately reflects the experiences of students of different class backgrounds. The most ambitious approach that Langhout and colleagues (2009) advocate is to create academic departments that focus on the study of social class (similar to women's studies) or hire faculty across the institution who conduct social class research, thereby ensuring that the curriculum reflects the diverse experiences of our society. These changes would also help the broader student population to develop a critical understanding of issues surrounding social class and how they affect all people throughout our society. An important dimension of higher education is to ensure that students with greater social power are exposed to opportunities to learn about diversity-related issues such as classism, particularly given that universities tend to be disproportionately populated by people from privileged backgrounds. Building well-informed content into the curriculum about social class can help to achieve this objective. At the University of Guelph, the Bachelor of Applied Science program takes this approach by integrating topics about food security into courses on human nutrition, and by offering courses specifically focused on child and family poverty.

Service-Learning Programs

Many of our co-curricular service-learning programs, such as Project Serve Canada and Project Serve International help to foster connections between real-world problems, social justice theory and classroom learning while promoting meaningful personal reflection. Given the small group approach of these programs and their fundamental grounding in the context, history and background of participants' lives, they are particularly well suited to first-generation students. They also promote practical skill development and the application of abstract knowledge. These programs resonate with the experiences of first-generation students and create a learning environment that is transformative for participants.

Educational Interventions: Student Engagement and Assessment

Whether curricular or co-curricular in nature, using student development theory as a framework to inform the design, implementation and evaluation of educational interventions can prove highly effective. King and Howard-Hamilton (2000) point out that student development theory can act as a useful conceptual framework for interpreting data on student satisfaction, learning and success. It can help garner useful data for examining how well institutions are achieving holistic goals of facilitating students' growth in areas such as making informed ethical choices, developing a healthy sense of identity, learning to be a good citizen and advancing a deeper appreciation for differences.

The cornerstone of any good intervention is a clearly defined set of intended outcomes that are closely tied to appropriate assessment strategies. While the ideal assessment employs the rigour of academic research, there are many cases where operational constraints result in assessments being undertaken that are not suitable for a peer-reviewed journal. Nevertheless, there are a variety of instruments available to support the implementation of robust assessment processes. The Council for the Advancement of Standards in Higher Education (CAS) provides a useful roadmap for many programs and services by organizing and synthesizing relevant literature in order to establish benchmarks and best practices. In Ontario, a review of post-secondary education (Rae 2005) recommended broader use of metrics that would allow for comparison across institutions, giving rise to much wider use of the National Survey of Student Engagement (NSSE). Using the results of NSSE, institutions can get a sense of where they excel in comparison with peer institutions and where additional effort might be exerted.

ORIENTATION WEEK

About five years ago some of the assessments we conducted at Guelph helped to build a strong case for renewed effort in promoting academic engagement in our orientation programs. Using this analysis as a guide, we have made a number of significant changes and some encouraging results are beginning to emerge. During Orientation Week, roughly 350 events take place over seven days to help introduce students to life on campus, both social and academic. One such program is "Profs are People Too," which utilizes a speed-dating format whereby students go from table to table, engage in a brief conversation with a faculty member for a couple of minutes and move on to the next table. The event takes place in one of the campus pubs/cafés, is quite informal and very popular. Two other events work in tandem: on a large scale, Academic Program Meetings (common to most campuses) are facilitated by Program Counsellors, focus on introducing students to key resources and are specific to each undergraduate degree. On a smaller scale, another event consists of more than 70 "First Meetings for Majors" which introduce students to classmates and to some of the faculty members who will be teaching them. The program provides an opportunity to discuss interesting research, controversial topics and career opportunities related to each field of study. There are even small-scale meetings like this for those students who have not yet chosen a major.

The objectives of these programs are further supported by Academic Community Groups to which every incoming undergraduate student is assigned. The groups meet at least three times throughout the week, are facilitated by approximately 90 upper-year student volunteers, and again provide a basis for students to initiate friendships with peers in the same academic program. These groups are then used strategically as a way of guiding students to other academically-themed events. This is particularly important as participation in Orientation Week at Guelph is entirely voluntary and much of the default community building occurs in relation to residence halls that are by-and-large not organized around academic programs.

Academic engagement is also promoted through an open-house style tour of the Library and Learning Commons that lasts about ten minutes and runs continuously throughout most of the day on Thursday and Friday—the days when first classes are taking place. First classes are an integral part of Orientation Week; social and informal activities on these days are built around classes and designed to promote curricular engagement. "Campus Scoop," where senior administrators help serve free ice cream to first-year students, is one such example. Our success in all of these ventures has depended on regular and frequent discussion about the "Orientation Mission and Objectives," which emerged from broad consultation with campus stakeholders. This living document emphasizes student development, as well as describes how Orientation Week is about much more than social activities and having fun. Support for this philosophical position, particularly among student groups, acts as a starting point and overarching guide for how we structure the week, which activities are highlighted and how we prioritize where we place our energy and resources.

All of these activities lay a foundation for developing a sense of identity as a student. In the summertime leading up to Orientation Week, there has been significant emphasis on the nature of the week as a learning-based program. First-generation students frequently misunderstand the nature of Orientation Week, so Guelph has placed great emphasis on teaching about what the week has to offer well in advance of its kick-off. Historically, many of the most vulnerable first-generation students saw the schedule for the first day of classes and without understanding the critical importance of Orientation, scheduled themselves to work at their off-campus employment while the week is underway. Heading-off this propensity is therefore vital to our success in supporting this group. What we have found through the use of an outcome-based survey instrument is that our efforts to promote academic engagement are having a positive effect. The web-based tools we use for this assessment allows us to create filters such that we can see how the results vary for those students who identify with key groups of interest, such as first-generation students.

At present, we are also working on developing a programming model that extends orientation across the first six weeks of the fall semester, helping students to become familiar with campus resources just as they are needed and promoting student-faculty interactions. Through all of these programs, there is a premium placed on activities that introduce students to the academic culture on campus.

A series of "special lectures" that are integrated within Orientation Week and feature faculty members who deliver a lecture on a topic of interest such as sociological theory and the media, hydration in elite athletes, re-thinking conflict, and how the recent collapse of honeybee populations has significant social implications. These events provide new students with an opportunity to experience engaging lectures before classes officially begin, and the faculty members debrief students as to what they should have learned, note taking techniques, and exam preparation strategies. In recent years we have seen a significant increase in the number of students attending these special lectures, with many being filled to capacity.

The cornerstone of our Orientation Week is a formal induction ceremony with all the pomp and circumstance of convocation. We emphasize the importance of academic success by offering events like this alongside hundreds of other activities such as games of ultimate Frisbee, barbeques, a large and enthusiastically supported pep rally and evening concerts. Roughly a thousand upper-year students, who are engaged in a wide variety of leadership roles on campus, volunteer throughout the week and actively promote the institutionally driven activities, helping to ensure that they are every bit as successful as those that are student-driven. Many of these events have enjoyed such high demand that there has been standing room only in the venues. To counter the broader social expectations that "Frosh Week" (sic) is about partying and intoxication, we were able to create learning opportunities that are engaging and have high voluntary participation rates. This illustrates how a focus on academic success can be connected to all aspects of campus life.

STUDENT-FOCUSED PERSPECTIVE

Focusing on the student as an individual is a core concept in strategic enrolment management (Kalsbeek 2006a). This approach emphasizes the importance of supporting and building partnerships with students prior to and throughout their time on a university or college campus, and encompasses future relationships with them as valued alumni. A central tenet of this orientation is early identification and intervention with students who are believed to be at risk, typically facilitated through intentional partnerships with Student Affairs professionals and other stakeholders.

When it comes to developing specific programs and services that meet the needs of first-generation students, Luckett and Luckett (2009) advocate for creating conditions that enable the emergence of personal and social identities that are aligned with being a successful student. Martinez and colleagues (2009) caution, however, that ascribing the label of "first-generation" to students must be undertaken judiciously. They argue that for the most part these students do not have a strong sense of affiliation with each other on the grounds of being first-generation, nor do they have a clear understanding of how such an identity can be seen as a sign of strength. As such, they may be vulnerable to inferring and easily internalizing negative messages associated with this construct. The authors suggest that treating the notion of first-generation status as merely a risk factor can have a deleterious effect whereas it may be beneficial to emphasize how the term denotes achievement and can be a source of pride.

MENTORING PROGRAMS

Participation in mentoring programs has been attributed to better first-semester adjustment by focusing on developing strong social support among peers and the formation of important social ties (Pittman and Richmond 2008). Padron (1992) suggests that the most common need among first-generation students is for more academic and personal guidance, and describes how many of these students are intimidated and bewildered by the system, and seem less aware of educational opportunities than their peers. Bui (2002) also supports the value of mentoring and describes a program that serves first-generation students by providing a combination of professional academic counselling, informal peer advising and academic tutoring. As previously described, this is precisely the approach of the mentoring programs offered by the Centre for New Students at the University of Guelph.

Research on mentoring relationships with first-generation students has found that the majority of participants respond better to mentors who can offer recognition, affirmation and some intimacy, and this is in contrast with those who generally only offer a professional style of interaction (Luckett and Luckett 2009). This might help to explain why some research makes the surprising suggestion that there may not be a strong connection between mentoring programs, GPA and graduation rates (*e.g.,* Sanchez *et al.* 2006). The way in which the program is constructed matters a great deal and this has not always been taken into account by some evaluative studies. Luckett and Luckett (2009) conclude that all first-generation students should be given personal mentors who will provide safe, unconstrained opportunities to negotiate and try out emerging identities.

At Guelph, a number of intervention programs for high-risk students use mentoring as a mode of engaging and creating individually tailored plans for those who are struggling. We have already introduced one such program, Bounce Back, which is built on the dual approach of building a friendly, informal rapport in concert with a semi-structured discussion that has specific objectives. Student mentors are carefully matched with program participants, beginning with a focus on compatible academic programs. They also receive considerable pre-service and on-going training. Mentors are encouraged to engage in conversations with participants aimed at addressing what has gone wrong to date, setting realistic goals, and developing strategies to achieve those goals. Once this foundation work is completed in the first or second meeting, participants are coached and encouraged through regular check-in meetings and follow-up email messages. As a result of their participation in Bounce Back, students have consistently demonstrated significant gains in academic performance, retention and satisfaction with their university experience.

ACADEMIC ALERT SYSTEM: REACHING OFF-CAMPUS STUDENTS

A similar example described by Padron (1992) involves an academic alert system that allows the institution to identify those students with low grades and sporadic attendance at midterm time. In response, individualized letters are sent out and advisors call the student at home. This helps to assure students that the institution is concerned about them as individuals and wishes to support their success, while promoting engagement by offering information about resources that might be of assistance. Drawing an analogy from the University of Guelph, we offer a program called Off Campus Connection (OCC) for first-year students not living in residence. The program was conceived in response to a realization that 90 percent of new students at our institution live in residence and many of our transition supports are provided in this context. We have found that first-generation students are more likely to live off-campus and that students who live off-campus in their first year often have a poor understanding of campus support services, involvement opportunities and how to navigate the academic system. In response, trained upper-year students call program participants on the telephone a couple of times each semester to answer questions and offer support. This ongoing connection with new students has proven to facilitate a stronger sense of engagement and satisfaction, particularly among those who identify as first generation.

One of the most common themes that comes up in conversations with OCC participants is a feeling of being completely overwhelmed. Training of the student mentors, therefore, aims at developing helping skills that first affirm the emotional dimension of this experience, and then focus on untangling the underlying difficulties. First-generation students in this program have taught us to be attentive to the complexity of the problems these students face, and that practical solutions (*e.g.* participating in stress management or time management workshops) are only the beginning of the intervention. The long-term success of these students rests on two things: building an identity as a successful University of Guelph student and actively making use of co-curricular supports. We have found that a critical prerequisite is having a sense that someone at the University knows them and is interested in how they are doing.

SUMMER PREPARATION PROGRAMS

Lasselle and colleagues (2009) describe a summer preparation program that was designed to boost the confidence of prospective first-generation students and helped to elevate their aspirations towards continuing their education. They point out that this is particularly important given that for the most part, the parents of these students often had very little personal knowledge of higher education. Although this program was intended to increase interest in any post-secondary education, it was found to be particularly successful in attracting applicants to the host institution. At the University of Guelph there are a number of programs designed for students who are undecided. For example, Spring Academic Open House targets students who have not yet accepted the University's offer of admission. These one-day events provide information and seminars specific to each degree program, and transition information from a variety of campus service providers for students and their families.

We have also found it helpful to offer a suite of pre-arrival transition programs over the course of the summertime. Some initiatives are integrated into services offered by other departments, such as a transition seminar about surviving first year delivered in conjunction with campus tours; others are designed for targeted populations, such as a one-day orientation program for first-generation students and their families; another for international students; and still another for Aboriginal students. Guelph also offers an online summer orientation program (startonline. ca), which helps to ensure that information, support and a strong sense of community is available to everyone in a low-threshold format. Reviews of similar programs at other institutions suggest that Guelph's solution was not only the first of its kind in Canada, but is also one of the most comprehensive. No doubt our success is in having a large pool of volunteers who help with everything from writing content to moderating synchronous and asynchronous discussion areas—returning students volunteer as moderators, and staff volunteer as "guests" on the site and as writers for articles about virtually all aspects of the student experience. Content is delivered in response to incoming students' needs at appropriate times in the summer (residence information when room assignments are announced, course selection information when students are choosing their classes for the fall, etc.). Content is also constantly being changed and updated, with an objective of keeping the site looking fresh on a daily basis. There are several ways that students can engage in theme-based discussions in the program, including an area reserved for first-generation students. All of this relies heavily on a community-based approach.

Our suite of pre-arrival programs also includes a transition event hosted in students' hometowns, which allows students and their families to have last-minute questions answered, meet other new students from their region and hear interesting stories from alumni that build excitement for the journey ahead. During the months leading up to the fall semester, we have also mailed math packages to every incoming student who is enrolled in math-related courses in their first year and made solution sets available online, thereby enabling us to track participation. More recently, we have launched a new initiative called "The Pursuit Project" whereby first-generation students with lower admission averages are invited to mentoring nights where they can engage in conversation with faculty members who have volunteered to participate.

In all, the University of Guelph's programs are designed to promote the building of relationships through peer-to-peer interactions, share resources and information, avoid user-fees, meet students on their own terms and allow individuals to pick-and-choose participation in the programs that best meet their needs and interests. In order to ameliorate some of the difficulties faced by first-generation students, an academic environment characterized by the presence of positive role models is critical. Ensuring that there is strong cultural diversity among faculty, staff and administrators demonstrates that perseverance can bring professional careers and recognition, while promoting inter-cultural competency and awareness on campus more generally. When it comes to a student-focused approach, Ting (1998) found that predictors of success for first-generation students include high social rank, leadership experience in high school and community service. These pre-existing conditions are often of great relevance in the context of Student Affairs work where opportunities to enhance academic engagement and success are facilitated through co-curricular learning. Partnerships across the institution, involving student affairs and academic units can help to ensure that the approaches that are undertaken are both integrated and holistic in nature.

Academic Success Perspective

Current conceptions of strategic enrolment management have shifted from a focus on the "admissions funnel" to a "student success continuum," whereby a host of institutional stakeholders share responsibility for the academic achievement and success of students (Bontrager 2004b; Wallace-Hulecki 2009). This approach has an important focus on the design of academic programs and modes of instructional delivery. It also helps to direct the way in which the institution meets the educational needs of the community, industry and society at large (Kalsbeek 2006a). We turn our attention then, to how the educational environment interacts with first-generation students' expectations of their education and themselves, their pre-arrival skills, and support from parents and families in navigating the academic environment. We also briefly return to new student orientation, and describe an innovative learning model that is responsive to students' needs, and we conclude by touching on personal financial constraints that interfere with academic life.

Lehmann (2009b) argues that access to role models who are experienced in higher education leads first-generation students to pursue concrete pathways from degree to profession. In this study, students were found to justify their academic pursuits and occupational aspirations by focusing on the instrumental nature of a university education, often using this notion as reassurance in an unfamiliar environment. The employment value of their education was of the utmost importance for these working-class students. As such, a professional degree in law or medicine was seen as better signifying employability than a vague degree in the social sciences, arts or general fields of science such as biology. This was corroborated by Terenzini and colleagues (1996) who found that first-generation students in their study took fewer courses in the humanities and fine arts.

In as much as post-secondary institutions are intermediaries between first-generation students and their career ambitions, it is incumbent on the institution to help match students' objectives with the demands of the marketplace. Curriculum, therefore, can be designed to help broaden first-generation students' understanding of career opportunities beyond the professions of physician, lawyer and teacher, by facilitating connections between abstract and theoretical knowledge, and the application of such knowledge. *Grounding the work of academia in real-world problems, a notion that we acknowledge is abhorrent to some enclaves within the academy, is criti-*

cal for engaging first-generation students. Education for its own sake or simply out of a love for learning, are not default positions for first-generation students (Padron 1992). Inspiring students in this regard, possibly by nurturing their natural curiosity, is a process that takes time and often begins with responding to the experiences and perspectives that students bring with them into the learning environment. Lehmann (2009b) argues that first-generation students do not reject theoretical, abstract knowledge but, rather, stress the importance of having a clear sense of how to apply their education. They tend to see a good middle-class job as the clearest indication of a successful return on their investment.

Some first-generation students have described how being placed in an academic stream in high school generally made non-academic post-secondary options unthinkable (Lehmann 2009a). At the same time, first-generation students have been known to express significant anxiety about the tremendous leap from the final year of high school to their first year of undergraduate study (Shields 2002). In Bounce Back, we have found that first-generation students at Guelph (as is common elsewhere) often attend university simply because it is what was expected of them, and not because they have a clear sense of where it will lead. Those who have struggled academically often cite a variety of explanations, with the difference between high school and university ranking near the top of their list. These students have described how they did not understand what was required of them academically, and that the expectations of their instructors were unfair or unrealistic. All three perspectives reflect the difficulties these students have with recognizing, internalizing and engaging in the challenges of a learner-centered, adult education model that requires them to be independent and self-directed.

There is some evidence to suggest that although first-generation students feel less prepared for university than their non-first-generation peers, this may have little long-term effect on feelings of success once they arrive on campus. Shields (2002) found that such perceptions are closely linked to the number of credit hours completed and grade point average, regardless of generational status. With regards to self-perception, the reason there is a difference between first-generation and other students is not the educational background of their families per se but, rather, their academic progression; and progression, in turn, can be affected by parental education level. In other words, there may be an indirect effect. When it comes to high school preparation, first-generation students indicated that expectations about the amount of work and its difficulty were not made clear to them and many felt let down by their high schools (Lehmann 2009a). Many first-generation students assert that because they are the first in the family to have this experience, they simply have no idea about what to expect at university (Engle *et al.* 2006; Engle and Tinto 2008).

Whatever vision or aspirations first-generation students might have when they first contemplate post-secondary education, the skills required for success is the next important consideration. Several researchers cite the need for greater academic preparation, suggesting that advanced mathematics, university preparation courses that address both intellectual/curricular skills and interpersonal skills, tutoring and summer bridging programs are particularly beneficial (Engle and Tinto 2008; Engle, Bermeo and O'Brien 2006; Wallace-Hulecki 2009). Likewise, programs designed to help first-generation students interact with other students, staff and faculty and become accustomed to a university or college environment prior to the first day of classes, such as through campus tours, short-term residential experiences and summer orientation programs, can be highly effective. Many programs at the University of Guelph seek to achieve these goals and help to ensure a well-rounded and integrated approach. They aim to emphasize that students have great capacity to help themselves and each other, and that they are supported in this endeavour by an entire community that is oriented toward their academic success.

Challenges in the Admissions Process

In addition to pre-entry skills, first-generation students sometimes face significant challenges in the admission process. Participants in research by Priebe and colleagues (2008) indicated that because their parents were not versed in the processes of applying to university, selecting a program and obtaining funding, first-generation students generally experienced a lack of parental guidance. This experience was shared by students who participated in a Pell Institute study who identified college and university staff as invaluable sources of guidance and support throughout the admission process (Engle, Bermeo and O'Brien 2006). Programs designed specifically for parents and supplemented by outreach activities and resource materials can help to educate families about academic processes while building stronger connections and demystifying the post-secondary experience (Engle and Tinto 2008; Lopez-Mulnix and Mulnix 2006 as cited in Wallace-Hulecki 2009).

Parents of first-generation students sometimes also struggle to help students navigate academic policies, procedures and pedagogy if this kind of information is primarily discussed inside the classroom (a context to which they have little or no access). This is particularly troublesome when students return home feeling frustrated or disillusioned. Student affairs professionals can enhance the success of the institution's efforts to build better academic and curricular systems by helping to educate parents about academic expectations and why the learning environment is structured as it is.

When engaging parents, the University of Guelph seeks to go beyond simply providing information about resources that are available on campus by also improving familiarity with university-style learning. This is achieved through information sessions during the admission process, a blog for parents and families and a direct mailing that includes a handbook written specifically for this audience.

Early Immersion in Innovative Pedagogy Fosters Positive Academic Experiences

Beyond orientation, it has been found that first-generation students frequently seem more receptive to innovative pedagogy than students from college or university-educated families, and they are more motivated in their academic pursuits (Padron 1992). Professionals who are engaged in strategic enrolment management, therefore, can help to advocate for new and more effective approaches to teaching and learning. One such example is the Problem-based Learning model advanced by Murray and Summerlee (2007), which has been used on our campus as a way of creating first-year seminars that are completely transformative. The model is based upon a small class experience, which contrasts sharply with the predominately large classes of many hundreds of students that typify the first year for most undergraduate students on our campus. It orients classroom learning towards *process* rather than relying primarily on outcomes measured by multiple choice exams and impersonal assignments. Students are taught a process for analyzing information that is presented to them in the form of a case study. The process guides students towards identifying learning issues that they divide among themselves, investigate between class sessions and report on when the group reconvenes. Progression through the case, therefore, depends on the contributions of every member of the class. Processing the group experience, reflection and providing feedback to peers about their performance (both in terms of what they contribute and how they do it) are core to every single meeting of the class as well as students' final grades.

The role of the "instructors" is rarely to inform but rather to act as a gatekeeper of the process and, ultimately, to recede into the background. Such innovative additions to the curriculum can serve as useful tools for recruitment and engagement, ultimately giving rise to learners who are more critical, insightful and self-aware. For first-generation students who all too often feel lost in a large and unfamiliar environment, such approaches make the learning experience more meaningful, bring it down to a human scale, and equip them with a wide variety of skills necessary for academic success.

First-Generation Students and Work

A consistent finding in many studies of first-generation students suggests that this population is more likely to work while enrolled in courses, to work part-time throughout their academic careers or, in some instances, to have full-time jobs (*e.g.* Martinez *et al.* 2009; Engle and Tinto 2008; Pike and Kuh 2005). Reducing first-generation students' inclination to undertake full-time employment while enrolled might also decrease their propensity to prematurely withdraw from their program of study. At Guelph our mentoring programs have encountered a number of first-generation students who have unrealistic expectations of themselves and the amount of time they can devote to both work and studying. Mentoring in these circumstances must delicately balance a non-judgmental approach that respects the student's autonomy while also helping to shed insight into the realities of what students must invest in their studies outside of class hours in order to be successful.

Terenzini and colleagues (1996) indicate that first-generation students tend to complete fewer course credit hours in their first year, spend fewer hours studying and work more hours per week off-campus than their non-first-generation peers. To address the financial constraints that compel first-generation students to secure employment, and to promote campus engagement, it has been suggested that providing a greater variety of on-campus employment and expanded work-study opportunities would be beneficial, particularly if connections can be made to a student's program of study (Engle *et al.* 2006; Engle and Tinto 2008; Canadian Council on Learning 2009b). Engle and Tinto (2008) also suggest that financial aid counsellors have a vital role to play in helping students to better understand the debt they are assuming, the number of hours it is reasonable to work, and the impact that their employment will have on their academic pursuits.

In an era of limited financial resources, the University of Guelph shares a struggle with many of our contemporaries: we frequently wrestle with creating paid versus unpaid student positions for the delivery of programs and services. We have found that increasing tuition and fees means that many of the most skilled and experienced student workers simply cannot afford to work without compensation. If we truly respect the heavy burden that can be imposed by the expense of a university education, then it seems incumbent upon us to offer meaningful employment whenever possible. Given that promoting enriching learning experiences—whether through volunteerism, service-learning, or internship opportunities—is a core value held throughout the University, we have ensured that a diverse range of employment and experiential learning opportunities are available.

In all of our programs there is a strong emphasis on ensuring that our staff and volunteer positions not interfere with a student's academic pursuits. As such, individuals are required to have a minimum GPA before taking on one of these roles, and to maintain or enhance their grades while in the position. This requires that the hiring unit is prepared to coach student-staff and volunteers on how to be academically successful in addition to executing the duties of their position. It also means that such positions must be built around academic pressure points—some of which can be anticipated, such as final exams, and some that arise unexpectedly such as when a particular class assignment is more taxing than originally expected. For first-generation students, such employment and volunteer experiences offer opportunities to develop a well-rounded set of skills, internalize institutional values relating to academic success, take on roles of responsibility that balance with (rather than compete against) curricular activities, be mentored by a supervisor, learn more about campus resources and address personal financial constraints.

Strategic Market Approach

The fourth and final dimension of strategic enrolment management considers how a college or university situates itself in relation to the broader community of post-secondary institutions (Kalsbeek 2006a; 2006b). This perspective is about differentiating a brand and competitive position in the marketplace of higher education. Although an institution's position is determined by the perceptions of those external to it, thus limiting direct control, a variety of initiatives can be undertaken to indirectly influence perceptions through investing in strategies that clarify, strengthen and enhance its competitive niche. Fundamental to these strategies are retention and graduation rates, with careful consideration of whether an institution delivers on its promise to students in a value-added fashion.

In the University of Guelph experience, these strategies are often carefully guarded because of the competitive nature of the marketplace. The literature points to using marketing and recruitment outreach strategies to spread the word about an institution's identity by engaging alumni and local employers at community events (Copper 2008). To this end, local chapters of the Alumni Association at the University of Guelph host 'send-off events' in some of the communities from which our incoming students originate. The events, hosted in mid-August, provide opportunities for alumni to speak about some of the highlights of their time at the university and how they have gone on to use their university education in their careers and personal lives. Bank executives, entrepreneurs, former Canadian ambassadors, and social workers (among many others) at a range of ages, whether recently graduated or retired, have participated in welcoming incoming students and their parents to the "University of Guelph family." As a partnership with the Centre for New Students, this program helps to clarify perceptions of the student experience on our campus and to establish preliminary connections with other new students, staff and members of the alumni community.

Customized marketing, recruitment and admission materials designed specifically for diverse populations such as first-generation students are critically important vehicles for conveying a sense of the institution's values and expectations, and facilitating a sense of belonging. They also communicate information that students need to make informed decisions. Information cited in the literature as being of particular importance includes: academic program descriptions, admission standards, residence information, visa requirements, health services, a breakdown of actual costs including compulsory fees, work-study opportunities, orientation programs, student life and campus culture, as well as future career prospects. Furthermore, demystifying the processes associated with admission and student financial aid assessments were noted as being equally important (Wallace-Hulecki 2009).

Targeted materials that are well-rounded, informed, attractive and engaging play a seminal role in promoting an accessible post-secondary education to first-generation students. In that spirit, Guelph has produced a handbook for international students that is mailed out prior to their arrival and a similar handbook for Aboriginal students. Both of these publications are of professional quality and are designed to guide students through the range of programs, services and resources available to them when they arrive on campus, and to introduce key expectations. For those with little pre-existing knowledge and few expectations of the richness of what's available on campus, creative, attractive and well-designed documents are what is most likely to catch a student's attention. First-generation students, therefore, benefit from careful attention to both the content and style of our materials.

In a similar fashion to print materials, an institution's Web site (and not just that of the admissions department) communicates key messages to prospective students. Simply posting a digital version of a book on a Web site is often insufficient for engaging the reader, and many publications need to be completely reconceived when moving to an online format. Once again, Guelph has followed the common trend of producing less print material in favour of these digital publications. This helps to address issues of access, immediacy and searchability, while ensuring that important information, updates and materials do not become lost.

In a world of Web 2.0 technologies, an institution's presence on social media such as Facebook, Twitter and YouTube helps to engage diverse populations. No doubt, these technologies can be scary for institutions that are used to exerting significant control over their public message. While all of these technologies permit a branded presence, they are fundamentally dependent upon word-of-mouth. For first-generation students, the informal approach helps to humanize the institution.

Like many units dedicated to supporting new students across North America, the Centre for New Students at the University of Guelph has a presence on all of the aforementioned social networking media and is beginning to venture into new technologies such as Foursquare. Part of the mandate of the Centre is to focus on the transition needs of those students who face greater challenges as they embark on their post-secondary education. Choosing to be present on students' own turf allows us to intervene when there are problematic messages (such as from local bars and clubs, or from misinformed students), clarify ambiguous information, ensure that questions are answered correctly, and have a first point of contact with those who are apprehensive about asking for help in person.

One of the many functions of the Centre for New Students is to monitor the student experience on both a broad-scale and at the individual level. It helps to ensure that students experience the University in a way that is consistent with its brand identity by connecting those who are having trouble with the various access points for help. The centre makes it easier for first-generation students to navigate the system, de-mystifying the many decentralized programs and services provided by the institution. Its approach is built on the assumption that well-crafted interventions for those with the greatest struggles create a strong safety net for everyone.

Strategic placement in the market is a continuous process that speaks to the way in which institutions are dynamic, living places. Work on retention rates, graduation rates and the public perception of the institution are therefore agendas that continue to evolve over time. The University of Guelph has long been a leader with regards to retention and graduation rates, consistently ranking near the top among its peers and well above the system average (University of Guelph 2008). Achievement in this area can be attributed to a myriad of factors, not the least of which is the wide range of opportunities and experiences the institution creates to meet the varying needs of a diverse population. By recognizing that there is not a "one size fits all" solution, we are able to adapt to new pressures, challenges and opportunities that develop from improved understandings of our students, including those who are first-generation.

CONCLUSION

The initial idea behind the writing of this chapter was to answer the question: is the notion of "first-generation students" a useful social construct or is it simply a convenient label to attach to a sub-population of non-traditional high-risk students? In particular, we wondered whether there was much distinction between first-generation students and those who are from low-income families. A review of the literature suggests that indeed there is considerable overlap between first-generation students and a variety of identity groups including those for whom English is a second language, Aboriginal students and immigrants. We found, however, that first-generation students do indeed have unique experiences that distinguish them within each of these identity groups.

Among many unique perspectives, first-generation students tend to question their place in the academy more, feel bewildered by large institutional systems, are focused on a utilitarian perspective when it comes to their education, and face a variety of personal barriers including a lack of family support and limited financial means. Through better understanding the experiences of first-generation students, we are able to apply the principles of strategic enrolment management in order to create a more collaborative, reflexive and robust system for recruiting, retaining and graduating a diverse student body. Increased participation is unlikely to occur, however, without universities and colleges preparing to meet the needs of under-represented groups. In partnership with a range of stakeholders including government, boards of education and community organizations, there is a need for multi-faceted networks of support that represent what has been coined a "life course" approach to post-secondary education (Berger and Motte 2007). In so doing, colleges and universities will be well positioned to respond to the growing demands for a strong workforce, educated public, and innovative solutions to the complex challenges we face.

*Nicole Lacasse, Patrick Mignault
and Johanne Morneau*

13

CASE STUDY: UNDERGRADUATE ACADEMIC AND CAREER SUCCESS AT UNIVERSITÉ LAVAL

/ **Chapter 13** /

Université Laval (Laval University) has, like other institutions of higher learning, devoted a great deal of effort over the last decade to recruiting new students, thus boosting its yield rate. Through strategic enrolment management (SEM), we have also focused on the various steps of the student path to graduation. For Université Laval, ethical, responsible SEM means providing an environment that encourages student engagement, persistence, and success, right from the first day on campus.

Université Laval has a good reputation for student retention and success in Québec. The campus attrition rate compares favourably with that of other francophone universities, and retention rates are roughly the Québec average (for both francophone and anglophone universities). However, globalization and the knowledge economy, which require a highly qualified labour force, mean that Université Laval, along with the Québec education system as a whole, must improve its graduation rate.

Support for academic and career success is a cornerstone of strategic enrolment management. In keeping with its educational mission and social responsibilities, Université Laval made academic success a core component of its strategic action plan in 2008 (Université Laval 2008a). The institution has emphasized two areas: helping students adjust to university life and developing academic guidance and support. These priorities complement others already in place. A number of reports, briefs, policies, and actions in these areas have been produced and implemented over the last decade at all academic levels.[21]

---

[21] All citations are available online at www.ulaval.ca: Commission des affaires étudiantes 2004a, *Pour mieux soutenir les étudiantes et les étudiants dans leur projet d'études : persévérance et réussite au 1er cycle,* ; Commission des affaires étudiantes 2004b, *Pour mieux soutenir les étudiantes et les étudiants dans leur projet d'études: persévérance et réussite et aux 2e et 3e cycles*; Commission des affaires étudiantes 2006, *L'accueil, l'encadrement et l'intégration des étudiants étrangers à l'Université Laval—Rapport synthèse*; Commission des affaires étudiantes 2010, *Les études et la vie étudiante : conciliation-flexibilité-adaptation*; Commission des études 2006, *Les*

Prior academic preparation and student motivation are the two main determinants of success (Kuh *et al.* 2005a; Kuh 2009). In this light, Université Laval considers that its role as an institution of higher learning is to support student engagement and persistence. Various interventions can be used: screening for at-risk students, orientation and integration activities, individual coaching of new students, social and academic student twinning, tutoring, learning assistance, learning centres, and so forth. The institution must support the student's academic plans based on the student's academic profile and personal, social, and cultural characteristics.

In 2009 Université Laval sought to determine those factors that affect student success and to identify and assist struggling students. Before adopting new programs, it was necessary to learn more about student needs and evaluate the effectiveness of interventions already in place. Various initiatives were undertaken to achieve this: collecting institutional data on changes in attrition and failure rates, analyzing new students' progress, conducting telephone interviews with newly enrolled international students, and surveying administrators to find out what measures were already in place to promote engagement, persistence, and success. These studies and surveys are already shedding new light on the effectiveness of strategies at the undergraduate level. The University plans to achieve its strategic objective of improving its support for student engagement, persistence, and success by 2012.

In this chapter we discuss the current state of undergraduate engagement, persistence, and success at Université Laval, the strategic enrolment management process the university has adopted to achieve its objectives, and the initiatives recently undertaken to support academic success.

UNDERGRADUATE ENGAGEMENT, PERSISTENCE, AND SUCCESS AT UNIVERSITÉ LAVAL

First-year dropout rates in American and Canadian universities range between 20 percent and 25 percent (Grayson 2003). In Canada, Barr-Telford *et al.* (2003) estimated that 24 percent of young people who start post-secondary studies abandon

études à l'Université Laval: Constats et perspectives. Rapport synthèse; Commission des études 2010, *S'éduquer au monde chez soi: La formation locale à l'international*; Université Laval 2001, *Politique d'accueil, d'intégration et d'encadrement des étudiants*, CU-2001–100; Université Laval 2002, *Politique d'intégration des personnes handicapées étudiantes à l'Université Laval*, CA-2002–36.; Université Laval 2004a, *Politique sur l'usage du français*, CA-2004–150.; Université Laval 2008b, *Politique d'encadrement des étudiants à la maîtrise avec mémoire et au doctorat*, CU-2008–37.

them within 18 months. In Québec the situation is slightly different; in 2005 the Québec Ministry of Education, Recreation and Sports (Ministère de l'Éducation, du Loisir et du Sport, or MELS) estimated the dropout rate of full-time university students at 20.2 percent (Sauvé *et al.* 2006). However, given the differences between Québec's school system and those in the rest of Canada and the United States, it is difficult to compare Québec data to Canadian and American figures.

Université Laval Compared to Other Québec Universities

Between 1994 and 2000, the average attrition rate at universities in Québec was 18.8 percent after the first year of studies and 28.7 percent after five years. Table 4 presents the respective performances of Québec's principal universities in this respect.

During this period, Université Laval's first-year attrition rate compared favourably to other universities. After five years, it was still better than that of most other universities. It should be noted, however, that between the first and fifth year, Université Laval's attrition rate increased nearly 11 percentage points. McGill University, which has very selective admission criteria, was the only university in Québec with an attrition rate under 20 percent after five years.

Table 5 (on page 264) presents the change in first-year retention rates of cohorts registered in a full-time bachelor's program between 1997–1998 and 2002–2003. The average retention rate at Québec universities rose from 82.0 percent for the 1997–1998 cohort to 85.8 percent for that of 2002–2003.

TABLE 4. STUDENT ATTRITION RATES IN QUÉBEC UNIVERSITIES FROM 1994 TO 2000

University	Dropout Rate After One Year (%)	Dropout Rate After Five Years or More (%)
Université Laval	15.3	26.2
Université de Montréal	20.1	26.5
McGill University	10.1	14.1
Université de Sherbrooke	26.6	27.7
Concordia University	17.5	39.5
Université du Québec à Montréal (UQAM)	23.3	37.9
Average	18.8	28.7

Source: Tremblay 2005

TABLE 5. FIRST-YEAR RETENTION RATES (%)
OF STUDENT COHORTS IN QUÉBEC UNIVERSITIES

University	1997–1998	1998–1999	1999–2000	2000–2001	2001–2002	2002–2003
Université Laval	84.0	84.4	84.7	83.7	84.0	84.8
Université de Montréal	83.4	81.3	79.9	82.0	83.2	83.7
McGill University	89.4	90.1	89.8	89.5	89.5	92.9
Université de Sherbrooke	75.0	76.7	73.4	75.6	82.7	87.0
Concordia University	80.5	81.3	82.5	83.7	84.8	85.3
Université du Québec à Montréal	79.7	80.5	76.7	80.9	76.7	81.3
Average	82.0	82.4	81.2	82.6	83.5	85.8

SOURCE: Tremblay 2005

Retention rates at Université Laval remained stable over all six cohorts. Although the university performed better than the Québec average up to 2001–2002, its retention rate was slightly below average in 2002–2003. Université de Sherbrooke's progress (from 75.0 to 87.0%) is the most striking trend in Table 5. This 12 percentage point improvement illustrates that it is possible to substantially boost completion rates.

Analysis of Université Laval Data

Data from MELS sheds light on Université Laval's undergraduate retention rates and provides a basis for comparison with other universities. However, the portrait presented by MELS needs to be supplemented and updated using the university's own figures. The following data (Figure 6) was retrieved on May 31, 2009.[22] According to our data, undergraduate retention rates[23] vary according to the student's academic profile at admission and the type of program taken (certificate, bachelor degree, etc.). The analysis indicates that for each year studied, and for all undergraduate programs combined, a little less than a third of students who are admitted directly from the College of General and Vocational Education (Collège

---

[22] On this date the cohorts studied were at different stages in their university programs so we lack complete or sufficient data on the most recent cohorts. This limitation obviously has an impact on the completion analysis over longer periods, for which only the oldest cohorts can be considered.

[23] The term "retention" refers to a student pursuing his or her program of studies from registration through graduation. Retention rate is the size of a cohort (newly registered students in a program) compared to the number of students who are still registered and/or have graduated within a prescribed time.

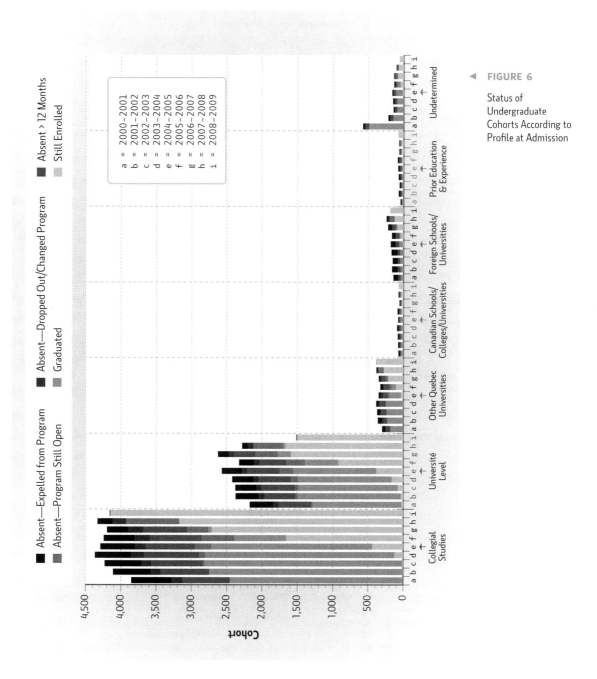

◄ **FIGURE 6**

Status of
Undergraduate
Cohorts According to
Profile at Admission

d'enseignement général et professionnel, or CÉGEP)[24] drop out. The same is true for students who transferred from one program to another at Université Laval. The attrition rate for students admitted from international schools is lower since the exclusion rate among these students is very high.[25]

STRATEGIC ENROLMENT MANAGEMENT AND ACADEMIC SUCCESS

The Competitive Environment

In Québec, as elsewhere, knowledge has become a key factor in social and economic development. Workforce training and knowledge development have taken on special importance, giving rise to the concept of the "knowledge society." A number of international organizations have studied the university's role in the new knowledge society since the 1990s: the Delors Commission (1996), the Conference of European Rectors (1997), the UNESCO World Conference on Higher Education (1998), the Council of Europe (1998), OECD (1998 and 2008), and Québec's Higher Council on Education (Conseil supérieur de l'éducation) (2010). In the new globalized economy, knowledge is viewed as key to maintaining and improving competitiveness internationally (Spring 2009). Université Laval has a key role to play in training highly qualified workers in Québec.

As a research university and member of the U15[26], Université Laval plays a major role in Canadian research and is called upon to meet the increasing demand for workforce training. The labour market is increasingly exacting with respect to such training. A Québec study in the early 2000s showed that 50 percent of the job growth between 1984 and 1999 occurred in "high knowledge" industries (Ministère de l'Industrie et du Commerce 2001).

---

[24] Québec has a unique educational system within Canada. Students graduate from high school after Grade 11 and then move on to the CÉGEP system where they may enroll in one of two streams: a two-year pre-university stream or a three-year technical/vocational stream.

[25] Students can be excluded from programs for various reasons: (i) Their cumulative average is too low; (ii) their French proficiency does not meet requirements; (iii) they fail the same learning activity three times; or (iv) they do not finish their studies by the prescribed deadline.

[26] The U15 is made up of the following Canadian universities: University of Alberta, University of British Columbia, University of Calgary, Dalhousie University, Université Laval, McGill University, McMaster University, University of Manitoba, Université de Montréal, University of Ottawa, Queen's University, University of Saskatchewan, University of Toronto, University of Waterloo, and University of Western Ontario.

The higher education market is also increasingly competitive. Students shop around for university programs as they do any other product. To remain competitive in the higher education marketplace, universities must offer attractive training programs and have a solid brand image. They must develop and implement strategies to structure their recruitment efforts and support students through to graduation.

Université Laval's competitive environment is exacerbated by demographic issues, both in Québec City and in its other traditional recruitment areas, as well as by the fact that it is a French-language university, which limits its potential market expansion. Québec's demographic history in the twentieth century was marked by two main periods: the baby boom era (between 1946 and 1966), when the birth rate skyrocketed by 55 percent, followed a period of twenty years (1966 to 1986) during which Québec's birth rate fell by 25.9 percent. Since 1986 the birth rate has stabilized at around 11.5 percent (Gauthier *et al*. 2004). The combined effect of the rise and fall of the birth rate, together with longer life expectancies, has transformed the population structure. A high proportion of Québec's population is now in the middle of the age pyramid, while the base of the pyramid (that is, the youth demographic) is eroding due to the aging of the population.

Québec's student body is expected to continue to grow until 2011 then decrease for the following ten years to reach 90 percent of its current size. Estimates are even more pessimistic for eastern Québec, where 85 percent of Université Laval's students are recruited. Université Laval attracts 80 percent of Québec City's CÉGEP students, but less than two percent of those from Montréal. In addition, the proportion of high school students that enter pre-university programs at CÉGEP continues to fall. Over a 15-year period, the proportion dropped from 44 percent (1992–1993) to 36 percent (2006–2007) (MELS 2008).

To compensate for the anticipated shrinkage of Québec's student population, Université Laval has made international initiatives and support for academic success strategic priorities. A variety of initiatives have been undertaken to create a favourable environment that fosters international student integration. Every year, Université Laval welcomes about 4,000 international students from 112 countries. Between 2001 and 2009, the university boosted the number of international students by 12 percent. However francophone universities are at a disadvantage recruiting from a number of international markets, including strategic areas such as

Asia, because allophone students (those whose mother tongue is neither English nor French) prefer university programs delivered in English. In 2008 less than 5 percent of Université Laval's international students came from Asia, the Middle East, or Oceania.[27]

Strategic Enrolment Management at Université Laval

Based on its organizational structure and its student recruitment and retention objectives, Université Laval has adopted a strategic enrolment management framework and SEM process for following students through their academic and career path (Figure 7). The purpose of this framework is to assist students through the various stages of their educational and career development, considering them as lifetime members of the university community. The process is a continuum divided into six distinct parts:

- Attractiveness: Develop the university's educational product and living environment by providing innovative, flexible services and training programs.
- Information and promotion: In order to positively influence students' career choices, establish relationships with potential applicants and assist them with their academic plans up to the moment they submit their applications.
- Admission and registration: Process applications rapidly and appropriately and follow up efficiently with university representatives and the student.
- Support for success: Establish programs to support student academic and career achievement.
- Graduation and placement: Help graduates break into the job market by forging ties with the professional community.
- Alumni relations: Maintain and develop ties with alumni, help them update their skills, and foster their advancement throughout their careers.

The university's SEM process has been guided by the university's faculties and a committee, known until recently as the Université Laval Student Recruitment Steering Committee (COSRÉUL). The committee is made up of the deans of the 17 faculties and representatives from the main administrative student services. In 2010 the

---

[27] Université Laval primarily recruits international students from the French-speaking nations of the Middle East (*e.g.*, Lebanon), Africa (north and west Africa), and Caribbean (*e.g.*, Haiti).

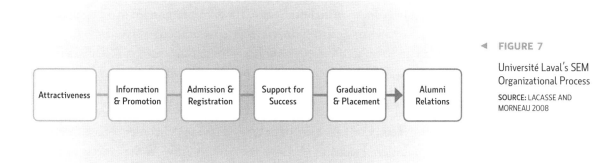

◀ **FIGURE 7**

Université Laval's SEM
Organizational Process

SOURCE: LACASSE AND
MORNEAU 2008

committee's name was changed to the Strategic Enrolment Management Committee to better reflect its new mission. Université Laval's decentralized organizational structure means that the faculties must be directly involved to ensure efficient management of the SEM process. The faculties are involved to various degrees in guiding and advising students, organizing supplementary workshops, and providing student services. The Office of the Vice-Rector of Academic and International Activities has organized joint activities with the faculties and services to present and discuss the SEM framework: SEM meetings, professional development days, and establishing a university-wide committee on supporting academic success. The new committee is tasked with (1) examining the research literature and the university's own data on academic success, (2) identifying winning strategies, (3) helping the faculties improve measures to support academic success, and (4) promoting knowledge transfer.

Strategic Enrolment Management and Student Retention and Success

One aspect of the university's mission is to equip people with the skills they need to contribute to society's advancement. Academic success is a measure of how well this mission has been fulfilled. The university, society, and students alike benefit when students complete their university education. By adopting a strategic enrolment management framework, Université Laval puts a strong emphasis on student retention and academic success.

Access to higher education has been a fundamental value in Québec since the 1960s. The Parent Commission marked the beginning of the first phase of improving access to higher education in the province. The Parent Report led to the establishment of a public system based on the universal right to education: everyone should have access to an education according to his or her aptitudes and interests (Conseil supérieur de l'éducation 1988). Between 1960 and 1970, Québec universities gradually opened their doors and dropped their elitist image. A second stage in educational reform began in the mid-1990s, with an aim of ensuring equal opportunity for academic success within programs (Conseil supérieur de l'éducation 1995). In order to raise Quebecers' level of education, graduation became the new objective in the process of democratizing education. Québec universities were encouraged to establish programs and services to improve their graduation rates (Conseil supérieur de l'éducation 2009). MELS signed performance contracts with each university outlining their institutional commitment to improve student support and boost student success.

In Québec, the focus on academic success has given rise to at least four research, intervention, and knowledge transfer groups: the Centre for Research and Intervention for Educational Success (Centre de recherche et d'intervention sur la réussite scolaire, or CRIRES), the Consortium on the Dissemination of Perseverance and Success in Higher Education (Consortium d'animation sur la persévérance et la réussite en enseignement supérieur, or CAPRES), the Centre for Research and Intervention on Education and Life at Work (Centre de recherche et d'intervention sur l'éducation et la vie au travail, or CRIEVAT), and the Canada Research Chair on Motivation and Academic Success. [28]

Founded in 1992 by Université Laval and the Labour Unions Group of Québec (Centrale des syndicats du Québec)[29], CRIRES studies student retention and academic success and supports schools in their efforts to promote academic achievement for all students.[30] Based at Université du Québec, CAPRES' mission is to disseminate knowledge and expertise on academic success to CÉGEPs and universities in Québec. CAPRES organizes various knowledge transfer activities with a view to creating discussion forums and reflection with institutions of higher learn-

---

[28] *See* <www.motivation.chaire.ulaval.ca/sgc/site/crcmrs/lang/en_CA/pid/73>.

[29] Centrale des syndicats du Québec (CSQ) used to be called Corporation des enseignants du Québec (CEQ) and Centrale de l'enseignement du Québec (CEQ).

[30] *See* CRIRES, <www.ulaval.ca/crires/>. This research and intervention organization comprises 38 full and associate researchers representing seven Québec universities. It comprises Université Laval, Université de Sherbrooke, Université du Québec à Trois-Rivières, Université du Québec à Chicoutimi, Université du Québec en Outaouais, Université du Québec à Rimouski, and McGill University.

ing.[31] CRIEVAT is the biggest research group in Canada studying the relationship between the individual, his or her training, and the workplace.[32] This multidisciplinary, interuniversity research team[33] aims to develop knowledge on bridging the gap between teaching institutions and the workplace. Through its research mission, members of CRIEVAT also supervise the research (papers and postgraduate theses) of a number of students.[34]

Research literature indicates that student engagement is the key to academic success and that prior academic preparation and student motivation are the two main determinants of a student's success or failure in post-secondary studies (Pascarella 1991; Pascarella and Tarenzini 2005; and Kuh *et al.* 2005a). Romainville (2000) classified the causes of university student failure into three interactive categories:

- Student characteristics at entrance (for example, course prerequisites, geographic origin, age, and academic history and plans).
- How students adjust to their new situation (how they relate to and engage in their studies).
- The quality of university teaching (development of teaching and pedagogical practices).

Admitting only students with the best academic records is considered only a partial solution to problems of academic failure. The university must continue to not only ensure that students master the knowledge and skills they need, but must also provide high quality university teaching.

For Université Laval, ethical and responsible admission is seen not just as a matter of accepting only the best students, but rather encouraging the engagement of the students it admits. That is, the university must not only recruit students, but also supervise and guide them toward success according to their individual personal, social, and cultural characteristics. Such support must be founded on key processes that foster (i) personal validation, (ii) self-efficacy, (iii) sense of purpose,

---

[31] *See* <www.uquebec.ca/capres/index.cfm>.

[32] *See* <www.crievat.fse.ulaval.ca>.

[33] CRIEVAT is made up of 19 full and 16 associate members from 11 different universities.

[34] *See* <www.crievat.fse.ulaval.ca/membres/etudiants>.

(iv) active involvement, (v) reflective thinking, (vi) social integration, and (vii) self-awareness in the students (Cuseo 2010).

The Student Recruitment Office recently conducted two surveys of current students in order to improve its recruitment strategy and to obtain a clearer idea of student expectations with regard to their studies. The first survey was intended to paint a sociographic picture of undergraduate and graduate students in all programs at Université Laval. It is anticipated that the study (whose results are still to come) will reveal the students' socioeconomic and cultural characteristics (such as parents' level of education; student nationality, cultural and ethnic group; income and debt levels; place and type of residence; interrupted studies; and social involvement). This survey will also shed light on the students' academic aspirations.

The second study is part of a survey conducted by the firm Customer Relationship Index (CRi) on first-year students at various Canadian universities. Université Laval was the only francophone university to take part in this study. The purpose of the survey was to establish a psychographic profile of first-year university students—their values, attitudes toward their studies, expectations, and so forth—and to identify any relevant differences in the participating universities' respective student populations. The results (which are also still to come) will give us a better understanding of the various aspects of the university experience.

Effective guidance that fosters academic success requires scientifically recognized best educational practices for improving student engagement (Astin 1993; Pascarella 1991; Pascarella and Terenzini 2005). Kuh *et al.* (2005a) divided these practices into five categories:

- Level of academic challenge
- Active and collaborative learning
- Student faculty interaction
- Enriching educational experiences
- Supportive campus environment[35]

The categories Kuh proposes for classifying educational practices are used in the Institute for Effective Educational Practice's National Survey of Student Engage-

---

[35] Best teaching practices can also be based on principles of academic success (Cuseo 2010).

ment (NSSE) questionnaire. Université Laval is taking part in the NSSE survey in order to document the reforms that have been undertaken. The initiatives presented in the following pages are based on these scientifically recognized practices.

Best practices for improving student engagement can increase students' level of satisfaction (Kuh *et al.* 2005a), which is closely linked to academic success. Noel-Levitz (2009) demonstrated the link between student satisfaction, their persistence, and academic success. Student satisfaction, particularly concerning the atmosphere on campus, can increase student retention and the likelihood that students will continue their studies at the same university (Noel-Levitz 2009).

Student Retention and Academic Success: Progress to Date

Thanks to the numerous programs and services provided by Université Laval over the years, students have enjoyed a campus environment that fosters academic success. The services are provided by various administrative units:

- Undergraduate Program Office
- Student Life Office
- Student Aid Centre[36]
- Scholarship and Financial Aid Office
- Registrar's Office
- Sports Services
- Job Placement Service
- Université Laval Alumni Association

To varying degrees the faculties have also implemented activities to support academic success, sometimes through their program offices: orientation activities, learning assistance centres in French and mathematics, twinning programs, and so on. A number of faculties have also supplemented the university scholarship and financial aid program (undergraduate admission scholarships, leadership scholarships, Ph.D. admission scholarships, exemption from extra tuition fees, and a financial aid program to support academic success).

---

[36] Previously called the Guidance and Counseling Centre. It was changed to Student Aid Centre in 2009.

A university orientation, guidance, and integration policy has been in effect since 2001, reflecting the importance Université Laval places on student success and achievement (Université Laval 2001). Applying to all employees, the policy incorporates all Université Laval policies and guidelines on the subject with a view to fulfilling the following objectives:

- Promote success in students' intellectual and career training programs, as well as their personal and social development, by providing a positive environment.
- Stress each person's responsibility to orient, assist, and integrate students.
- Encourage and maintain dialogue among all members of the university community and stimulate reflection on the prerequisites to student orientation, assistance, and integration.

However, as statistics on undergraduate student retention and success demonstrate (Section 1), this overall framework in and of itself did not result in a significant increase in the retention rate at Université Laval. In 2004 Université Laval's Student Affairs Committee noted this state of affairs in a brief on the effectiveness of existing support measures (Commission des affaires étudiantes 2004a and 2004b). The Committee issued recommendations with concrete examples of how to encourage students to complete their studies. A working group was then tasked with examining how the Student Affairs Committee's brief should be followed up. Priorities were then set by the working group.

As part of its SEM process, Université Laval made the implementation of activities supporting academic success one of the cornerstones of its strategic action plan in 2008 (Université Laval 2008a)[37]. The aim was to improve its annual performance in this regard by 2012. One of the objectives of the plan was to better integrate the various activities and interventions put in place by the university and its faculties and to share best practices. The university has emphasized two areas: activities to help students integrate into the university, and assistance and teaching support for academic success.[38]

---

[37] In 2008, Université Laval also ratified a special agreement on academic retention and success. The purpose of the agreement is to rally partners in the Québec City area who are concerned with academic success in all fields and the development of university programs and careers in science and technology. *See* <http://perseverancecapitale.ning.com>.

[38] Improving the quality of university teaching is also a strategic concern at Université Laval, but will not be covered in this chapter.

RECENT STRATEGIC ENROLMENT MANAGEMENT INITIATIVES

Before changing its academic success support activities or adopting new ones, Université Laval sought to better understand academic success on its own campus. Three initiatives were designed to achieve this:

- Collecting institutional data on changes in attrition and failure rates.
- Analyzing how international students integrate into campus life by conducting telephone interviews with newly enrolled students.
- Surveying administrators on the application and effectiveness of activities promoting engagement, persistence, and success.

Data Collection

As a first step toward better understanding the effectiveness of current support activities, Université Laval collected data on academic success, focusing on undergraduate students whose retention rate had not sufficiently improved. In 2009 we extracted and organized data from our database in order to analyze persistence and graduation rates. The resulting data has allowed us to examine changes in persistence rates for undergraduate and graduate students by faculty throughout the university.[39] We have also been able to identify the courses—known as "killer courses"—with the highest failure rates.

With this information, academic success support interventions can now be targeted to programs with the highest attrition rates. For example, in fall 2008 the data showed that those programs with very strict enrolment limits like medicine, dentistry, and pharmacy had failure rates below two percent. It was determined that academic success is not a problem in these programs and therefore they should not be a focus for the university.

The database also allowed us to conduct a cross analysis of failure rates with student admission characteristics known to be potential causes of failure, such as course prerequisites, year of study, academic history, geographic origin, age, and gender (Romanville 2000).

A number of research studies have identified first-year students as an at-risk group (Coulon 1997; Romainville 1998 and 2009). In their first year, students must

---

[39] In winter 2006 the deadline for dropping out without a failing mark was moved further back in the academic semester to the Friday of the tenth week of the term. This lowered the failure rate and raised the "withdrawal without failure" rate.

learn the skills they need to be successful students. They must adapt to a new world and understand its codes, requirements, and customs. Université Laval compared the failure rate of new students (those with no university experience) to more experienced students (those who had taken at least 24 credits at the time they registered for a course). Data on the 2008–2009 cohort indicated that experienced students generally fared better than new students. However, this is not true for all faculties. In more than a third of the programs, new students do better than the more experienced students.

Academic history is another useful factor for studying student success (Romainville 2000). Université Laval did a cross analysis to track the status of students admitted to the university based on their R-scores.[40] This analysis makes it possible to determine the relationship between R-scores and student status (classified as *dropped out*,[41] *still enrolled*, or *graduated*). The Université Laval data bore out the conclusions of previous studies that established a direct link between previous academic performance and success or failure at university (Chapman 1996). The cross analysis showed that students who do best are those with high R-scores at admission. In some programs the enrolment restrictions neutralize the impact of R-scores on students' performance at university since all the students admitted have high R-scores. However, in programs that do not limit enrolment, R-score impact on academic performance is significant. In these programs CÉGEP students admitted to Université Laval with lower R-scores are an at-risk group that require special attention if they are to succeed.

In many industrialized countries, including Canada, more male than female students run into problems at university (Bouchard, Boily, and Proulx 2003). Thus we examined whether gender had a significant effect on failure rates on campus. The data shows that the current failure rate for male students (10.4%) is 4.4 percent higher than that of female students (6.0%). However, this is not true for all departments and faculties. In about a dozen cases, male students have lower failure rates than female students. Most of these cases are in the Faculty of Science and Engineering.

---

[40] The R-score is an academic record evaluation method used by most Québec universities for admission to certain programs.

[41] *See* note 25.

Thus the above statistical analysis made it possible to identify at-risk student groups in specific programs where support interventions should be provided: first-year students, those with low R-scores, male students, and international students.

Operation "How are you doing?" for International Students

In fall 2009 the university's Academic Success Committee, funded by the Office of the Vice Rector, Academics and International Activities, launched Operation *How are you doing?,* targeting newly enrolled international undergraduate students. The Student Aid Centre developed a model telephone interview for contacting newly enrolled international students in their first semester. The objective of this semi-structured interview was to see how the students were doing and to help them take appropriate steps if they were having difficulty. The telephone interviews were conducted by experienced graduate students selected by faculty staff and trained by personnel at the Student Aid Centre.

Operation *How are you doing?* had three objectives:

- Engage in discussion with students from the target population about how they were adapting to life at Université Laval from a social, academic, and linguistic perspective.
- Inform the students of resources available to help them deal with the problems they identified.
- Collect data to help plan the support interventions to put in place.

A total of 115 students in six faculties were contacted at mid-term in fall 2009. Nearly half of the respondents (44.4%) were from the Faculty of Science and Engineering and 34.8 percent from the Faculty of Arts. The other students came from the Faculty of Social Science (7.8%); the Faculty of Agriculture and Food Sciences (6.1%); the Faculty of Forestry, Geography, and Geomatics (5.2%); and the Faculty of Business Administration (1.7%).

The telephone interviews included a number of open questions in order to identify the main ways the students had adjusted since their arrival at Université Laval. Adaptations to the physical and cultural environment—particularly the language, pace of life, food, and Québec's cold climate—seemed to be the most prominent issues identified. Upon enrolment, international students have very little time to get to know their new environment, the campus, and the city. A number of respondents also mentioned interpersonal relations as an issue because of their separation from their family, the difficulty of establishing a new social network, and the discrimination they faced as international students. Challenges posed by differences in the education system also were identified: the complexity of enrolment procedures, upgrading and remedial sessions, the degree of academic autonomy required, and adjustment to the academic program. Time management was also identified as a major issue. For all students, adaptation is hampered by the time they have to put into their studies.

A more in-depth analysis of the survey results revealed that more than half the respondents (52.9%) mentioned social integration issues, which were caused by a number of factors:

- Distance from family/homesickness.
- Lack of knowledge about their environment and sometimes late arrival.
- Cultural differences: language, nonverbal communication, climate, and pace of life.
- Difficulty approaching others and in building a social network.
- Tendency to associate only with other students of the same origin.
- Attitudes toward international students: distant, distrustful, cold, prejudiced.
- Lack of time to devote to their social life and people's lack of availability because they are focused on their studies.

All of these obstacles to effective cultural and social adjustment affect how well international students adapt to their academic environment. As in the social sphere, half the respondents (49%) said they had trouble with their studies due to a number of causes:

- North American university academic style: participative learning, fast pace, work load, required autonomy, class size.
- Student-related difficulties: inadequate academic background, inappropriate choice of courses, difficulty with certain subjects, study methods, lack of motivation, falling behind in class, poor academic results.
- Language: rapid delivery and accent of native speakers.
- Lack of contact with other students in the class.
- No contact person in the faculty.

In the interviews the students were asked who they turned to for learning assistance. The respondents could give more than one answer. Half of the international students (51%) said they went to their professors for help. Other sources of assistance were other students in the same program (27.5%), faculty staff (17.6%), and the program head (17.6%).

The survey enabled us to collect invaluable data on difficulties newly-enrolled international students face and helped us plan future support measures to facilitate students' cultural, social, and academic integration. The results show that measures already in place, such as mentoring, learning communities, and student twinning, should be encouraged because they meet student needs.

Survey of Program Administrators on Academic Success Support

In the Winter of 2010, the Academic Support Committee surveyed undergraduate program administrators from all faculties about their use of 29 interventions known to foster student engagement, persistence, and academic success. The list of interventions was drawn up based on the literature on academic success and the program heads' own experience.[42] The objective of the survey was to evaluate existing support activities at Université Laval and explore how the program administrators evaluated their effectiveness and how interested the faculties were in developing new interventions. When respondents said they used an intervention, they were asked how effective it was. Inversely, if a measure was not used, they were asked if they were interested in developing such an intervention and to estimate its potential effectiveness.

The online questionnaire was sent to 139 people (program directors, vice deans, and faculty heads). The participation rate was 32 percent (44 respondents).

APPLIED MEASURES

The two most frequently used interventions were student orientation (81.8%) and information on professors' availability provided in the course outlines distributed to students at the beginning of term (81.8%). Orientation activities were considered to be an effective measure by 91.7 percent of those who used them. Use of univer-

---

[42] *See* sidebar on the next page for a list of the 29 measures used in the survey.

MEASURES PROMOTING ENGAGEMENT, PERSISTENCE, AND SUCCESS

* Pre-university years and regular preparatory courses
* Orientation activities
* Activities to familiarize students with university facilities and services
* Identification of at-risk students upon admission
* Early screening of students experiencing academic difficulty
* Identification of students at risk following one or more failures or course withdrawal without failure
* Identifying and following up with students who have withdrawn from a program (to understand the reasons and/or circumstances)
* Mechanisms to support specific student populations
* Reduced semester course load for certain students
* Pedagogical measures aimed at larger groups
* Specific support measures for the first semester of a program
* Activities to ease the transition from CÉGEP to university, bachelor's to master's, etc.
* Activities to facilitate program learning
* Success contracts
* Tutor or adviser
* Individual guidance
* Notice of professor's availability to students
* Ongoing feedback on learning evaluations
* Upgrading and remedial sessions
* Sessions to prepare for exams
* Twinning of students, peer support
* Organized study groups
* Repeat/remedial courses tailored to observed weaknesses (in small groups)
* Summer session to repeat or spread credits over 3 academic sessions
* Writing and reading activities

CONTINUES ON NEXT PAGE ▶

sity services (77.3%) and information to familiarize students with university facilities and services (72.7%) were also common interventions. However, a quarter of the respondents who organized these activities considered them to be ineffective. Required preparatory training (preparatory year and courses) (92.3%), lighter course loads (88.9%), and early screening for students in difficulty (88.0%) were also identified as effective measures by those who used them.

Other interventions less frequently used by respondents were remedial courses (4.5%), academic success contracts (9.1%), organized study groups (13.6%), and activities to ease the transition from CÉGEP to university (13.6%). Although study groups were quite rare, two-thirds of respondents acknowledged their effectiveness, and even though few respondents use measures to identify at-risk students at admission (29.5%), they consider this measure effective (92.3%). The recently implemented database on academic success should encourage the screening of at-risk students at the point of admission in the future. (*See* Table 6, on page 281.)

Respondents generally showed a marked preference for applying interventions targeting all students rather than specific groups through remedial courses, academic success contracts, and so forth. Although a number of respondents said they promoted active learning (47.7%), they were little inclined to apply "active and group learning" practices. Organized study groups (13.6%), student twinning (20.5%), and learning assistance in large groups

(29.5%) were little used. Yet, those who did use these interventions often found them to be effective.

INTEREST IN USING NEW INTERVENTIONS

A number of respondents showed interest in developing new interventions for helping at-risk students: identifying at-risk students following one or more failures or withdrawals in a course (11/13), identifying students who have dropped out of a program (16/26), and early screening for students in difficulty (15/19). Many respondents were also interested in student twinning (24/35) and designating a faculty member responsible for supporting academic success (19/34). Two interventions are considered to be particularly effective by those who use them: student twinning (8/9) and identifying a faculty member responsible for supporting academic success (9/10). (*See* Table 7.)

Interventions that were less frequently used by respondents spurred little interest on their part. The effectiveness of two such interventions—summer term (6/9) and organized study groups (4/6)—should be analyzed in more depth given the small number of respondents who use them and the mixed reaction as to their effectiveness.

Respondents were more interested in identifying students who are at risk or having difficulty. However, once the students are identified, what actions should be taken to help them? The respondents were interested in few of the new measures proposed. Designating a faculty member responsible for supporting academic success could be part of the solution. This person's main task, apart from setting up an early screening process for struggling or at-risk students, would be to ensure the application of effective support measures acceptable to the faculty.

CONTINUED FROM PAGE 280

* Support center for languages, math, French, basic subjects (difficult courses - specify)
* Promote active learning, the use of ICT, interactive software to engage students in studies
* Use of institutional services for students. Identification of a resource person to aid students in your program
* Other support measures (specify)

TABLE 6. EFFECTIVENESS OF APPLIED MEASURES

Most Effective	Least Effective
■ Preparatory year and regular preparatory courses (24/26) ■ Screening for at-risk students at admission (12/13) ■ Orientation activities (33/36) ■ Lighter course loads for some students (24/27) ■ Early screening of students in difficulty (22/25)	■ Learning assistance in large groups (8/13) ■ Summer term to make up courses or spread credits over three terms (6/9) ■ Organized study groups (4/6) ■ Activities to familiarize students with university facilities and services (24/32)

TABLE 7. INTEREST IN USING NEW MEASURES

Most Interest	Least Interest
■ Identifying at-risk students following one or more failures or dropouts in a course (11/13) ■ Early screening for students in difficulty (15/19) ■ Student twinning (24/35) ■ Identifying students who have dropped out of a program (16/26) ■ Designating a faculty member responsible for supporting academic success (19/34)	■ Faculty assistance center (3/34) ■ Remedial courses (6/42) ■ Organized study groups (7/38) ■ Summer term to make up courses or spread credits over three terms (7/35) ■ Academic success contracts (8/40)

Developing Support for Students

Over the past decade, various measures have been used at Université Laval to improve retention and graduation rates. Since 2008, the following efforts to support academic success have been implemented:

■ Internal consultation on academic success: An Academic Success Committee was formed, advisory groups worked on various issues, and "think tanks" were organized with faculty heads, program directors, and directors of the main student service units.[43]

■ International student twinning program: Run by the Student Life Office, this program offers new international undergraduate and graduate students the opportunity to be matched with a more experienced student to help them become familiar with their new living and academic environment.[44]

■ Enhanced orientation activities: Some faculties have improved their student orientation by making it longer in duration (a week rather than a day) and more diversified to promote student academic and social integration. There has also been greater cooperation with student associations in organizing and promoting these activities.

■ Hiring of an Aboriginal student advisor: As a result of work by Université Laval's Inter-University Centre of Studies and Aboriginal Research (Centre interuniversitaire d'études et de recherches autochtones, or CIÉRA),[45] an Aboriginal

---

[43] See "Strategic Enrolment Management at Université Laval," on page 268.

[44] See <www.bve.ulaval.ca/accompagnement_des_etudiants_etrangers/services_et_activites/programme_de_jumelage_des_etudiants_etrangers/>.

[45] See <https://depot.erudit.org/bitstream/003190dd/1/Texte.pdf>.

student advisor was hired to work on Aboriginal student orientation and integration services.

- New courses promoting student integration and success:
  - ▶ Discover Québec: Your new living environment: This course gives international students the opportunity to learn about many different historical and contemporary aspects of Québec's main regions and Québec City in particular.
  - ▶ Integrating into a North American Francophone University: The purpose of this course is to help students from international school systems and various cultural and educational backgrounds to integrate into the university by familiarizing them with university culture in a North American francophone environment.
  - ▶ Succeeding at University in the Digital Age: The objective of these four 15-hour training workshops is to familiarize students with the use of information technologies in their research and papers.[46]

    These courses are in addition to the training workshops that the Student Aid Centre has offered for a number of years to help students learn the skills they need to succeed as students. The training workshops address learning strategies, common learning difficulties, and academic stress and anxiety.[47]

- Newly designed preparatory year: Five preparatory programs (administration, arts, music, science, social science) were developed to enable international students to:
  - ▶ Take the prerequisite courses for their programs.
  - ▶ Develop appropriate language skills for university studies.
  - ▶ Learn the tools and learning methods they need for university.
  - ▶ Acquire the level of knowledge necessary to succeed at university.[48]

- *Operation 'How are you doing?'*: As described earlier in this chapter, Operation *How are you doing?* was created in 2009 for newly enrolled international undergraduate students.[49] It was continued in 2010 and was extended to new students from certain regions of Québec. The regions were selected based on indicators

---

[46] *See* <www.distance.ulaval.ca/fad/cours/EDC-4000.htm>.

[47] *See* <www.aide.ulaval.ca/sgc/pid/1075>.

[48] *See* <www.futursetudiants.ulaval.ca/admission/admission_au_1er_cycle/candidat_etranger/annee_preparatoire/>.

[49] *See* "Operation *'How are you doing?'* for International Students," on page 277.

related to student recruitment and persistence/graduation rates: Bas-Saint-Laurent, Saguenay-Lac-Saint-Jean, Outaouais, Abitibi-Témiscamingue, Côte-Nord, Nord-du-Québec, and Gaspésie-Îles-de-la-Madeleine.

- *Early screening for students in difficulty:* In fall 2010 the Faculty of Science and Engineering, with support from the Student Aid Centre, introduced a new intervention program to help struggling students. Using the Digital Learning Environment,[50] the program targets students who are in difficulty in mid-semester and urges them to identify what problems they are having in an online questionnaire so they can be guided to the relevant tools and resources at the Student Aid Centre.

The university's Academic Success Committee is currently examining the possibility of extending this initiative to the entire university community. A consultant has been hired to help ascertain how to:

- ▶ Implement the early screening process currently being tested at the Faculty of Science and Engineering to all faculties.
- ▶ Develop early intervention strategies for at-risk students using predictive analyses based on various aspects of the student's academic history (CÉGEP marks, attitudes, previous out-of-country education, number and type of courses in which the student is enrolled, and so on) before the beginning of the course or in the first weeks of term.
- ▶ Develop tools to ensure ongoing follow-up based on various engagement indicators (class attendance, submission of work on time, dropout rate early in the semester, failure rate, and so on).

- *Webfolio*: To promote academic engagement, the Job Placement Service developed a web-based tool that gives students a chance to think about their future careers. Four modules of online exercises and activities allow students to learn about themselves, better understand the job market, and develop clear career plans as soon as they enter university. After completing the modules, students receive their webfolios, which can be viewed by employers who recruit at Université Laval.

---

[50] The digital learning environment is an integrated teaching portal for designing and publishing Université Laval course Web sites. *See* <www.ena.ulaval.ca>.

The Academic Success Committee is now looking to foster other support interventions that can be used at various points in the academic term and at critical periods in the student life cycle to enhance student success. The idea is that a combination of ongoing and time-specific interventions could be offered to students to meet their needs and encourage engagement in their studies.

Figure 8 (on page 286) presents a chart of possible academic success support initiatives for a typical term. The chart was developed taking into account possible support measures, key periods for students, and the university calendar. It includes existing and potential support interventions at Université Laval. At enrolment students require guidance in selecting their courses. Early screening for at-risk students could be performed at this point. Linguistic and cultural integration workshops could be offered in the weeks before school starts. Before classes begin, the university welcomes students to help them adjust to their new academic environment: orientation day/week, campus tours, and presentation of the main university services. Similar activities can also be organized in the various faculties: faculty tours, staff introductions, meetings with advisors.[51] Around mid-September, after classes start, the faculties or university-wide services can offer ongoing support: through "learning to be a student" workshops, learning assistance centres, advising sessions, twinning programs, study groups, webfolios, and so on. After the first exam or term paper, the student should receive feedback on their academic performance. This can be accompanied by a self-assessment tool which students can use to evaluate their learning strategies and the problems they are having adjusting to student life. This would also be a good time to have a second meeting with an advisor. A learning support workshop can be offered to students who are struggling. It is also important to follow up with students who withdraw from their course(s) or program. At the end of term, students should receive further feedback on their academic performance and meet with their advisors to review the semester. For compulsory courses, giving students the right to rewrite exams may help students to pass their courses and improve retention rates.

---

[51] The concept of the "resource teacher" can help define the advisor's role. In France, resource teachers were introduced at universities to provide students with personalized assistance as a response to the Ministry of Higher Education and Research's 2008–2012 multiyear plan to promote undergraduate success. See <http://media.enseignementsup-recherche.gouv.fr/file/Communiques/01/8/orientationlicence_21018.pdf>. The resource teachers' role is to establish a relationship of trust with students who they do not evaluate. The teachers help students get their bearings, identify their personal and academic difficulties, and support them in their educational plans. Follow-up consists of at least three half-hour interviews at key points in the academic term.

A UNIVERSITY-WIDE GOAL: BOOSTING RETENTION RATES

Academic failure and withdrawal have serious human and socioeconomic costs. Université Laval is keenly aware of the important role universities play in the knowledge society and has made academic and career success one of its main strategic objectives since 2008. The university wishes to boost student retention rates, which have not significantly improved in recent years. Using its new SEM process, the Office of the Vice Rector of Academic and International Activities is actively working to create an environment that provides effective support for academic success with a view to improving the university's performance in this regard. To further document the issues and challenges with respect to academic success on campus, the

FIGURE 8 ▶

Possible Measures
for Supporting
Academic Success
During a Typical
Undergraduate Term

SOURCE: BASED ON
MORNEAU & LACASSE 2010

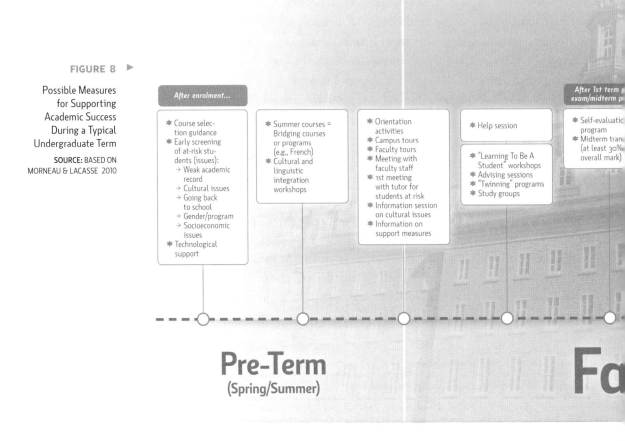

university started by (1) collecting university data (2) analyzing how international students adapt to their new environment, and (3) surveying university administrators. The resulting data and analyses guided the development of new measures to promote academic success adapted to specific needs: twinning activities, courses and workshops to ease integration, design of preparatory year programs, and early screening of students experiencing academic difficulty.

Université Laval is now working on a framework to guide university and faculty initiatives in support of academic success. The aim is to coordinate university-wide efforts as seamlessly as possible at the undergraduate level. Central administration will then work in conjunction with the faculties to adapt the framework to their

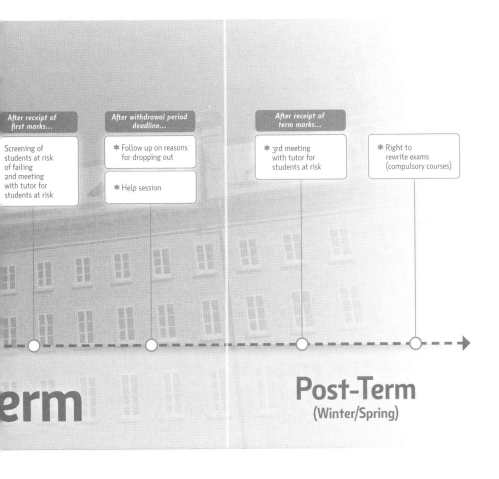

After receipt of first marks...

Screening of students at risk of failing 2nd meeting with tutor for students at risk

After withdrawal period deadline...

✱ Follow up on reasons for dropping out

✱ Help session

After receipt of term marks...

✱ 3rd meeting with tutor for students at risk

✱ Right to rewrite exams (compulsory courses)

...erm

Post-Term
(Winter/Spring)

distinct needs and realities. Given that financial and human resources are limited, measures to support academic success will first be applied in faculties that have the lowest retention rates. The new measures proposed in the plan will be based on students' specific needs and the existing interventions already in place in each faculty. Special attention will be paid to sharing responsibilities between the faculties and university-wide services.

Ultimately Université Laval's goal is to make engagement and support for academic success two values shared by students and all staff. Students have a fundamental role to play in ensuring their own success at university and in their careers. Engagement remains the key. We must have high expectations regarding student academic engagement and performance and we must furnish the necessary support. Implementing measures to provide students with individual guidance on achieving their academic goals will also require the enthusiastic support of all those in the university community with a stake in academic success.

E. Jane Fee, William Radford,
Sarah Dench and Steve Marshall

14

INTERNATIONALIZATION
AND SEM AT
SIMON FRASER UNIVERSITY

/ **Chapter 14** /

INTERNATIONAL STUDENTS IN CANADA: A BRIEF HISTORY

International students have been coming to Canadian universities since before confederation. Would-be priests from far and wide attended the (formerly) Catholic universities from their inception, New Englanders crossed the border to take classes at the small Maritime universities, and scholars from around the world were part of the founding classes of our oldest city universities. In the post-WWII move towards massification of higher education and the rise of international development initiatives, international students from around the world, and the global south in particular, came to Canada in increasing but modest numbers.

The changing patterns of migration in the 1960s and 1970s gave rise to many community colleges delivering English language classes to immigrants. This provided a platform for colleges to recruit large numbers of international students, a trend that continues to this day. Throughout the '80s and '90s and into the first half of the past decade, modest numbers of international students continued to be admitted to Canada's universities. Meanwhile, in some countries, globalization coupled with changes in funding formulae and immigration policies resulted in a massive increase in efforts to recruit international students with a consequent rise in numbers and associated revenues. In Australia, for example, educational services now vie with mining as the major source of foreign income. Developments in Australia exemplify what is seen by many commentators as the commodification of higher education, a shift that has created a schism with those who believe that "internationalization" should be driven by the loftier notion of global citizenship.

Until quite recently there has been a typically Canadian scenario on the international student front, both in terms of federal-provincial responses and the sociopolitical discourse. On the one hand, public sector education has only occasionally (and usually apologetically) been seen as a commodity to be traded. "Internationalization," whereby international students have been recruited for their role in teaching and learning about the world, has been viewed as laudable but only supported in a rather lukewarm manner. This appears to be changing, at least in regard to the recruitment and management of international students, as they increasingly become an intentional and integral component of a strategic enrolment management (SEM) approach within a given institution.

The shift is being driven by a number of colluding factors: a downward trend in domestic student numbers, increased skilled immigration, less money from the public purse for operational costs, prodding from governments to be more entrepreneurial, and a monumental rise in global demand for higher education, particularly from countries with emerging economies. Countries around the world are purchasing educational services in the trillions of dollars and the market opportunities and (some argue) international scholarly obligations have attracted many august institutions into the market.

Across Canada, the international student file is shifting rapidly and incrementally in myriad ways, as diverse as the country itself. Education is a provincial responsibility in Canada and little collective national activity occurs in education, international or domestic. As far as international education is concerned, each province should be considered to be a sovereign entity, with the exception of national level marketing and visa and immigration policy and services. The federal government, through the Department of Foreign Affairs and International Trade (DFAIT), provides a marketing initiative that attempts to brand Canada as a study abroad destination. Compared to the robust national initiatives of other countries, Canada's efforts are fairly feeble. A handful of NGOs and membership associations attempt to advocate and act as a surrogate for a national international education mechanism, but these tend to lack the breadth and resources of similar organizations in the United States.

Where the federal government does play a major role is in the issuing of visas and the creation and enforcement of policies governing international student sojourns in Canada. Although Immigration Canada has improved in recent years, the time required to process visas is still much greater than those of competitor countries and the process is less than consistent across the various Canadian posts around the world. Where Canada differs from other countries with respect to policy is in the fact that many international students are, in effect, offered the chance to work and immigrate upon completion of their studies. The opportunity to immigrate is rarely offered by other countries to international students and this differentiator may well be the main factor in increasing numbers to Canada. The word is out around the world that for the price of an undergraduate degree, students also have a good chance of getting a Canadian passport; this opportunity more than makes up for the limited marketing efforts and the amateur recruitment machinery of the Canadian post-secondary sector.

With the federal government acting as marketer and passport purveyor, most of the business of recruitment and enrolment management of international students occurs at the provincial and institutional level. The amount a particular province does and how much is left to the institutions themselves varies widely across the country. In Atlantic Canada, there is a fledgling marketing effort, named EduNova, which attempts to market Nova Scotia institutions in a collective manner. In Quebec, as with most public sector services, there is a robust recruitment, enrolment and retention system provided by government services and the institutions themselves. Ontario has no provincial marketing "machine" and each institution acts alone; although this may change as the Ontario government has recently called for a doubling of international student numbers as a partial cure for its fiscal deficit. Manitoba has a robust marketing and recruitment scheme that is linked to its plans for attracting and retaining skilled immigrants. Saskatchewan has no collective effort of any significance and Alberta has a fledgling government department assigned to the portfolio. British Columbia has a rather more robust mechanism at the provincial level than other provinces, with the exception of Quebec. It is to this example that we now turn.

INTERNATIONAL STUDENTS IN BRITISH COLUMBIA

In British Columbia (B.C.), there has been a provincially sponsored international education agency since the early 1990s. The British Columbia Council for International Education (BCCIE) was founded in 1990 and initially acted as an agency supporting internationalization at B.C. institutions, with international recruitment and retention being the least of its foci; its efforts are mostly concentrated on internationalization of campus and community. Although over the years it has waxed and waned in response to provincial government interest or lack thereof, BCCIE has remained in place, albeit in different forms. At present, it is an arms-length society, funded by the provincial government with its primary focus being the international marketing of the B.C. education sector worldwide. BCCIE's purview includes K–12 education and private providers as well as higher education institutions.

Institutions in B.C. have a long tradition of recruiting and managing international student flows and retention programs, either alone or in concert with BCCIE. Generally speaking, smaller universities and colleges and the K–12 school system appear to derive more benefit from BCCIE's marketing efforts than the three larger universities that have their own recruitment and retention initiatives, international marketing divisions and international recruitment partnerships. The B.C. research universities enrol more international students proportionally than other universities in Canada. We surmise that this may be due to a myriad of factors including British Columbia's position on the Pacific Rim, links between diasporas and their countries of origin that act as a marketing proxy and international student portal, and the relative success of B.C.'s top universities in international and domestic league tables. Another factor may well be the relatively benign B.C. physical climate that undoubtedly attracts many foreign students away from other parts of Canada. It is also apparent that the college to university transfer system, unique to B.C., has a positive impact on international student flows.

Current self-reported data indicate that British Columbia's three largest universities enrol approximately 16 percent international students (combined undergraduate and graduate). Indications are that these numbers will continue to rise and it is anticipated that within three years 20 percent of students will be international students. This phenomenon clearly begs many questions with respect to SEM. Is this the right proportion? If so, how can it be sustained? Should international student revenue be built into base budgets? If the proportion is too high, how should it be reduced? Should universities be concerned about disproportionate numbers from particular countries? How do we prevent "ghettoization" and how do we get the right mix? How should we provide appropriate retention supports with respect to linguistic and academic preparation as well as cultural transition? How should we support immigrant students who demonstrate many of the same integration characteristics as international students, yet do not have access to many of the support systems available to international students? These questions are woven throughout our narrative as we present a case study of Simon Fraser University's history with international students over the past 20 years, with a particular focus on the past five years.

INTERNATIONAL STUDENTS AT SIMON FRASER UNIVERSITY

For many years in British Columbia support for international students, and immigrant students who did not speak English as a first language, was exclusively provided by community-based immigrant centres and the community college system. Colleges received substantial funding from the government to fund Adult Basic Education and English as a Second Language (ESL) programming. However, as the B.C. post-secondary system evolved and many of the colleges and university colleges were transformed into regional degree-granting institutions, the exclusive reliance on colleges to support students with English as an additional language (EAL) diminished. Over the past few years Simon Fraser University (SFU), like the other research-intensive universities, has begun to develop new programs and policies that address the particular needs of the changing student body, as well as the general challenges presented by students' varied English language academic preparation upon entry.

SFU was created in the mid 1960s as part of the provincial government's education accessibility agenda. Known as the "radical campus", SFU prides itself in its tempestuous beginnings, flexible programming, and a tutorial system that provides for more intimate faculty-student interactions. SFU is often described as having an "organic" culture where interesting and innovative ideas are allowed to bubble up and flourish. SFU enrolments have expanded dramatically over the past 10 years, and as is the case with many Canadian institutions, the university has found it challenging to keep pace with enrolment growth.

Approximately 32,000 students are currently enrolled across SFU's three major campuses, each located in a different community in the Greater Vancouver Region. The main campus sits atop Burnaby Mountain, a 45-minute commute from central Vancouver; SFU Vancouver is housed in a collection of heritage buildings located in the core of downtown; and SFU Surrey, the newest campus, is located in a striking modernist high-rise in the heart of Surrey, B.C.'s fastest growing community. SFU Vancouver has had a profound impact on SFU's influence within the downtown community, an effect that continues with the addition of the Woodward's Contemporary Arts complex, in the infamous "downtown Eastside." SFU Surrey has also been a strategic addition to the SFU network of campuses given its location in a rapidly growing community with a historically high immigrant population and low participation rates in post-secondary education. This three-campus structure serves students from across a wide range of communities in B.C., as well as across Canada and the world at large.

Currently SFU provides services to more than 3,700 international fee-paying students, representing about 15 percent of the undergraduate student body and 25 percent of the graduate student body, an increase of approximately three percent over the previous year. Approximately 20 percent of the international undergraduates transferred to SFU from Fraser International College (FIC), a private college located on SFU's main Burnaby campus (FIC is described in greater detail later in this chapter). A small number (around 50 per year) transfer in from the English Bridge Program (EBP), housed within the Department of Linguistics in the Faculty of Arts and Social Sciences. EBP offers a 10-week program of academic English support for students who do not have sufficient English language skills for entry but are otherwise admissible. The majority of new international students are recruited from a variety of countries by university recruiters, agents, or senior university officials; some transfer in from local colleges; and a growing number come from B.C. high schools catering to international students and B.C. high school programs offered abroad. The B.C. Ministry of Education licenses offshore high schools, primarily in China, to offer a B.C. curriculum and allow students to graduate with a "Dogwood," B.C.'s high school completion diploma. This development has not been without controversy, evidenced by the fact that at any one time a number of these offshore schools are being investigated for questionable delivery of the curriculum and grade inflation.

International students at SFU come from a variety of countries through a combination of passive and active recruitment practices; however, students coming from the Pacific Rim remain the largest demographic, with students from China making up the majority of international students at SFU (*see* Figure 9, on page 297).

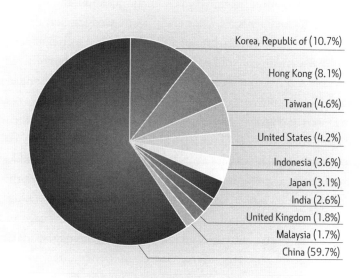

◀ **FIGURE 9**

International Student
Population at SFU

SOURCE: SFU
INSTITUTIONAL RESEARCH
AND PLANNING 2009

A large, single country can impact the classroom experience in a significant way, and even challenge the pluralism that we strive for through internationalization, if a single linguistic or cultural group dominates. There is also potential financial risk since reliance on large numbers from particular countries means that international student enrolments are vulnerable to events such as political shifts, natural disasters and other events affecting student flows. Furthermore, in certain contexts, having a large group of students from a single country can lead to the "ghettoization" of this particular minority group within the academic arena and social settings, with consequential institutional and social ramifications.

The increase in international student applications to SFU does not appear to be a temporary phenomenon. We expect that it will continue given the combination of exponentially increased global demand for higher education places, limited supply in many countries, and the fact that SFU's brand has global presence. Since SFU is located in a global city region that is already diverse and highly multilingual (Statistics Canada predicts that by 2017 more than 50 percent of Vancouver's population will belong to a visible minority, thereby negating the term), there are relatively few concerns expressed within the university community about the notion of admitting international students per se. It is generally acknowledged that the diverse nature of the student body provides richness to the classroom experience at SFU, which is itself a positive recruitment tool for students, faculty and staff. There is even tacit acceptance that international student tuition revenue is welcome and even essential in the current economic climate.

Simon Fraser University's growing international student population is clearly the result of a growing global reputation, an effective recruitment program, the mutually beneficial relationship with Fraser International College as well as SFU's location in the heart of a cosmopolitan, polyglot community. However, the number of international students cannot be taken as a proxy for the real percentage of SFU undergraduates who speak English as a second, or additional, language and have been educated to some degree outside Canada. Some reports suggest that between 40 and 50 percent of SFU's undergraduates are recent immigrants who have emigrated within the past five years, but who now have Canadian citizenship or are permanent residents and hence are domestic-fee-paying students. This mix of students, while creating a vibrant multicultural student community, presents particular challenges in the provision of support services and retention initiatives.

'INTERNATIONALS' AND SEM AT SFU: CURRICULUM, DIVERSITY, AND LITERACY

SFU's response to the increase in numbers of international students and immigrants is best understood within the broader context of the university's response to the changing student demographics that come with immigration, multiculturalism, and multilingualism in Metro Vancouver as a whole. According to recent census figures for Metro Vancouver, 41 percent of the population speaks languages other than the two official languages of Canada (Statistics Canada 2007, p. 11), with 20 percent of the population self-identifying as Chinese (Statistics Canada 2008c, p. 32). It will come as no surprise, therefore, that the multicultural and multilingual nature of our cosmopolitan city is also reflected in the demographic make-up of students at SFU. How, then, does this diversity relate to the presence and needs of students at SFU?

University Discourses and Misconceptions of "International ESL" Students

At the coffee bar and in faculty workshops on campus, a frequent comment to be heard from instructors is "What can I do? Nearly my entire class is international ESL students." Central to the formation and maintenance of such discourses of so-called "international ESL" students are traditional paradigms that are losing their validity in the multicultural, transnational realities of student life at SFU. The notions that are being called into question are those that differentiate between learners who are categorized as "ESL" or "native speaker," or as "domestic" or "international." Such discourses are often characterized by a misunderstanding of what the term "ESL" means. This can be seen in the mistaken application of the "ESL" label to students for whom English may be a joint first language, or a third or fourth language rather than second. Equally, the associated discourses or remediation and deficit that come with the ESL label fail to recognize the many multilingual and intercultural assets that students given the label bring to our universities (Marshall 2010). Another problematic characteristic of such discourses is the over-generalization of the term "international" to students who are not; for example, students who may fit a visual/linguistic stereotype of international-ness but who are, in fact, multilingual landed immigrants or Canadian citizens. What is evident in these two examples is a frequent mismatch or disconnect between the visa criteria that are used to define international students for enrolment purposes at universities and the related discourses of university instructors (and of many students themselves) that are based on classroom experience and observation. As a result, an instructor may identify a student as "international ESL" who is in fact a third generation Canadian-born Chinese monolingual English-speaker. The discourse of the "international ESL" student can be further complicated by the presence on campus of international students from countries where the English language has some kind of official status (for example, India and the Philippines), as well as domestic students from Québec whose first or primary language is French.

CURRICULUM, LITERACY, AND SUPPORT SERVICES

One of the earliest SFU initiatives to address changing student demographics and academic preparation was the University Curriculum Initiative. Begun in 2000, this process set out to re-examine the nature of SFU's undergraduate curricula in order to ensure that all undergraduates received a relevant, effective and coherent education. The recommendations of the appointed Task Force, which were implemented beginning in Fall 2004, reflected the intellectual and educational values that SFU should foster, the intellectual qualities that all SFU undergraduates should share, and the skills and experiences that would best prepare SFU undergraduates for successful and fulfilling global futures. The Task Force recommendations added new English language proficiency and quantitative requirements for admission to SFU, as well as graduation requirements ensuring that all graduates had effective communication, critical thinking and quantitative reasoning skills as well as a breadth of coursework. Two Foundational courses were also created, to better filter and support students admitted to SFU who required some additional preparation in quantitative readiness and academic literacy. One of the courses, Foundations of Academic Literacy, was developed to assist students needing further development of their writing skills (discussed in detail later in this chapter).

According to the Writing, Quantity and Breadth (WQB) degree requirements that came into full effect in September 2006, all undergraduates at SFU are required to take courses designated W (writing-intensive), Q (quantitative reasoning), and B (breadth, or outside of their main discipline) in order to graduate. The aim of the new degree requirements was both to include effective pedagogies in learning situations across the university and for the university to produce comprehensively-educated graduates with literacy and numeracy skills that would be adequate for their future employment. This aim relates to a key factor that emerged during the long consultation process that preceded implementation of the curriculum, namely, the view of certain faculty members and employers that graduates were entering the workforce with inadequate literacy and numeracy skills. Students who meet SFU's literacy and numeracy requirements (most commonly, Grade 12 English and Math scores of 75 percent and 70 percent, respectively) are able to enrol directly in W and Q courses. Those with scores below these minimums are required to take foundational courses in academic numeracy and academic literacy.

In terms of meeting the needs of international students with English as an additional language (EAL) who are making the transition to undergraduate studies at the university, and for domestic EAL students, enrolment into courses designated W (writing-intensive) has presented the university with several challenges, and exacerbated the demands on SFU's EAL and supplementary academic supports.

The pedagogy of writing-intensive learning at SFU can be understood in terms of two complementary concepts that are core to the teaching and learning of academic literacy in higher education: *writing to learn* and *learning to write.* Writing to learn can be most simply understood as learning through writing. This writing-intensive approach differs from more traditional forms of writing in the disciplines that involve departments setting up academic writing courses in which their own students receive explicit instruction on how to write in ways that are typical of that discipline. A key distinction is that writing-intensive approaches within a discipline incorporate writing pedagogy of regular course content so that students learn the content *through writing.* It is hoped that, by engaging with course content through writing, receiving considerable feedback and review of work, and through writing more, students will also *learn to write* more effectively. And herein lies a potential problem for this form of writing-intensive pedagogy: a student has to be able to read and write well enough to benefit from it, and as such, it could be argued that writing-intensive learning best suits the needs of an "idealized native speaker" (Leung, Harris, and Rampton 1997) of English. A particular challenge that the university has faced is the fact that a large number of multilingual SFU students are not ready for the rigors of writing-intensive learning and need extra assistance in developing their foundational academic literacy skills.

Related to the curriculum changes and in recognition of the need to better support students academically, the Student Learning Commons (SLC) was created as part of the Library in late 2005. The SLC offers some limited EAL support services as well as general writing support programs for all SFU students. Support is largely delivered by Student Mentors, senior undergraduate and graduate students trained and supported by staff coordinators.

In 2007, a Student Success Program (SSP) was created to allow SFU to be more proactive in supporting students who are struggling academically. Operated out of Student Services, the SSP offers students on academic probation or required to withdraw the support they need to recapture academic success at the university. The first two "cohorts" accepted into the SSP were international students and students from the Faculty of Applied Sciences. This priority start for international students occurred because data collected by the university had begun to show that a larger than expected percentage of international students was struggling with their studies and at risk for failing.

In the spring of 2010, revised English language admission requirements were approved by the Senate requiring that students entering SFU in Fall 2011 and thereafter show evidence of having spent a minimum of three years in an English-speaking educational institution before being accepted for admission. Based on a similar move by UBC, and reflective of past admission requirements at SFU, these revised requirements are meant to ensure that all students, regardless of their basis of admission, have the linguistic competency necessary to thrive at SFU.

Recently, the newly formed Teaching and Learning Centre (formerly the Learning and Instructional Development Centre), housed within Continuing Studies, has agreed that part of its mandate is to help the SFU community engage in a series of conversations about the changing student demographics, and in particular, the increasing number of EAL students. Faculty members at SFU continue to voice concerns that they feel challenged in teaching to the changing population of students, and they seek greater support and expertise.

Foundations of Academic Literacy

One response to these concerns was the creation in 2006 of a course, Foundations of Academic Literacy (FAL). Students who meet SFU's language and literacy requirements gain what is referred to as a FAL equivalency credit, allowing them to register directly in W (writing-intensive) courses. Students can gain a "FAL equivalency" by attaining any one of the following: a Grade 12 English score of 75 percent; 6.5 IELTS (for students with English as an additional language); required grades in the Language Proficiency Index examination; a C- grade in a college English course (for transfer students); or adequate scores on a number of other alternative national and international examinations (although these are rare). Students who do not meet these requirements must enrol in Foundations of Academic Literacy, a 13-week first-year foundational academic literacy course, during their first 45 credits of study. Students are required to gain a minimum C grade in the course in order to be able to register in writing-intensive courses. If students fail to attain a C grade after their first attempt at the course, they will be unable to enrol in writing-intensive courses. If they fail after two attempts, their registration to all courses at

SFU is blocked and students must leave SFU until they can demonstrate that, either through a test score or academic work at the college level, they are adequately prepared for academic work in English. Enrolment in FAL is also a component of the Student Success Program, for those who have not previously completed the course.

It is clear that the programs and support mechanisms outlined in the preceding paragraphs are valiant but inadequate efforts to support student success. Clearly a student body, composed of a majority of students for whom English is an additional language, is in SFU's near future. If we are to adequately serve the needs of the "new student body," the programs we currently provide will have to be expanded and woven into a comprehensive teaching and learning strategy that provides remedial programming as well as support for faculty, staff and students.

THE FIC APPROACH TO SEM

In 2005, SFU began discussions with IBT Education Ltd. (now Navitas Education Ltd.), regarding the development of a partnership to recruit international students to Simon Fraser University. IBT, a publicly traded company on the Australian Stock Exchange, was established in Australia to develop partnerships with the university sector. SFU sought to supplement in-house international recruitment activities, to identify and develop new markets for international students, and to improve retention of international students through better support for transition to studies in Canada. At the time, senior leaders at SFU were concerned that there were significant risks on the horizon for international recruitment to Canadian universities, and there were equally strong concerns that SFU was struggling to improve the retention rates of international students.

The recruitment and academic pathway model employed by Navitas with partner universities was a form of SEM, designed to attract international students who require some level of academic and English upgrading in order to gain entry to university. The pathway 'colleges' developed by Navitas provide a personal, supportive learning environment over a one-year period of study, and a supported transition to the partner university. SFU considered that the company's focused approach to these issues was cost-effective and not something SFU could replicate, even with a significant investment of funds into similar in-house services.

SFU representatives visited a number of the universities partnered with Navitas to understand first-hand the organization of the colleges and to assess the success and suitability of this model for SFU. Following discussions with their university counterparts and Navitas representatives, the Vice-President Academic, the Associate Vice-President Students and International, and the Associate Dean of Faculty of Arts and Social Sciences, were all convinced that a partnership to establish a pathway college at SFU would be worthwhile for international students and a good fit for SFU. Subsequently, a proposal to this end was developed and community consultations were undertaken at SFU.

The proposed partnership was to establish a private college for international students, located on the SFU Burnaby campus. The college would be set up an arm's length from SFU but co-branded with SFU, charging the same international student tuition rate as SFU and offering a selection of SFU-specific lower division courses taught by qualified instructors hired by the college. SFU faculty members were to act as "course coordinators," providing academic oversight of the course offerings and instructors to ensure on-going quality assurance and full articulation of courses. The college would also offer English language support classes and other supplemental instruction. Students attending the college would have access to SFU services such as the library, health and counseling services, student housing, and other university services, and representatives from SFU departments and faculties would be able to encourage the students at the college to consider selecting particular disciplines for further study. Completing a minimum of 30 pre-approved, university-level credits (10 courses) at specified GPA levels, students would be offered a guarantee of admission to SFU in one of three programs: Arts and Social Sciences, Business Administration, or Computing Science.

The SFU community reaction to the partnership proposal was mixed, and at times, heated. SFU had never previously entered into a public-private partnership of this nature. Concerns were expressed about intellectual property, the potential impact of an economic imperative on academic standards, faculty workload, working conditions, the commodification of international education, and other related issues. Conversely, many others in the SFU community saw that oversight of the curriculum and pedagogy would be advantageous in that SFU would have assurance regarding the quality of teaching at the college and greater confidence in the transferability of courses toward SFU degrees. With the new partnership in place, students attending the new college would receive more personal and intensive academic support than those immediately admitted to SFU and, it was hoped, the time spent in adjustment to the Canadian educational context would reduce culture shock and improve retention. The ability to use the new college as a means to manage international student flows was seen as a significant advantage of the relationship. In March 2006, a five-year contract between SFU and Navitas was signed to establish Fraser International College (FIC).

FRASER INTERNATIONAL COLLEGE IS BORN

The first intake of students at Fraser International College was in the Fall 2006 semester. An appropriate suite of courses was chosen as the first offering for the three disciplinary streams. A senior staff person from the VP Academic's office was tasked as the SFU liaison to oversee and facilitate SFU's interests and responsibilities and to work closely with the FIC College Principal. Eighty-four students were admitted as the first group attending FIC. College staff was on hand to meet and greet the new students, assist them with transition to the Canadian post-secondary setting, and to provide academic and personal support.

From 2007 to 2010 the college grew quickly. Enrolment targets were met 18 months ahead of schedule, and as of Fall 2009, 34 courses were being offered and more than 1,000 students were enrolled at FIC. The largest group of students originated from China, mirroring the situation with direct recruitment to SFU. However, FIC was successful in recruiting students from countries and regions from which SFU had not previously attracted students.

In Spring 2010, more than 450 students had successfully transferred from FIC to SFU. Their academic progress was tracked as part of annual reports provided to the SFU Senate. FIC was highly successful at supporting and retaining students at the college, and, following transfer to SFU, the students were slightly more academically successful (as measured by average CGPA) than other international students. In early 2010, SFU conducted an external review of the academic operations of the partnership with FIC; the results were very positive, and in October 2010 a new ten-year contract was signed between SFU and Navitas Education Ltd.

The partnership with the college has afforded SFU the opportunity to improve its approach to the strategic enrolment management of international students, and to learn about SEM from an organization for which international SEM is a primary function. SFU has been able to observe first-hand that a small community of well-supported students will improve and succeed academically in a carefully chosen and challenging curriculum. SFU departments and faculties have had the opportunity to work with college staff and the FIC students in order to develop relationships, and to promote the range of programs and degree options available. Academic English programming is contracted to FIC through the English Bridge Program, an already existing academic unit within SFU, which further strengthens academic connections between SFU and FIC. SFU has also had the opportunity to explore relationships with international recruitment agents that have already been screened and "road-tested" by another body. Given perceptions in Canada about variability in the quality and reputation of recruitment agents, this was an important opportunity for SFU to build relationships with agents, but also to manage risk to reputation.

The international student population at FIC pre-transfer to SFU is a defined, supported, and well-prepared group of prospective students. The partnership has provided SFU with an opportunity to see first hand that a flow of international students can be recruited and retained through relationship building, appropriate support, and with the right provision of information to the students. Whether this supportive approach is scalable to larger groups of international students who enrol directly in the larger university remains an important question and something to be considered given the challenges presented by our changing community demographic and transformed student body.

THE GENERAL SEM CONTEXT AT SFU

Since 2007, when it became publicly apparent that student demographics across Canada were changing, SFU began taking steps toward a more strategic institutional approach to how students are recruited and retained. In early 2007, Student Services hosted two Enrolment Management Summits to highlight the enrolment challenges that SFU might face in the future. The primary purpose of the summits was to introduce concepts of SEM to the wider enrolment community at SFU, and to begin a consultation process to address how the impending challenges to enrolment could be most effectively addressed. The major outcome of these summits was the creation of an Enrolment Management Coordinating Committee (EMCC), chaired by the Registrar, whose mandate it is to improve communications and better coordinate enrolment practices. A small subgroup of the EMCC was tasked with analyzing the current state of undergraduate student recruitment at SFU, seen as a high priority action. A report of critical issues and recommendations on student recruitment was presented to the EMCC in January 2010.

In the meantime, it was also acknowledged that student retention issues were of critical importance to the ultimate success of enrolment management at SFU. Again in 2007, a self-identified group of interested parties from Student Services came together in a committee known as *Retention 101* to better educate themselves on issues of retention and student success, participate in professional development activities, share best practices, implement early retention intervention strategies and compile survey data concerning the retention landscape at SFU. In April 2008 a report detailing findings was drafted.

The worldwide economic downturn of 2008 unexpectedly relieved some of the immediate recruitment pressures on the university. Ironically, however, the same economic downturn forced a new environmental challenge on the University, namely the need to significantly reduce operating budgets. The time was right for re-invigoration of the concept of strategic enrolment management at Simon Fraser University, with an eye to bringing together student recruitment and retention initiatives. A third SEM event was held in late September 2009. At that event, with the President, VPs, Deans and other senior administrative staff in attendance, a public commitment to move forward with SEM was made. A recommendation was made that a small committee be struck to put forward an action plan for incorporating a SEM approach at SFU. Soon after, the VP Academic announced the creation of the Strategic Enrolment Management Planning Committee (SEMPC) consisting of two senior Student Services officers, a Dean and an Associate Dean. This Committee was charged with quickly putting together a SEM action plan for SFU.

The Committee analyzed the feedback collected from the stakeholders, met with all Dean's Offices and used the information collected to determine how the Committee would proceed with its work. Three primary themes were identified as being SEM priorities at SFU:

■ *Vision and Strategy*—The need for better articulation of the institutional vision, as well as clarification of what the composition of the student body would be to best reflect this vision.

■ *Community, Collaboration and Communication*—A desire to ensure that existing enrolment management committees and structures operate as effectively as possible, and are in alignment with SEM vision and goals.

■ *Data and Business Intelligence*—Ensuring that appropriate and timely business-intelligence is available to decision makers to support SEM processes and practices. In conjunction with the SEM Planning Committee, a new set of retention tables were developed to help pinpoint which factors have a particular influence on academic success for all categories of undergraduate students at SFU.

The recommendations of the SEM Planning Committee have recently been approved by the Vice-President Academic and are being operationalized beginning in Fall 2010. The increasing international enrolment picture at SFU has helped to spur on the approval of these SEM recommendations, as the University realizes that it must become more strategic in its approach to international students. There are growing concerns that SFU is simply not doing enough to ensure that international students have the English language competency and transitional support to be successful in their studies. The various support initiatives that have been created over the past few years must be re-examined to ensure that they are planned and coordinated in an effective and efficient manner. Recently, the VP Academic has established a review committee to respond to faculty concerns about the growing EAL population at SFU and to ensure that EAL/ESL programs and services are effective in meeting the needs of enrolled and prospective SFU students. This committee will look at the needs of EAL students, and examine the business plans and reporting relationships of each EAL/ESL program to ensure that it effectively meets student needs. Faculty discussions are also beginning to formally take place concerning what impact the growing international population has on learning, pedagogy, and curricula.

This new focus on SEM is leading to discussions about how we plan and manage the flow of students into SFU, how strategic we are being in our methods of student recruitment and support for these same students, how well we coordinate between all the various services and approaches currently in place at SFU, how well we understand the composition of our student body and how teaching and learning must adjust to the new reality. A SEM approach would suggest that each of these issues should be discussed in the broader context of a plan for internationalization—a plan not yet in existence.

INTERNATIONALIZATION ON CAMPUS AND BEYOND

Each institution of higher learning must decide on its own unique response to globalization—the economic, social and cultural pressures and changes that are taking place around us and within our midst. In the past, internationalization at SFU has meant providing faculty and students with opportunities for gaining international experience so they can function effectively in the larger world. Now, the success in recruiting international students to SFU has been helpful in ensuring that SFU's classrooms reflect global realities and that internationalization activities occur both on our campuses and externally.

Regarding both SEM and international students in Canada, there is an absence of strategy at the national level, a weak effort in some provinces and fledgling initiatives at SFU, such as the FIC partnership, that may be replicated elsewhere. We propose that a lack of strategy is no longer acceptable, either nationally, provincially or institutionally. We posit that the demographic shifts to which we have already alluded, together with sustained and potentially increased immigration flows—as well as the continued significant proportions of international visa students—call for a paradigmatic shift in the very notion of internationalization that must underpin SEM at SFU.

It appears to already be the case at SFU that the number of students who identify as EAL and were educated, to some extent, outside Canada equals and likely outweighs those who speak English as a first language and were educated exclusively in Canada. SFU, and most other Canadian universities, were built, designed, organized and structured around the concept of a normative student who used English as their first language, was educated in Canadian schools and was raised in mainstream Caucasian culture. SFU is a dramatic illustration that this reality is no longer true: the "new student" is a polyglot, polymath intercultural citizen. We propose that this seismic shift in who we are at SFU presents the central challenge for both internationalization and SEM.

This is an opportune time at SFU to rethink internationalization while anchoring emerging SEM structures and processes in the context of a globalized intercultural and polyglot student body. Our task is to develop a clear and articulated vision for internationalization, a coherent and collaborative approach to planning and coordination of the many international activities across the institution, as well as the institutional research capacity, to ensure that these activities are supported by up-to-date and relevant data and information. Grappling with a SEM approach to the internationalization question at SFU should lead us toward a better understanding of the most effective overall SEM practices for SFU. It is a work in progress.

*Devron Gaber, Jody Gordon and
Yves Jodoin*

15

BEYOND TRANSFER:
THE MOBILE STUDENT

/ **Chapter 15** /

Traditional strategic enrolment management (SEM) models describe a student's experience in cradle-to-grave language—a student commences at institution 'A' in order to graduate from there in a set period of time. Yet today we are seeing a growing number of students who start at institution 'A' and transfer to institution 'B' before graduating. The growth in the number of transfer students is reflected in the proliferation of specialized support services such as transfer student orientation, transition publications and increased staffing in articulation departments. Institutions that have embraced the philosophical underpinnings of SEM—to break-down institutional silos and ensure a smooth transition through each stage of a student's post-secondary education experience—are well positioned to receive transfer students.

The provinces of Québec and British Columbia (B.C.) are rich in student transfer history. Historically, they represent two unique approaches to increasing student mobility and student accessibility within the post-secondary system. Alberta also has a well-developed transfer system, similar to the one in B.C., dating back to the inception of the community college system in Alberta in the 1960s. Recently, the colleges and universities in Atlantic Canada signed a Memorandum of Understanding encouraging "greater collaboration among institutions and improving completion times, enabling students to have a more seamless educational experience in attaining their post-secondary credentials" (PCCAT 2010). However, in Saskatchewan, the *Campus Saskatchewan* partnership, including the Saskatchewan Council for Admissions and Transfer, was shut down in 2010 because its Board of Directors decided it had fulfilled its mandate, although the province still does not have an integrated transfer system.

TRANSFER SYSTEMS ACROSS CANADA

A transfer system has not developed at the national level in Canada, perhaps because post-secondary education falls under provincial and territorial jurisdiction. Each jurisdiction has developed its post-secondary system in unique ways to meet the needs of the province or territory. While some provinces like Québec, B.C. and Alberta have well-developed transfer systems, others do not. A main reason for the lack of transfer systems in some provinces, like Ontario, is that the post-secondary system was developed under a different framework with colleges delivering trades and technology programs and universities being designed to offer degree level programming (Skolnik 2010). There was little or no academic or general education coursework taught in the colleges and, therefore, less need to arrange transfer opportunities between colleges and universities. The systems in Québec, B.C. and Alberta, on the other hand, were established with *Collège d'Enseignement Général Et Professionnel* institutions (CÉGEP) or colleges providing students with an opportunity to do university level academic coursework. This meant that a transfer system had to be developed so that students could receive credit for appropriate coursework when transferring to a university to complete a degree.

Although post-secondary education falls under provincial jurisdiction, efforts to develop inter-provincial transfer systems have been made in the last decade to address the issue of students moving between post-secondary institutions across provincial boundaries to continue their education and receive credit for previous learning. In 1995 the Pan-Canadian Protocol on the Transferability of University Credits was finalized, and in 1999 a protocol for college-to-college credit transfer was developed by the Association of Canadian Community Colleges. Despite this level of cooperation between institutions both within and across provinces/territories, Canada still lacked a national system of credit transfer. In 2002, the Council of Ministers of Education (CMEC) formed the Credit Transfer Working Group with representatives from provinces and territories. The mandate of the Working Group is to identify workable pan-Canadian actions or strategies to improve credit transfer for recommendation to Ministers and to identify priority areas for action.[52]

---

[52] One of the first tasks for the Working Group was to develop a set of principles for credit transfer, which resulted in the Ministerial Statement on Credit Transfer in Canada being approved by the CMEC in October 2002 (revised in November 2009 and available at www.cmec.ca/Publications/Lists/Publications/Attachments/216/ministerial-statement-credit-transfer-2009.pdf).

In 2006, the Pan-Canadian Consortium on Admissions and Transfer (PCCAT) was formed:

The purpose of the Consortium is to facilitate the implementation of policies and practices that support student mobility both within and among Provinces and Territories and granting of transfer credit in order to improve access to post-secondary education in Canada (PCCAT 2010).

Membership in the Consortium includes those working in support of the mobility of students and transfer of credit within post-secondary institutions, government organizations, agencies and associations (PCCAT 2010). PCCAT meets once a year to further its agenda and has established a Research Subcommittee to begin exploring issues relating to inter-provincial transfer. Thus, student mobility is no longer seen as a regional or even provincial matter. It is a national concern.

In this chapter, we take a look back at how two robust transfer systems—in Québec and B.C.—developed. We will then discuss transfer as it exists today in these two provinces and how mobility data in B.C. is yielding a rich understanding of student mobility within the province. We conclude by discussing implications of student mobility for post-secondary education in Canada.

THE HISTORY OF TRANSFER IN BRITISH COLUMBIA AND QUÉBEC

British Columbia

Prior to 1910 in B.C., there were two main providers of post-secondary education—Victoria College, which was affiliated with McGill University, and a private provider, Sprott-Shaw. In 1910, with the passing of the *University Act*, the University of British Columbia was created. No other public institution was created in B.C. until the Macdonald report of 1962. John B. Macdonald, the president of UBC at the time, took it upon himself to conduct a province-wide study on the future of education in B.C. Titled *Higher Education in British Columbia and a plan for The Future*, the Macdonald report would significantly shape the future of public post-secondary education in B.C.

The Macdonald report, influenced by the post-secondary structure in California, defined a system of transfer as "possible between institutions but it should be based not on identity of courses but on performance of students. Admission policies should be concerned less with prerequisites and more with evidence of ability when students seek transfer from one institution to another" (Macdonald 1962, p. 23). Macdonald (1962, pp.55–56) recommended:

- One new four-year degree granting college (he specifically noted that the new institution was not to be a university meaning that they should not offer graduate work);
- Two-year colleges located where they would serve the largest number of young people in the province (regional colleges); and
- All two-year colleges could offer transferability for their students flowing into UBC only.

The B.C. government, which had not commissioned this report, acted quickly on some, but not all, of Macdonald's suggestions. They established regional colleges across the province based on evidence of community support through local plebiscites. However rather than making Victoria College a four-year institution, the provincial government established a new full university, the University of Victoria (UVIC), in 1963 and then created a third university, Simon Fraser University (SFU), in 1965. These two new universities were granted the right to offer both undergraduate and graduate programming and were instructed by the B.C. government to accept transfer students from the fledgling colleges. The first community/regional college opened in 1965 and by 1974, ten were in operation with a transfer system to all three established universities, not just UBC (Knowledge Network 2008).

In 1968 students occupied SFU's administration office to protest the lack of transfer opportunities for Vancouver City College students despite the creation of a transfer system. Although government did not directly intervene to solve perceived problems in the transfer system, post-secondary institutions understood that if they did not work together to resolve transfer problems, government would intervene to solve the problems for them (Gaber 2002). Post-secondary institutions therefore created the first discipline-based articulation committees at a conference in December 1968 to resolve transfer issues. Six years later the Post-Secondary Articulation Coordinating Committee was formed with the role of overseeing transfer and articulation in B.C. Membership included the senior academic officer from each public college and university and registrar from each university. This oversight committee evolved into the B.C. Council on Admissions and Transfer (BCCAT) in 1989. Today B.C. continues to be a leader in transfer, not only in Canada, but across North America.

The system, originally designed with sending institutions, or colleges, and receiving institutions, or universities, in mind, began to blur by the early 1990s with the conversion of five colleges into hybrid institutions. University colleges were formed to respond to the growing need for baccalaureate degree graduates in the work force and a lack of access for some students (either due to where they lived, their lack of financial means or their grades in high school) to a traditional university. University colleges were granted the authority to offer four-year baccalaureate degrees as well as continuing to offer a full array of programs offered in community colleges. University colleges, now needing to attract students wishing to complete a four-year credential as well as traditional one- and two-year credential completers, turned their attention to colleges for that supply. Graduates of two-year colleges could be laddered into the university colleges' four-year degree through a two-plus-two model while other students could start at the university college and make their way towards the completion of a range of credentials, including baccalaureate degrees.

University colleges thus moved towards a dual role within the transfer system—both as senders and receivers of students. While this change in university colleges' function added to the complexity of the transfer system, student choice also increased. No longer would students have to leave their home community to complete a baccalaureate degree. Students could now study at a university college at a tuition rate considerably lower than at the more traditional universities.

In 2003, the B.C. government passed the Degree Authorization Act which gave public colleges the authority to grant applied baccalaureate degrees and university colleges the authority to grant applied Master's degrees. The same act also expanded degree-granting authority to private institutions in the province through a degree quality approval process. The Act was instrumental in increasing student choice for degree completion and thus had a further impact on traditional transfer flows. By 2010, 22 of 25 public institutions in B.C. grant one or more degrees, and there are now ten degree-granting private institutions in the transfer system.

In 2005 the provincial government changed the status of two of the five university colleges by splitting one into a college and a research university (the Okanagan campus of UBC) and turning another into a regional university. In 2008, the provincial government announced that the three remaining university colleges, one college and one Institute, would become teaching-intensive universities under the province's *University Act* legislation.[53] These five institutions became, through the stroke of a legislative pen, universities. Thus the system of transfer in B.C., which had started as a binary system based on a sending and receiving dichotomy, had reached a critical fork in the road.

Québec

Prior to the 1960s, the Province of Québec had six main universities located in the three largest metropolitan areas of the province. Due to the vastness of the land mass of Québec, it meant that an important portion of the population did not have easy access to post-secondary education. Access to universities was also made difficult by the fact that most French-speaking high school students had to go to liberal arts colleges ("collèges classiques"), which were limited in numbers and run mainly by religious orders, before being admitted to universities.

In 1961, facing growing demand for a better post-secondary education system, the Québec Government instituted a royal commission to consider the matter and develop suggestions for change. In 1963, Le rapport Parent (Parent Commission) recommended, amongst other things, the creation of a new type of post-secondary institution to supplement and eventually replace the existing liberal arts colleges, thus increasing substantially access to university education. All of these Parent Commission's recommendations came to fruition in the following years.

In 1967, the Québec government established a new level of post-secondary education between high school and university called the CÉGEP[54]. This pre-university level of education had programs that were centrally controlled by the Québec Ministry of Education and were thus similar from one CÉGEP to another in the province. Students could, therefore, move from one CÉGEP to another CÉGEP freely without losing credits.

---

[53] Except for the Institute, these initiatives were to retain the comprehensive program base that included certificate and diploma programs.

[54] A student earning a Bachelor's degree in Quebec has the same number of total years of schooling as in the rest of Canada: 6 years in primary school, 5 years in high school, 2 years in CÉGEP and 3 years at university for a total of 16 years.

In 1968, facing growing demand for university education from the baby-boomer generation who were graduating from the new CÉGEP system, the Québec government created a network of nine new universities, called Université du Québec, with a central head office overseeing the various campuses. As the years went by, a number of programs were created with similar course content that were easily transferable from one campus to another. The Université du Québec network was modeled partly on the California State University system. From six universities prior to 1960, access to university education by the late 1970s expanded to 18 campuses spread over eight urban areas and one distance education virtual campus. This meant that university level education was now available in smaller cities and areas where the long established universities had never been. University tuition fees, which were established at similar levels around the province, were frozen at 1970 rates until the 1990s, thus making tuition fees in Québec amongst the lowest in North America. Many have argued that this served to further enhance student accessibility to postsecondary education. Universities attracted students based on their program offerings and seat availability in classes.

Thus the evolution of transfer mobility in B.C. and Québec differed—with similar results. While Québec's system was modeled after the California centralized system (one university helping to serve multiple locations around the province), in B.C. smaller independent colleges were established in both rural and urban areas to ensure students could transfer to any of the three major universities. Both provincial systems were designed with student mobility in mind and the recognition that baccalaureate attainment can be enhanced and achieved through transfer of credit from one institution to another. As a result, students in Québec and B.C. moved between institutions (colleges to university in B.C. and CÉGEP to university in Québec) with relative ease.

TRANSFER TODAY IN QUÉBEC AND B.C.

Québec

Unlike B.C.'s course-by-course transfer system between individual institutions, in Québec there is no automatic recognition of credits when a student transfers from one university to another. Each case is treated on an individual basis by universities, taking into account the course syllabus and the grade that was obtained by the student seeking to transfer credit "in." This hampers mobility.

In Québec a different system, called Authorization to Transfer Credits, was developed by the Conference of Rectors and Principals of Québec Universities (CREPUQ). This system is equivalent to the system of "Letters of Permission" in universities across Canada. The home institution was responsible for approving the course choices made by students ahead of time, and the receiving institution had the final say in approving the transfer before the student started his or her coursework. The aim was to provide easy mobility for students who wanted to take courses at another university for a variety of reasons: subject matter, availability, location. From a strategic enrolment viewpoint, students could stay enrolled in their home institution while taking courses at another institution. In some cases, it meant that a student might try a new academic discipline in another institution before deciding to apply to that institution, having assurance that credits would be recognized. For the provincial government, which provided most of the funding for all Québec universities, it meant that a certain rationalization of the program offerings through government approval and evaluation of programs could occur.

This system, which first began as a paper-based system in the late 1980s allowing transfer of academic credits between universities, evolved in 2003 to a computer-based tracking system.[55] In 1988, 0.8 percent of Québec students (1985 students) used the system. By Fall 2008, 1.9 percent of university students (5064 students) in Québec used the system, and 79.7 percent of all transfer requests in 2008 received approval. On a yearly basis, over 15,000 undergraduate and graduate students use the system. Out of the 5,000 students taking courses at another institution in the Fall 2008 semester, 50 percent did so in the greater metropolitan area of Montreal. Since Montreal has a large concentration of higher education institutions, the system makes it easy for a student to take a course at McGill University while being registered as a regular student at Concordia University, a short walk or a few subway stops away, and then return to his or her other classes at Concordia the same day. It is worth noting that in 2008, 34 percent of the course transfers were at

---

[55] *See* <https://dbs.crepuq.qc.ca/mobilite-cours/4DSTATIC/ENAccueil.html>.

Télé-Université, the distance education institution that is now part of Université du Québec à Montréal (UQAM).

After 30 years of a centralized system, the Québec government gave CÉGEPs greater autonomy in the 1990s. They were allowed to create their own courses in certain elective disciplines other than general education courses. This has resulted in decreasing mobility slightly for CÉGEP students in particular programs. In order to make themselves more attractive, CÉGEPs and universities developed one-to-one articulation agreements thus permitting mobility within a comprehensive program starting at CÉGEP and ending with a university bachelor's degree.

British Columbia

B.C. has developed a course-to-course transfer system in which sending and receiving institutions, all of them fully autonomous, agree beforehand which courses are equivalent and will be assigned credit when the student arrives at the receiving institution. These courses are then published in the B.C. Transfer Guide, thus giving students a level of predictability when planning their transfer paths. The system enables students to exit and re-enter participating post-secondary institutions and get credit for previous coursework that has been deemed transferable beforehand.

The B.C. Transfer Guide (www.bctransferguide.ca), the official transfer site used by about 50,000 unique visitors a month for transfer information, contains close to 70,000 course articulations which have been negotiated between institutions. This is dominated primarily by college-to-university agreements, but also now includes university-to-university articulations.

Another type of transfer common in B.C. is block transfer agreements. These agreements are "an efficient vehicle for credit transfer where course content is sufficiently different that course-to-course equivalencies cannot be established" (McIvor 2010, p. 2). Furthermore, block transfer agreements "are flexible, variable and follow different models. They can cover entire years or portions of a degree..." (McIvor 2010, p. 2), and they provide some guarantee to students that the course work they have completed will count towards a higher credential.

Degree partnerships "describe a variety of models that provide a guarantee to students who maintain adequate grades in a college program of continuation of degree studies at another institution" (Gaber 2006, p. 1). They provide students with assurance that course work completed at one institution will count at another. Such partnerships include guaranteed admission once minimum requirements are met. This not only brings assurance for course transfer credit but also ensures a smooth transition from college to university. Degree partnerships are becoming increasingly popular in B.C. as they provide more predictability to sending and receiving institutions for enrolment planning purposes.

Another recent trend in the B.C. transfer system is the growth in Flexible Pre-Major Agreements (FPM). A FPM is a set of flexible requirements delivered by "sending institutions and acceptable to receiving institutions and deemed to fulfill the lower level requirements for the major" (Orum 2010, p. 2). The benefits to students are obvious:

> *With FPM agreements in place across many sending and receiving institutions, students can plan their first and second year courses to leave open multiple options for transferring into various B.C. institutions and for entering the major at the third year level. If students have planned to attend a particular university and end up not doing so, completion of the FPM requirements for their chosen major will provide them with possibilities. Completion of the FPM requirements will also mean students should not be required to pick up 'missing' courses for their major in their third and fourth years, or repeat content they have already covered* (Orum 2010, p. 2).

It is important to note that of the three alternate forms of arranging transfer described above, only block transfer agreements have the ability to reduce the reliance on course-to-course transfer whereas both degree partnerships and FPMs rely heavily on a well-developed course-to-course transfer system. A key benefit of these new approaches is providing both institutions and students with more certainty about available transfer routes.

In summary, with the addition of five new universities, the authority of colleges to offer applied baccalaureate degrees and private institutions as partners in the transfer system, the lines have become blurred between what is a receiving institution and what is a sending institution. The increased complexity is taxing the system of course-to-course articulation. The next section explores the data being mined in B.C. to re-examine what constitutes a mobile student and to improve institutional enrolment management planning.

STUDENT MOBILITY—BEYOND TRANSFER

In B.C., significant effort has been expended in the last few years to increase the understanding of student transitions and mobility from a longitudinal and system-wide perspective. The examination of student mobility has been carried out under the auspices of the Student Transitions Project (STP). Those students who transfer to research universities are a sub-population of the broader mobile student population studied by the STP. The STP began in 2005 and is a collaborative effort of B.C.'s Ministries of Education (K–12) and Advanced Education and Labour Market Development, B.C.'s public post-secondary institutions and BCCAT. The purpose of the STP is to collect, analyze and report on data from the K–12 and post-secondary education systems to answer research questions on student transition and mobility.[56]

The work of the STP is made possible because B.C. has a unique student identifier, called the Personal Education Number (PEN), which is assigned to all students who enter the K–12 and public post-secondary education systems in B.C. The PEN allows researchers to track students as they move towards Grade 12 graduation, on to a post-secondary institution and among post-secondary institutions. Because of the longitudinal nature of STP data, questions can be answered on a province-wide basis on the number of registrants, the length of time in a post-secondary institution, the programs that were enrolled in and the number of graduates, drop outs from the system and stop outs who leave for a period without having graduated but then return to the public post-secondary system. This information is updated on an annual basis with each new submission of data and is disseminated through reports, newsletters and Excel pivot tables.

One branch of STP research is to follow the movement of students among post-secondary institutions once they have enrolled in the system. Figure 10 (on page 324) provides a visual of the movement of all students across years within the B.C. system. STP states that "roughly 26,000 of the continuing registrants moved between B.C. public post-secondary institutions from 2006/07 to 2007/08, moving

---

[56] The goal is to provide reliable information at predictable times and in a timely manner to assist institutions and government with planning. Information about the STP and its recent publications can be found at <www.aved.gov.bc.ca/student_transitions/>.

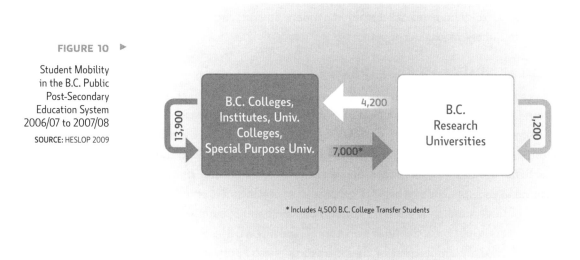

FIGURE 10 ▶

Student Mobility
in the B.C. Public
Post-Secondary
Education System
2006/07 to 2007/08

SOURCE: HESLOP 2009

in multiple directions and along various pathways" (Heslop 2009, p. 1). Of these students, approximately 4,500 or 17 percent were the traditional transfer students who move from a college or other sending institution to one of B.C.'s research universities. Of the remaining students, the bulk of movement is between institutions other than research universities.

Data like those presented in Figure 10 are causing educators in B.C. to think more about student mobility rather than student transfer, which has traditionally been defined as those students who move to research universities with transfer as the basis of admission. In a "student mobility" system, it is important to understand the longitudinal movement of different student populations, the kinds of programs they move among, the kinds of credit they have achieved at their previous institution and whether they are given credit for previous coursework. Unlike research universities, the colleges, teaching intensive universities and institutes in B.C. do not have transfer as a basis of admission, so it is more difficult to identify and track these students.

In order to learn more about a broader student mobility system, BCCAT held a Visioning Session in November 2009 with key post-secondary and government personnel to explore the sub-populations whose mobility patterns they would like to learn about, the kinds of questions they would like answered about those sub-populations and the barriers to finding out the information being sought. The participants identified a host of sub-populations, including students moving between public and private institutions, student "movers" with credentials, students with some credits moving among post-secondary institutions other than traditional transfer students and stop-outs as some of the priority sub-populations to explore in the evolving research agenda (BCCAT 2010). Thus the transfer system in B.C. is being redefined based on the available evidence of student movement in multiple directions. The theory is that B.C. is well positioned to provide maximum opportunities for transfer, regardless of what kind of institution the student comes from or moves to, because of the long history and culture of transfer in the province.

A robust transfer system is good for students. It increases their choices and maintains assurance for the applicability of coursework completed. For universities and colleges the impact of the transfer system, and of a mobile student population, can be summarized threefold: competitive, collegial and collaborative. The system encourages collaboration between institutions to create such options for students as degree partnerships and flexible pre-majors. Collegiality exists not only in the review of curriculum but between student services who work across institutions to smooth transition through educational advising support for students prior to transfer and through records systems that electronically exchange transcript information. Yet the transfer system, coupled with changing demographics, does place institutions in a competitive environment, each fighting for a slice of the mobile student pie. Competition, it is argued, is not necessarily a bad thing for students nor is it bad for institutions. But it does result in colleges and universities marketing their programs across other's catchment areas and treating the student as a consumer of education. The implications have been vast for strategic enrolment management planning in post-secondary education.

STRATEGIC ENROLMENT MANAGEMENT AND IMPLICATIONS FOR STUDENT MOBILITY

As experiences in Québec and B.C. have demonstrated, students, when provided the opportunity, will continue to pursue a post-secondary education even if it means attending more than one institution to do so. Had B.C. and Québec not developed systems that provided students with the option of mobility, many students may have gone underserved in pursuing a post-secondary credential. Yet students transfer, even in the more informal sense, from one institution to another all across Canada. While provincial systems of transfer, such as those developed in Québec, B.C. and Alberta, support student mobility within those provinces, other provinces do not have well-defined transfer systems and there is no national system of transfer. Thus students have no guarantee against credit loss. Many post-secondary students in Canada already face many barriers to persistence:

> *The proportion of post-secondary students who are from families with no previous history of post-secondary education, from families with moderate or low incomes and of average or even below-average academic achievement has grown. So, too, has the number of post-secondary students who are Aboriginal. These types of students not only face greater barriers to access but potentially are also more likely, for academic, financial or cultural reasons, to abandon their studies before graduation* (Parkin and Baldwin 2009b, p. 1).

A student may drop out or 'stop-out' from his or her education for many reasons, some more positive than others. Yet when "we can prevent this from occurring by providing timely and coordinated support, we are facilitating the most singularly impactful process on the future of students' lives" (Gordon and Mitchell 2010). Flexible pre-majors, allowing students to complete courses at another university when not offered at their home institution, block transfer agreements and course-to-course articulations are just some of the ways we can ensure successful graduates.

The mobility data discussed here suggests that the number of students moving among post-secondary institutions is substantial. In B.C. mobile students (defined as movement among different types of institutions in any direction) outnumber the traditional transfer students (defined as college to university). What we lack is a national picture of student mobility. Understanding the complexities of student movement within a province positions us to better understand student mobility on a national level. National mobility data could also shape the structure of academic programming to ensure flexible points of entry and exit.

PCCAT seeks to "facilitate the implementation of policies and practices that support student mobility both within and among Provinces and Territories and granting of transfer credit in order to improve access to post-secondary education in Canada" (PCCAT 2010); it is a call to action for all post-secondary institutions across the nation to improve student access. The foundation of SEM requires us to examine how we support student transition, especially for those students who move in and out of the post-secondary system and among institutions. Unnecessarily delaying students from completing their credential postpones their entry into the work force, increases their financial debt and could decrease a student's overall satisfaction with their post-secondary education experience.

The principles of SEM create opportunities for dialogue on how to improve the student experience at our respective post-secondary institutions. Now more than ever post-secondary institutional leaders across the nation must work together to find ways to improve the experience of the growing number of mobile students in Canada. The very essence of SEM requires it.

Susan Gottheil and Clayton Smith

16

LOOKING FORWARD

A GUIDE TO
THE CHALLENGES AHEAD

/ **Chapter 16** /

The experience of Canadian SEM practitioners over the past ten to fifteen years has shown us that strategic enrolment management has a place within the Canadian educational landscape. Constrained budgets, changing demographics and increased competition have highlighted the need for intentional planning and collaborative leadership. The changing student body has put a focus on the learner and enhancing student success and outcomes. The widespread use of student satisfaction surveys (and the reality that rankings and provincial key performance indicators are not disappearing) has led many of our institutions to a re-examination of curriculum and pedagogy, as well as highlighting institutional priorities such as enhancing the student experience and increasing student engagement. "Branding" and marketing efforts may still evoke critiques of the apparent corporatization of post-secondary education but are nonetheless accepted as almost inevitable as institutions compete for students, research grants and donors.

The preceding chapters of this book have demonstrated how the various SEM components have been applied in Canada. In some respects we have adopted or adapted SEM theory, tactics and strategies from our colleagues in the United States. However, the unique nature of the Canadian educational system(s), Canadian history and values, and the specific demographic make-up of our population have led to innovations and particular SEM applications and strategies that are different and new.

As we have analyzed our internal and external environments, many of us have benefited from the insights provided by Canadian literature reviews and research studies produced by the Canadian Millennium Scholarship Foundation, Canadian Council on Learning, Educational Policy Institute, MESA Project, and Statistics Canada. The Higher Education Quality Council of Ontario (HEQCO) has also funded institutional projects as well as system-wide studies which are helping us to understand the complexities of post-secondary access and success, and are pointing to programs that may help achieve institutional SEM goals.

Canada's changing demography, the decline in the number of students in the traditional post-secondary age range, and competition from other post-secondary institutions (as well as from the private sector and online providers) creates an imperative for us to continue to re-evaluate what we are doing, how we are doing it, and who we are doing it for. SEM planners and practitioners must keep an eye to the future and help their institutions and students prepare for a rapidly changing world.

What lies ahead?

THE CHANGING CANADIAN POST-SECONDARY LANDSCAPE

The post-secondary landscape has changed significantly over the past five years. Pressures from provincial governments and institutions have resulted in a blending/overlap of college and university roles as well as pressure for more seamless pathways and collaborative programs. Occasionally, reports are produced (such as the recent O'Neill report in Nova Scotia) suggesting the merger of institutions. Yet at the same time branding initiatives and competition have led to increased institutional differentiation on the basis of size, institutional mandate, types of programs offered, how teaching and services are offered ("bricks and mortar" versus online delivery), research breadth and focus, and student populations served (faith-based, First Nations, rural/urban, francophone). It is likely that provinces will continue to examine and re-examine the delivery of education to enhance access, increase student mobility and try to eliminate unnecessary duplication in program delivery to gain fiscal efficiencies.

Fiscal pressures have had and will continue to have an impact on all Canadian post-secondary institutions. Increasingly cash-strapped universities are being forced to "do less with less." Colleges and universities will continue to see decreased government grants, targeted funding with more strings attached, an increased reliance on student tuition and fees, and increased operational costs. This will lead us to continue to innovate and to do things differently. For many, the budget realities will mean fewer course offerings and possible program elimination, larger class sizes, and more sessional and part-time instructors. SEM practitioners will need to think carefully of how these fiscal realities will impact student marketing, recruitment, academic program development and service support and will need to continue to work strategically to serve students.

CHANGING DEMOGRAPHICS

Elementary and secondary school enrolments across Canada are now shrinking just as the "echo boom" generation finishes moving its way through the educational system and graduates from our colleges and universities. Most demographers predict a gradual decline in the post-secondary youth population beyond 2016. It is unclear the extent to which Canada's low birthrate will be offset by immigration and increasing educational participation rates in sustaining post-secondary growth. Any continued rise in post-secondary enrolment will need to come from new markets (through international recruitment or expanding career development opportunities), by enhancing the access and academic success of historically under-served and under-represented groups (such as Aboriginal students, francophones, students with disabilities), and/or by increasing student persistence and retention.

Since the future prosperity of Canada lies with a knowledge-based economy, continuing to increase access to post-secondary education is a social and moral imperative. A number of provinces are providing financial incentives to encourage colleges and universities to broaden access to Aboriginal, college transfer and first-generation student populations. Other demographic groups may yet emerge that require special attention. For example, post-secondary institutions have been experiencing a steady increase in the ratio of female to male students. Although high school dropout rates are decreasing generally, the male share of dropouts has been increasing. With the exception of certain programs such as engineering and business, recruiting men to post-secondary programs is becoming a greater challenge, though thus far few initiatives have been directed towards this imbalance.[57] Males enrolled in college are more likely than females to drop out of their studies, although male and female university students leave at the same rate (Finnie *et al.* 2010d).

---

[57] The University of Alberta's president, Indira Samarasekera, gained international publicity last year when she highlighted the issue of gender imbalance in post-secondary education. In December 2010, Line Beauchamp, Quebec's Minister of Education, Recreation and Sports, announced a campaign to promote the academic success of boys.

SEM planners have been keeping a watchful eye on where the Canadian population growth (and decrease) is occurring across the country. The greater Toronto and Vancouver urban centres are witnessing enrolment pressures as immigrants—who tend to have high educational aspirations for their children—settle in these larger cities. The Maritime provinces have seen their markets shrink over the past 15 years as the birthrate has decreased and young people have left to seek work (and education) elsewhere. The potential for growth in the western provinces—especially in Manitoba and Saskatchewan—is high where the Aboriginal youth population is quickly expanding.[58] The key in those provinces is to work with communities to overcome access and success barriers such as academic under-preparedness as well as the legacy of the residential school system.

Within a competitive environment many established colleges and universities will need to define and expand their markets. Some institutions are already exploring ways to differentiate themselves in the marketplace while offering innovative ways of delivering programs. For example, Algoma University has been exploring a "block plan" whereby students would enrol in one course at a time delivered in 3 week blocks (similar to the Quest University model). In areas with traditionally low university participation rates, institutions are renewing a commitment to increase the local market while expanding their national and international profile (UBC–Okanagan, Mount Royal University, and Thompson River University). And a number of Ontario colleges are working in partnership with small urban and rural municipalities to develop new campuses (much like Wilfrid Laurier University did with their Brantford campus).

DATA

As we have noted in repeated workshops and presentations, data is what makes enrolment management strategic. It gives us key information to support our analyses of the internal and external environments, helps identify the issues and priorities facing our institutions, and aids in assessing the programs and services we choose to implement. Yet in an attempt to be data-driven, we have collectively been challenged by having both too much data and not the right kind of data. We need to

---

[58] The Canadian Aboriginal population is proportionately younger and growing at three times the national average. Manitoba (15.5%) and Saskatchewan (14.9%) already have a high proportion of Aboriginal peoples in their provinces.

turn large, complex data sets into pieces of actionable insight and we must create richer meaning from the data we gather. This is an issue that SEM practitioners and planners must tackle within each of our institutions and collectively across the country together. Simply, we need more accurate and reliable data. *See* Chapter 2, "Using Data for Strategic Enrolment Management," for further discussion.

A key concern nationwide is that Canadians lack a common data set and a uniform approach to data collection.[59] The availability of information to establish baseline measures and to link student information from different databases is limited by our regulatory and legislative environments. The use of student self-identification (for Aboriginal students and students with disabilities) and inconsistent use of definitions (for example, for "first-generation" students) makes it difficult to accurately identify under-served populations and to track our success in attracting and retaining them in the post-secondary system.[60] It is difficult to assess the success rates of students who enter our institutions to study part-time (many of whom are enrolled in colleges and who are mature students from nontraditional backgrounds) when data reports include only those individuals who are full-time students.

The implementation of provincial centralized application centres has helped provide some jurisdictions with helpful comparative data for applicants—but this only provides information for students who are at the front end of the student life cycle (or at "the top" of the enrolment funnel). A number of provinces are now implementing provincial student numbers that will follow a student from primary school through their post-secondary studies. Although this will help to more accurately track students, what is needed is a national—and not just provincial—mobility tracking system.

As we develop SEM plans and appropriate strategies to achieve our enrolment goals, SEM professionals must identify key performance indicators that will help focus our tactics and evaluate the effectiveness of our strategies. As Richard Levin has indicated in his chapter on student recruitment (*see* Chapter 5, on page 79), it

---

[59] The U15 institutions—Canada's research intensive universities—have also been collaborating to exchange data on students as well as teaching staff, institutional resources, libraries, capital resources and research revenues. This data is used for benchmarking purposes and is not shared outside of the U15 group. In November 2010 the Association of Atlantic Universities published the first Atlantic Common University Data Set—allowing students, parents and others to access and compare data based on common definitions and displayed in a similar format.

[60] The addition of a "first-generation" question to OUAC/OCAS application forms will provide better data for Ontario.

is still common for Canadian universities and colleges to invest significant sums of money into recruitment efforts with no systematic evidence supporting their probable effectiveness or a means of evaluating their success. For example, few institutions allocate resources to mine Web analytics to determine what's working on key institutional Web pages and what's not.

RECRUITMENT

All individuals who are involved in the post-secondary choice process (prospective students, parents, guidance counselors, teachers, and friends) rely to a large extent on digital sources of information to make their decisions. It is clear that SEM professionals must understand how to harness the benefits of instantaneous 24x7 communication and interactive technologies—and be prepared to use them to enhance post-secondary access and success. Our Web sites must give accurate, up-to-date, instantaneous and interactive information and services. We must develop mobile-friendly Web sites, enhance our student portals, develop podcasts and invest in appropriate mobile apps. As Levin has indicated, we are unlikely to see any decline in the pace of technological advancement, nor is the shape of this factor predictable. We will need to be prepared to constantly adapt our recruitment strategies to "stay ahead of the curve."

New technologies such as social networking have already altered consumer decision making and student behaviour. Although Web sites provide key recruitment messaging and program information, they have promoted the "stealth" marketplace and encouraged "secret shoppers." The opportunity to "visit without visiting" is certainly a convenience for the prospective student but it is also a missed opportunity for institutions to promote academic programs and have students experience their campus community "face-to-face." It also means that we cannot identify prospective students to give the personalized attention that students expect and that, with the help of customized communication (CRM) tools, most colleges and universities are now primed to do.

ADMISSIONS

With the increase in competition for students—and an imperative to be student-centred and operationally efficient—Canadian post-secondary education has shifted its admission philosophy from that of "gatekeeper" to one of "facilitator." Admission professionals have altered policies and processes to personalize the admissions process, build relationships and enhance communication with applicants. For example, some institutions are offering conditional admission to candidates who self-report their grades. This alleviates the need to wait for paper records from schools and allows institutions to send out offers earlier (which is seen as a competitive advantage).

Institutions such as the University of British Columbia, Simon Fraser University, and University of Calgary have implemented the use of broad-based admissions questionnaires, in addition to grades and test scores, to better predict which students will succeed and be a "good fit" at their institutions. As Canadian colleges and universities seek ways to attract non-traditional students, this approach (although more time-consuming) may help identify and select applicants on the basis of leadership, initiative, and other personal characteristics that are not always reflected in high school grades.

FINANCIAL AID

The role of financial aid in Canadian post-secondary institutions has been in transition, steadily shifting from that of an essential student support service to that of a key strategic enrolment management activity. This has been driven by rising tuition fees, increasing competition for students, and an increasing awareness by students themselves of their choices in the higher education marketplace. Many institutional awards programs are still largely donor driven and are only incidentally related to influencing the behavior of either prospective or in-course students. This is now changing. A few Canadian institutions have begun to use institutional funds to "leverage" enrolment. The lack of government support and the pressure to achieve SEM goals may lead more of us to consider such strategies in the future.

As Peter Dueck has noted in his chapter on financial aid, there is already somewhat of an 'arms race' underway in Canadian universities in efforts to attract top students with guaranteed entrance awards (that is, merit-based scholarships) (*see* Chapter 7, "Financial Aid: Balancing Access and Excellence," on page 117). Most institutions do not want to be left out of the competition. As a result, no real competitive advantage may be gained. It may be useful, as UBC is doing, to try something different with limited financial aid dollars and to test the effectiveness of a new approach to student support.

It is troubling that governmental and institution-based financial aid programs are not reaching many of those who might benefit from them the most—low-income youth.[61] In 2006 the government of Ontario mandated that the province's colleges and universities implement the Student Access Guarantee and provide enough financial aid to cover the assessed needs of their students for tuition, books, and mandatory fees if these are not fully met by the provincial student aid program (OSAP). It is too early to tell whether or not this policy has positively impacted student access and—just as importantly—retention.[62]

Student debt levels continue to rise as the costs of pursuing post-secondary education increase. Students, parents and advocacy groups are exerting pressure to reform the existing Canada Student Loan Program to improve student financial assistance. It will be interesting to watch coming federal budgets as a combination of considerable tuition increases and the impact of the recent economic slow-down has been challenging the Canadian financial aid system. It may well be that the post-secondary institutions themselves will need to find more money—through operational budgets or fundraising—to enhance initiatives (including bursaries, emergency loans, work-study opportunities, and even food banks) that will help attract students and prevent them from withdrawing for financial reasons.

KEEPING OUR STUDENTS: ENGAGEMENT AND RETENTION

Although many institutions have adapted a SEM framework, the enrolment objective of many colleges and universities has been principally to attract more students through new and innovative marketing and recruitment initiatives. Only lately has attention turned to enhancing the student experience on campus. It has now become clear that if students leave dissatisfied with their academic program and the campus support they have received, enrolment goals will not be sustained in the long run.

As institutions analyse the behaviour of their own students some common patterns have emerged across the country. Students from special populations—those

---

[61] The United States provides more financial support to low-income families compared to Canada, whereas middle-income families in Canada receive a greater share of need-based aid than in the States (Belley, Frenette and Lochner 2011).

[62] The province of Manitoba recently implemented a similar initiative (the Student Success Grant program) that shares costs with its post-secondary institutions to help fund undergraduate students who have unmet financial needs beyond their combined bursary and maximum student loan amounts.

who are the focus of specific SEM targets (such as Aboriginal and rural students, students with disabilities, and some first-generation students)—are more likely to drop out of their studies. As well, many students appear to be studying less, working more, and taking longer to complete their credentials. How can we engage and keep more of our students? Research is needed on why students stay at, or leave, our campuses. We need to understand how best to identify and track "at risk" students so that we can provide appropriate intervention measures to prevent attrition. Although financial support is critically important, non-financial barriers to access and persistence appear to be just as important as financial ones.[63]

Good work has been done on many campuses. For example, some institutions have already successfully developed programs that help students focus on completing their studies (the four-year graduation guarantee at the University of Calgary and University of Regina's job guarantee). Supportive spaces for students to gather and receive culturally-sensitive services have been established at many colleges and universities to support students with disabilities, international students, Aboriginal learners, LBGT (lesbian, gay, bi-sexual and transgendered) students, and students with different spiritual and faith backgrounds. Attention is now also being placed on establishing one-stop student success centres that provide academic advising, orientation and transition programs, learning skills workshops, and career counseling—as well as providing encouragement to students to engage in campus life.

The concept of student engagement (coined by George Kuh and his colleagues) has recently been embraced by many Canadian institutions as a proxy for academic persistence and success. It has enabled the academic community to see that they have a critical role to play in developing more sophisticated retention strategies, ones emphasizing high impact academic and classroom-based as well as co-curricular components. The development and expansion of experiential and co-curricular programs such as service learning, study abroad, and co-op has broken down silos and enhanced collaboration between academic and student affairs units. This partnership needs to continue to develop.

Budgetary pressures have led to growing class sizes and a decreasing number of full-time instructors. If this trend continues, what will be the impact on student

---

[63] Half of all students in Canadian post-secondary education do not borrow at all (through government or bank loans) to fund their studies.

engagement and persistence? How much classroom innovation, including new forms of pedagogy and interactive modes of course delivery, will be possible under these circumstances?

INCREASING STUDENT MOBILITY

There has been a general increase in the mobility of students transferring between colleges and universities over the past few years. Yet many students continue to complain that the process is unwieldy and unsatisfactory. Information on transfer programs is difficult to obtain and course credit (and comparable work experience) goes unrecognized (often forcing students to extend their time in post-secondary studies unnecessarily). In addition, since post-secondary education falls under provincial mandates, it is difficult to move across the country. What is needed is a nation-wide approach to help students as they seek alternative educational opportunities and pathways to success. Students need clear, accessible and consistent information about the transfer process.

If universities, in particular, wish to increase their under-represented student populations they must make it easier for students to transfer into their institutions from the college system(s). In Ontario (and, it is probably safe to extrapolate, to other jurisdictions), Aboriginal students, students with disabilities, first-generation students and low-income students are more likely to be college transfer students than direct-entry students (Kerr, McCloy and Liu 2010).

It is unlikely that post-secondary institutions will quickly address issues such as transfer credit equivalencies and prior learning assessment (PLAR) without some explicit government direction and incentives. As the Council of Ministers of Education has made a commitment to increase student mobility we will likely soon see other provinces following the lead of Ontario. In January 2011 the Ontario provincial government announced a new centralized system that will facilitate transfers between institutions. Mobility targets will be set for each institution, encouraging more credit transfer agreements. As well, a new Credit Innovation Fund is being set up to help make pathways smoother between colleges and universities by providing advisors in the form of an interactive Web site and orientation programs for students.

SPECIAL STUDENT POPULATIONS

Regardless of provincial incentives and institutional efforts to increase access, one need only walk through the hallways of any college or university in the country to see that the student population is already becoming increasingly diverse. Yet as all SEM professionals know, special attention is being paid—and will need to continue to be paid—to attracting groups in our general population who are still under-represented and under-served. Below, we turn our attention to some of the groups that have become the focus at institutions across Canada.

Aboriginal Students

The Association of Universities and Colleges of Canada (AUCC) and the National Aboriginal Achievement Foundation have identified the crisis of First Nations, Inuit and Metis education as one of the most compelling national issues facing Canada. Although the proportion of Aboriginal peoples in the overall Canadian population is 3.8 percent, only 35 percent of the overall Aboriginal population aged 25 to 64 has completed post-secondary studies compared to 51 percent of the overall Canadian non-Aboriginal population (Statistics Canada 2006). This difference in participation rates between Aboriginals and the total population is almost completely driven by differences in high school completion rates (Mendelson 2006).[64]

The 2006 Aboriginal Peoples Survey indicated that a much higher proportion of the Aboriginal population is attending colleges (42%) and technical institutes and trade schools (20%) than universities (16%) (ACCC 2010, p. ii). In fact, the percentage of Aboriginals with a college certificate or diploma is almost on par with the non-Aboriginal population and the percentage with apprenticeship or trades certificates is higher than that for the non-Aboriginal population (ACCC 2010).

Although Aboriginal peoples are not a homogenous group, Aboriginal students are more likely to be older with family responsibilities (and thus are in greater need of childcare services and affordable family housing), first generation, studying part-time, and living away from home with no community support nearby. These students experience lower campus engagement and—because of insufficient academic preparation—have a tougher time adjusting to the demands of post-secondary studies.

---

[64] Recent Aboriginal high school graduates are 23 percent less likely than their non-Aboriginal peers to go on to post-secondary studies within two years after high school graduation (AUCCa 2010).

Aboriginal learners often face a more complex range of barriers and challenges than non-Aboriginal learners, and therefore targeted strategies and additional supports are required. If Canadian colleges and universities are serious about meeting the challenge presented by the National Aboriginal Achievement Foundation, resources will have to be allocated to create a culturally-appropriate, welcoming and supportive learning environment. Access and bridge year programming with targeted scholarships and bursaries can help with access. However we will need to ensure we have appropriate role models—faculty, staff and elders—who understand the barriers faced by Aboriginal students in their daily lives to increase persistence. Increased Aboriginal enrolment will not be achieved without outreach efforts and collaborative partnerships with the K–12 education system, Aboriginal communities and community groups.

First-Generation Students

The concept of "first-generation student" is relatively new in Canada and has not been widely adopted nationwide. Until recently there was not much Canadian research in this area and few institutions provided specific programs targeted to this group of students. More recently the province of Ontario has provided incentive funding to initiate access and retention programs for first-generation learners. The Higher Education Quality Council of Ontario has sponsored research to evaluate the programs' effectiveness. It is unclear if first generation status in and of itself impacts student persistence and experience.

Contrary to long-held assumptions, once enrolled, these students are not any more likely than their peers to encounter problems and leave their studies (Finnie, Childs and Wismer 2010b). Other factors—such as socio-economic status and family income, family ethos, motivation or membership in a particular ethno-cultural community—may be larger factors.

This does not mean that SEM practitioners should ignore first-generation students as a group. As Barry Townsend and Laurie Schnarr note in Chapter 12 (on page 215) on first-generation students, through better understanding the experiences of first-generation students we can create a more collaborative, reflexive and robust system for recruiting, retaining and graduating a diverse student body. The challenge for us is to reach out to first-generation families and bring students to our doors. It is then our obligation to provide the supports to help them succeed.

International Students

Over the past decade there has been a monumental rise in the global demand for higher education, particularly from countries with emerging economies. Although Canadian educational institutions have lagged behind their American, Australian and British counterparts, colleges and universities have entered the international marketplace with the hopes of attracting new students. Provincial support for international student recruitment has been uneven. Yet the number of international students studying in Canada has tripled since 1998 and in 2010/11 alone the number of international students studying at Canadian universities increased by 10 percent (AUCC 2010b).

International students often embark from their home countries alone, arriving in Canada with no social supports to face new cultural mores, inclement and changing weather conditions, and differing academic expectations. Compounded with studying in, and often learning, a new language many students find themselves homesick and struggling to continue their studies. Many find it difficult to make friends and become engaged in campus life. It is clearly not enough to recruit international students to our institutions—we need to provide services and supports to help them thrive in their new surroundings and to succeed.

Although not without controversy, "pathway programs" such as Navitas (which have been established at Simon Fraser University and the University of Manitoba) are becoming increasingly popular for students who lack the English language proficiency needed for direct entry into post-secondary studies. This represents a new approach to teaching first-year international students and features a hybrid of English language instruction, learning and academic support services and workshops, and university-level credit coursework. Some critics view this approach to the recruitment and integration of international students as the outsourcing of teaching and support for first-year students on campus. Others see it as a "soft landing"—a place to begin and adjust where students can make progress towards their credentials and address weaknesses in English language skills at the same time. It is likely that more institutions will need to adapt this approach to help their international students, whether they partner with an external agency or provide a transition program themselves.

As we increase the numbers of international students on our campuses, we must also prepare our campus communities for the change we will experience in classrooms and in co-curricular interactions. The arrival of students from other countries presents an opportunity for personal growth and intellectual exploration. International centres for students can help engage the campus in conversations about changing student demographics and help support international and cultural exchanges. Although instructors may be challenged in teaching a changing population of students in their courses, teaching and learning centres can help provide support and expertise in adapting curriculum and pedagogy and addressing cross-cultural understanding.

CONCLUSION

This book affirms that many colleges and universities across Canada have embraced the SEM planning framework to help address institutional enrolment goals. Changing demographics, increased competition regionally and nationally, and economic pressures have spurred the post-secondary sector and provincial governments alike to take a hard look at who we are serving and how we are educating our students. SEM professionals will continue to play a key role in helping their institutions adapt to new societal pressures and institutional fiscal realities. However, the Canadian SEM experience is still new. More research is needed and best practices must continue to be shared at workshops, conferences and through professional networks.

A key lesson learned is that strategic enrolment management does not belong to one academic or administrative department or to one professional organization. If we are to address emergent issues in our colleges and universities we must work together and break down institutional and disciplinary silos. The challenges facing SEM professionals in Canada may appear daunting; however the rewards of collaborating with academic and administrative partners across our campuses and our country to help our students enter our doors and succeed are enormous.

/ References and Resources /

REFERENCES

Ariely, D. 2008. *Predictably Irrational*. New York, NY: HarperCollins.

Association of Canadian Community Colleges and Human Resources and Social Development Canada. *Pan-Canadian Study of First Year College Students: Report 1 Student Characteristics and the College Experience*. 2007. Publication No. 978-0-662-46059-6. Gatineau, Quebec: Human Resources and Social Development Canada. Available at: <www.hrsdc.gc.ca/eng/publications_resources/learning_policy/sp_787_08_07e/sp_787_08_07e.pdf>.

Association of Canadian Community Colleges. 2010. *Colleges Serving Aboriginal Learners and Communities*. Ottawa: ACCC.

Association of Universities and Colleges of Canada. 2007. *Trends in Higher Education Volume 1: Enrolment*. Ottawa: AUCC.

———. 2008. October 6. *Canada Launches an Education Brand*. Retrieved March 4, 2011 from: <www.universityaffairs.ca/canada-launches-an-education-brand.aspx>.

———. 2010a. *Answering the call: The 2010 inventory of Canadian university programs and services for Aboriginal students* Ottawa: AUCC.

———. 2010b. Value of a Degree in the Global Marketplace. www.aucc.ca/value.

Astin, A.W. 1977. *Four Critical Years: Effects of College on Beliefs, Attitudes, and Knowledge*. San Francisco: Jossey-Bass.

———. 1993. *Assessment For Excellence: The Philosophy And Practice Of Assessment And Evaluation In Higher Education*. New York: American Council on Education, Oryx Press.

Auclair, R., P. Bélanger, P. Doray and M. Gallien. 2008. *Transitions—Research Paper 2—First-Generation Students: A Promising Concept?* Montreal: The Canada Millennium Scholarship Foundation. Retrieved January 4, 2011 from: <www.cirst.uqam.ca/Portals/0/docs/projet_transitions/TransitionsNote2-en-Final.pdf>.

Barr-Telford, L., F. Cartwrith, S. Prasil, and K. Shimmons. 2003. *Accès, persévérance et financement: premiers résultats de l'Enquête sur la participation aux études postsecondaires (EPÉP)*. Ottawa: Statistics Canada. Retrieved February 12, 2010 from: <www.statcan.gc.ca/pub/81-595-m/81-595-m2003007-fra.pdf>.

Barr, R.B., and J. Tagg. 1995. From teaching to learning—a new paradigm for undergraduate education. *Change*. 27(6): 13–25.

Belley, P., M. Frenette, and L. Lochner. 2011. *Post-Secondary Attendance, Parental Income, and Financial Aid: Comparing the U.S. and Canada. CIBC Centre for Human Capital and Productivity, 2011*. Retrieved April 4, 2011 from: <http://economics.uwo.ca/centres/cibc/wp2010/Belley_Frenette_Lochner03.pdf>.

Bennett, S. 2003. Redesigning libraries for learning. *Libraries Designed for Learning*. Washington, D.C.: Council on Library and Information Resources.

Berger, J. 2009, November. Participation in postsecondary education: Recent trends, in *The Price of Knowledge: Chapter 2*. Ottawa: Canada Millennium Scholarship Foundation.

Berger, J., and A. Motte. 2007. *Mind the Access Gap: Breaking Down Barriers to Post-Secondary Education.* Ottawa: Canada Millennium Scholarship Foundation.

Berger, J., and N. Baldwin. 2009. Student financial assistance in Canada: Past, present and future. *The Price of Knowledge: Access and Student Finance in Canada, Fourth Edition.* Montreal, QC: The Canada Millennium Scholarship Foundation, 151–180.

Bischoff, P.A. 2007. *Strategic Enrolment Management: Concepts, Structures and Strategies.* Retrieved November 20, 2010 from: <www.douglas.bc.ca/__shared/assets/SEM_Concepts__Structures_and_Strategies-Dec200750580.pdf>.

Black, J. 2008. University Enrolment Management. Keynote speech at Annual Meeting and Conference of the Ontario University Registrars' Association. Niagara Falls: OURA.

Blouw, M. 2010. *President's Welcome: Inspiring Lives of Leadership and Purpose.* Wilfred Laurier University. Accessed December 8, 2010 from: <www.wlu.ca/homepage.php?grp_id=2295&pv=1>.

Bolton, P., T. Pugliese, and J. Singleton-Jackson. 2009. Advancing the promotion of information literacy through peer-led learning. *Communications in Information Literacy.* 3(1): 20–30.

Bonikowska, A., and F. Hou. 2011. *Reversal of Fortunes or Continued Success? Cohort Differences in Education and Earnings of Childhood Immigrants.* Ottawa: Statistics Canada, Analytical Studies Branch Research Paper Series.

Bontrager, B. 2004a. Developing an enrolment management organization. In *Essentials of Enrolment Management: Case Studies in the Field*, edited by J. Black and Associates. Washington, D.C.: American Association of College Registrars and Admission Officers.

———. 2004b. Strategic enrolment management: Core structures and best practices. *College and University Journal.* 79(4): 9–15.

Bontrager, B., and B. Clemetsen. 2009. *Applying SEM at the Community College.* Washington, D.C.: American Association of Collegiate Registrars and Admissions Officers.

Bontrager, B., and C. Smith. 2009. *Strategic International Enrollment Management: A Preconference Workshop.* Presented at the Association of International Educational Administrators Conference, Atlanta, GA.

Bontrager, B., and K. Pollack. 2009. Strategic Enrollment Management at Community Colleges. In *Applying SEM at the Community College,* edited by B. Bontrager and B. Clemetsen. Washington, D.C.: AACRAO.

Bouchard, P., I. Boily, and M.C. Proulx. 2003. *La réussite scolaire comparée selon le sexe: catalyseur des discours masculinistes.* Ottawa: Status of Women Canada. Retrieved February 12, 2010 from: <http://dsp-psd.tpsgc.gc.ca/Collection/SW21-103-2003F.pdf>.

Braxton, John M., A.S. Hirschy, and S.A. McClendon. 2004. Understanding and reducing student departure. *ASHE-ERIC Higher Education Report.* 30(3).

British Columbia Council on Admissions and Transfer. 2010. What is a mobile student? Broadening the research framework beyond traditional transfer students. Vancouver: B.C. Council on Admissions and Transfer. Retrieved March 30, 2011 from: <www.bccat.ca/pubs/mobilitydiscussion.pdf>.

British Columbia Ministry of Regional Economic and Skills Development. 2011. *The Student Transitions Project.* Available at: <www.aved.gov.bc.ca/student_transitions/>.

British Columbia Transfer Guide. 2011. Available at: <www.bctransferguide.ca>.

Bui, K.V.T. 2002. First-generation college students at a four-year university: Background characteristics, reasons for pursuing higher education and first-year experiences. *College Student Journal.* 36 (1): 3–11.

Butlin, G. 1999. Determinants of post-secondary participation. *Education Quarterly Review.* 5(3): 9–35.

Canada Millennium Scholarship Foundation. 2005. *Changing Course: Improving Aboriginal Access to Post-Secondary Education in Canada.* Retrieved February 1, 2011 from: <http://qspace.library.queensu.ca/bitstream/1974/5735/1/mrn-changing-course-en.pdf>.

Canadian Council on Learning. 2009b. *Post-Secondary Education in Canada: Who is Missing Out? Lessons in Learning.* Retrieved on April 1, 2011 from: <www.ccl-cca.ca/CCL/Reports/LessonsinLearning/>.

———. 2010. Tallying the costs of post-secondary education: The challenge of managing student debt and loan repayment in Canada. In *Challenges in Canadian Post-Secondary Education.* Ottawa: Canadian Council on Learning.

CASE/Lipman Hearne. 2007. *CASE/Lipman Hearne 2007 Integrated Marketing Survey.*

Chapman, K. 1996. Entry qualifications, degree results and value-added in UK Universities. *Oxford Review of Education.* 22(3): 251–264.

Chen, X., and D.C. Carroll. 2005. *First-Generation Students in Post-Secondary Education: A Look at Their College Transcripts.* Washington D.C.: National Center for Education Statistics, Department of Education.

Chickering, A.W., and A.F. Gamson 1987. Seven principles for good practice in undergraduate education. *AAHE Bulletin.* 39: 3–7.

Chickering, A.W., and L. Reisser 1993. *Education and Identity, 2nd Ed.* San Francisco: Jossey-Bass.

Christensen Hughes, J., and J. Mighty. 2010. *Taking Stock: Research on Teaching and Learning in Higher Education.* Kingston, ON: McGill-Queen's University Press.

Cline, F.W., and J. Fay. 1990. *Parenting with Love and Logic: Teaching Children Responsibility.* Colorado Springs, CO: Pinion Press.

Commission Des Affaires Étudiantes. 2004a. *Avis de la commission des affaires étudiantes: Pour mieux soutenir les étudiantes et les étudiants dans leur projet d'études. Persévérance et réussite au 1er cycle.* Québec City: Université Laval. Retrieved February 12, 2010 from: <www.ulaval.ca/sg/greffe/Avis/version-1e1.pdf>.

———. 2004b. *Avis de la commission des affaires étudiantes : Pour mieux soutenir les étudiantes et les étudiants dans leur projet d'études. Persévérance et réussite aux 2e et 3e cycle.* Québec City: Université Laval. Retrieved February 12, 2010 from: <www.ulaval.ca/sg/greffe/Avis/version-2e-3e1.pdf>.

———. 2006. *Avis sur l'accueil, l'encadrement et l'intégration des étudiants étrangers à l'Université Laval.* Québec City: Université Laval. Retrieved February 12, 2010 from: <www.ulaval.ca/sg/greffe/AvisfinalCAE.pdf>.

———. 2010 *Les études et la vie étudiante : conciliation-flexibilité-adaptation.* Québec City: Université Laval. Retrieved April 11, 2010 from: <www.ulaval.ca/sg/greffe/AvisCAE2010.pdf>.

Commission Des Études. 2006. *Les études à l'Université Laval: Constats et perspectives. Rapport synthèse.* Québec City: Université Laval. Retrieved April 11, 2010 from: <www.ulaval.ca/sg/greffe/etudes_constats_et_perspectives.pdf>.

———. 2010. *S'éduquer au monde chez soi: La formation locale à l'international.* Québec City: Université Laval. Retrieved May 12, 2010 from: <www.ulaval.ca/sg/greffe/formationlocale_a_linternational.pdf>.

Conseil Supérieur De L'éducation. 1988. *Le rapport Parent, 25 ans après. Rapport annuel 1987–1988 sur l'état et les besoins de l'éducation.* Sainte-Foy: Conseil supérieur de l'Éducation.

———. 1995. *Pour la réforme du système éducatif. Dix années de consultation et de réflexion.* Ste-Foy: Conseil supérieur de l'Éducation.

———. 2009. *L'accès à l'éducation et l'accès à la réussite dans une perspective d'éducation pour l'inclusion.* Consultation document, Québec City : Conseil supérieur de l'éducation.

———. 2010. *Rapport sur l'état et les besoins de l'éducation 2008-10: Conjuguer équité et performance en éducation, un défi de société.* Québec City: Conseil supérieur de l'éducation.

Constantineau, P. 2009, July. *The Ontario Transfer Credit System: A Situation Report.* Council of Ontario Universities.

Copper, B. 2008. Changing demographics: Why non-traditional students should matter to enrollment managers and what they can do to attract them. *SEM Source.* November. Washington, D.C.: American Association of Collegiate Registrars and Admissions Officers.

Corak, M., G. Lipps, and J. Zhao. 2003. *Family Income and Participation in Post-Secondary Education.* Ottawa: Statistics Canada.

Coulon, A. 1997. *Le métier d'étudiant: l'entrée dans la vie universitaire.* Paris: Presses Universitaires de France.

Council of Ministers of Education. 2009. *CMEC Ministerial Statement on Credit Transfer in Canada.* Toronto: Council of Ministers of Education.

———. 2010. *Education Indicators in Canada: An International Perspective.* Ottawa: Statistics Canada.

CREPUQ. *See* Conference of Rectors and Principals of Québec Universities.

Currie, S., and D. Leonard. 2009. *Report on the Data-Readiness of Post-Secondary Access and Retention Programs for Under-Represented Groups.* Montreal: Canada Millennium Scholarship Foundation. Retrieved August 4, 2010 from: <www.srdc.org/en_publication_details.asp?id=236&mode=1&ret=%2Fen%5Fsearch%2Easp>.

Cuseo J. 2010. *Student Success: What Defines It? What Promotes It? What Really Matters?* Antwerp: Fifth European Conference on the First-Year Experience.

De Brouker, P., and L. Lavallée. 1998. Getting ahead in life: Does your parents' education count? *Canadian Social Trends*. 49.

Deloria, V. Jr., and D. Wildcat. 2001. *Power and Place: Indian Education in America*. Golden, CO: Fulcrum Publishing.

Dolence, M.G. 1993. *Strategies in Enrolment Management: A Primer for Campus Administrators*. Washington, D.C.: American Association of College Registrars and Admission Officers.

Dooley, M.D., A.A. Payne, and A.L. Robb. 2008. *Guaranteed Merit-Based Scholarships and the Characteristics of Entering Students at Ontario Universities* (Working Paper). Department of Economics, Hamilton. Ontario: McMaster University.

———. 2010. *Merit-Aid and the Distribution of Entering Students across Ontario Universities* (CLSRN Working Paper #57). Hamilton, ON: Department of Economics, McMaster University.

Drewes, T., and C. Michael. 2006. How do students choose a university?: An analysis of applications to universities in Ontario, Canada. *Research in Higher Education*. 47(7): 701–800.

Drolet, M. 2005. *Participation in Post-Secondary Education in Canada: Has the Role of Parental Income and Education Changed over the 1990s?* Ottawa: Statistics Canada.

Engle, J., and V. Tinto. 2008. *Moving Beyond Access: College Success for Low-Income, First-Generation Students*. Washington D.C.: The Pell Institute for the Study of Opportunity in Higher Education.

Engle, J., A. Bermeo, and C. O'Brien. 2006. December. *Straight from the Source. What Works for First Generation College Students*. Washington D.C.: The Pell Institute for the Study of Opportunity in Higher Education.

Environics Institute. 2010. *Urban Aboriginal Peoples Study: Main Report*. Toronto: Environics Institute. Retrieved June 28 from: <http://uaps.twg.ca/wp-content/uploads/2010/04/UAPS-FULL-REPORT.pdf>.

Finnie, R., R.E. Mueller, A. Sweetman, and A. Usher. 2008. *Who Goes? Who Stays? What Matters? Accessing and Persisting in Post-Secondary Education in Canada*. Kingston, ON: McGill-Queen's University Press.

———. 2010a. New perspectives on access to post-secondary education. *Education Matters: Insights on Education, Learning and Training in Canada*. 7(1). Retrieved December 4, 2010 from: <www.statcan.gc.ca/pub/81-004-x/2010001/article/11152-eng.htm>.

Finnie, R., S. Childs, and A. Wismer. 2010b. *Introduction to the Longitudinal Survey of Low-Income Students*. A MESA Project. Toronto: Canadian Education Project.

———. 2010c. *First Generation Post-Secondary Education Students* (version 02–24–10). A MESA Project L-SLIS Research Brief. Toronto: Canadian Education Project.

Finnie, R., S. Childs, K. Korducki, and A. Wismer. 2010d. *Gender and Post-Secondary Education* (Version 11–18–10), A MESA Project L-SLIS Research Brief. Toronto: Canadian Education Project.

Fisher, J. 1977. *Money Isn't Everything: A Survival Manual for Non-profit Organizations*. Toronto: Management and Fund Raising Centre, Pub. Division.

Gaber, D. 2002. *Provincial Coordination and Inter-Institutional Collaboration in British Columbia's College, University College, and Institute System* (doctoral dissertation). Corvallis, OR: Oregon State University.

———. December 2006. *Degree Partnerships in the BC Context: A Special Report*. Vancouver: B.C. Council on Admissions and Transfer. Retrieved March 30, 2011 from: <www.bccat.ca/pubs/sr_dec06.pdf>.

Gauthier, H., S. Jean, G. Langis, Y. Nobert, and M. Rochon. 2004. *Vie des générations et personnes âgées: aujourd'hui et demain, Vol. 1*. Québec: Institut de la statistique du Québec. Retrieved February 12, 2010 from: <www.stat.gouv.qc.ca/publications/conditions/pdf/VieGeneration Vol1.pdf>.

Gauthier, L. 2007. *Retention and Persistence: A First Nations Perspective*. Unpublished master's thesis. Minneapolis, MN: Department of Education, Capella University.

Gofen, A. 2009. Family Capital: How first-generation higher education students break the intergenerational cycle. *Family Relations*. 58: 104–120.

Goff, J., and J.E. Lane 2007. *Building a SEM Organization: The Internal Consultant Approach.* Conference Paper, AACRAO SEM Conference.

Gordon, J., and J. Mitchell. 2010. Partnering for success: A collaborative approach to student persistence. *AACRAO SEM Source.* Spring. Retrieved March 30, 2011 from: <www.aacrao.org/sem/>.

Grant, A. 1995. The challenge for universities. In *The Circle Unfolds: First Nation's Education in Canada,* edited by M. Battiste and J. Barman. Vancouver: UBC Press.

Grayson, J.P. 1997. Academic achievement of first-generation students in a Canadian university. *Research in Higher Education.* 38(6): 659–676.

Grayson, P. 2003. *Les recherches sur le maintien et la diminution des effectifs étudiants.* Montréal: Canada Millenium Scholarship Foundation. Retrieved February 12, 2010 from: <https://qspace.library.queensu.ca/bitstream/1974/5794/1/maintien_final.pdf>.

Hango, D., and P. de Broucker. 2005. *Post-Secondary Enrolment Trends to 2031: Three Scenarios.* Ottawa: Statistics Canada.

Hauserman, C., and S. Stick. 2005. The history of post-secondary finance in Alberta—An analysis. *Canadian Journal of Educational Administration and Policy.* Issue #42.

Hayes, T.J. 2009. *Marketing Colleges and Universities: A Services Approach.* Washington, D.C.: Council for Advancement and Support of Education.

HeavyRunner, I., and R. DeCelles. 2002. Family education model: Meeting the student retention challenge. *Journal of American Indian Education.* 41(2).

Henderson, S.E. 2005. Refocusing enrolment management: Losing structure and finding context. *College and University.* 80(3): 3–8.

Heslop, J. 2009. *Student Mobility in B.C.'s Public Post-Secondary Education System.* Victoria, B.C.: Student Transitions Project. Retrieved March 30, 2011 from: <www.aved.gov.bc.ca/student_transitions/documents/stp_highlights_dec09.pdf>.

Hoover, E. 2006. The rise of 'stealth applicants'. *The Chronicle of Higher Education.* 52(30): A40.

Hossler, D. 1986. *Creating Effective Enrolment Management Systems.* Newark: College Entrance Examination Board.

Hossler, D., and D. Kalsbeek. 2008. Enrollment Management and Managing Enrollment. *College and University Journal.* 83(4): 2–9.

Hossler, D., and J.P. Bean and Associates. 1990. *The Strategic Management of College Enrollments.* San Francisco: Jossey-Bass.

Hossler, D., J. Schmit, and N. Vesper. 1999. *Going to College.* Baltimore, MD: The John Hopkins University Press.

Inman, W.E., and L. Mayes. 1999. The importance of being first: Unique characteristics of first generation community college students. *Community College Review.* 26(4): 3–22.

Indiana University. 2010. *National Survey on Student Engagement.* Retrieved July 30, 2010 from: <http://nsse.iub.edu>.

Ivan, S., and S. Kernahan. 2010. *Streamlining the Enrolment Process through a Legal Lens: Legal Issues and Duty to Accommodate in Admissions and Enrolment.* 2010 AACRAO SEM 20 Conference presentation.

Junor, S., and A. Usher. 2007. *The End of Need-Based Student Financial Aid in Canada?* Toronto: Educational Policy Institute.

Kalsbeek, D.H. 2003. *Redefining SEM: New Perspectives & New Priorities.* Keynote presentation at AACRAO's SEM XIII, Boston MA.

———. 2006a. Some reflections on SEM structures and strategies (part one). *College and University.* 81(3): 3–10.

———. 2006b. Some reflections on SEM structures and strategies (part two). *College and University.* 81(4): 3–10.

Kamanzi, P.C., S. Bonin, P. Doray, A. Groleau, J. Murdoch, P. Mercier, C. Blanchard, M. Gallien, and R. Auclair. 2010. *Note 9: Academic Persistence Among First-Generation University Students.* Montreal: Centre interuniversitaire de recherche sur la science et la technologie (CIRST).

Keeling, R.P., A.F. Wall, R. Underhile, and G.J. Dungy. 2008. *Assessment Reconsidered: Institutional Effectiveness for Student Success.* Washington, D.C.: International Centre for Student Success and Institutional Accountability.

Kerr, A., U. McCloy, and S. Liu. 2010. *Forging Pathways: Students Who Transfer Between Ontario Colleges and Universities.* Toronto: Higher Education Quality Council of Ontario.

Kim, Y.K., and L.J. Sax. 2009. Student-faculty interaction in research universities: Differences by student gender, race, social class and first generation status. *Research in Higher Education.* 50: 437–459.

King, P.M., and M.F. Howard-Hamilton. 2000. Using student development theory to inform institutional research. *New Directions for Institutional Research.* 108: 19–36.

Kinzie, J. 2010. Student engagement and learning: Experiences that matter. In *Taking Stock: Research on Teaching and Learning in Higher Education*, edited by J. Christensen Hughes and J. Mighty. Kingston, ON: McGill-Queen's University Press.

Kirkness, V. 1999. Aboriginal education in Canada: A retrospective and a prospective. *Journal of American Indian Education.* 9(1).

Knapper. C. 2010. Changing teaching practice: Barriers and strategies. In *Taking Stock: Research on Teaching and Learning in Higher Education*, edited by J. Christensen Hughes and J. Mighty. Kingston, ON: McGill-Queen's University Press.

Knighton, T., and S. Mirza. 2002. Post-secondary participation: The effects of parents' education and household income. *Education Quarterly Review.* 8(3): 25–32.

Knowledge Network. 2008. *The Graduates: A History of Higher Education in B.C.* Video documentary.

Kotler, P., and K.A. Fox. 1995. *Strategic Marketing for Educational Institutions, 2nd Edition.* Englewood Hills, NJ: Prentice-Hall.

Kuh, G.D. 2009. *Conditions et pratiques éducatives qui favorisent l'engagement de l'étudiant et le succès dans ses études.* Montréal: Carrefour de la réussite au collégial.

Kuh, G.D., J. Kinzie, J.H. Schuh, and E.J. Whitt. 2005a. *Student Success in College: Creating Conditions That Matter.* San Francisco: Jossey-Bass.

———. 2005b. *Assessing the Conditions to Enhance Educational Effectiveness: The Inventory for Student Engagement and Success.* San Francisco: Jossey-Bass.

Lacasse, N., and J. Morneau. 2008. *Principaux enjeux du recrutement à l'Université Laval et gestion des effectifs étudiants.* Powerpoint Slideshow, December 5, 2008. Québec: Université Laval.

Langhout, R.D., P. Drake, and F. Rosselli. 2009. Classism in the university setting: Examining student antecedents and outcomes. *Journal of Diversity in Higher Education.* 2(3): 166–181.

Lasselle, L., F. Keir, and I. Smith. 2009. Enhancing pupils' aspirations to university: The St. Andrews

Sutton Trust School experience. *Journal of Further and Higher Education.* 33(4): 395–410.

Lauer, L.D. 2002. *Competing for Students, Money, and Reputation: Marketing the Academy in the 21st Century.* Washington, D.C.: Council for Advancement and Support of Education.

Lehmann, W. 2007. "I just don't feel like I fit in:" The role of habitus in university drop-out decisions. *Canadian Journal of Higher Education.* 17(2): 89–110.

———. 2009a. Becoming middle class: How working-class university students draw and transgress moral class boundaries. *Sociology.* 42(4): 631–647.

———. 2009b. University as vocational education: Working-class students' expectations for university. *British Journal of Sociology of Education.* 30(2): 137–149.

Leung, C., R. Harris, and B. Rampton. 1997. The idealised native speaker, reified ethnicities, and classroom realities. *Tesol Quarterly.* 31(3): 543–558.

LEVEL5 Strategic Brand Advisors. 2010. *University of New Brunswick "Building for the Future" Integrated Marketing Plan.* Toronto: Bruce Elliot.

London, H.B. 1989. Breaking away: A study of first-generation college students and their families. *American Journal of Education.* 97(2): 144–170.

———. 1992. Transformations: Cultural challenges faced by first-generation students. *New Directions for Community Colleges.* 80: 5–11.

Luckett, K., and T. Luckett. 2009. The development of agency in first generation learners in higher education: A social realist analysis. *Teaching in Higher Education.* 14(5): 469–481.

Macdonald, J.B. 1962. *Higher Education in British Columbia and A Plan for the Future.* Vancouver: The University of British Columbia.

Macleans. 2010. *University Rankings.* November 22.

Malatest and Associates, R.A. 2009. *Access to Opportunity First Generation Initiative: Evaluation of Selected Projects.* Toronto: Ministry of Training, Colleges and Universities.

Marshall, S. 2010. Re-becoming ESL: Multilingual university students and a deficit identity. *Language and Education.* 24(1): 21–39.

Martinez, J.A., K.J. Sher, J.L. Krull, and P.K. Wood. 2009. Blue-collar scholars? Mediators and moderators of university attrition in first-generation college students. *Journal of College Student Development.* 50(1): 87–103.

McElroy, L.A. 2006. *The Impact of Bursaries: Debt and Student Persistence in Post-Secondary Education*. Montreal: Canada Millennium Scholarship Foundation. Retrieved August 4, 2010 from: <www.library.carleton.ca/ssdata/surveys/doc/pdf_files/millennium_2006-07_rn-4_en.pdf>.

McIvor, R. 2010. *Block Transfer: A Private Career College Student's Ladder into the BC Transfer System*. Vancouver: B.C. Council on Admissions and Transfer. Retrieved March 30, 2011 from: <www.bccat.ca/pubs/sr_block2010.pdf>.

MELS. *See* Ministère de l'Éducation, du Loisir et du Sport.

Mendelson, M. 2006. *Aboriginal Peoples and Post-secondary Education in Canada*. Ottawa: The Caledon Institute of Social Policy.

Mendelson, M., and A. Usher. 2007. *The Aboriginal University Education Round Table*. The University of Winnipeg. Retrieved August 18, 2010 from: <www.uwinnipeg.ca/index/cms-filesystem-action?file=pdfs/conferences/2007/Aboriginal-rt-spring-report.pdf>.

Meuller, R.E. 2008. Access and persistence of students in Canadian post-secondary education: What we know, what we don't know, and why it matters. In *Who Goes? Who Stays? What Matters? Accessing and Persisting in Post-Secondary Education in Canada*. Kingston, ON: McGill-Queen's University Press.

Ministère de l'Éducation, du Loisir et du Sport. 2008. *Indicateurs de l'éducation*. Québec: Ministère de l'Éducation, du Loisir et du Sport.

Ministère de l'Industrie et du Commerce. 2001. *L'économie du savoir 1984–1999*. Québec: Ministère de l'Industrie et du Commerce.

Mohawk College of Applied Arts and Technology in Ontario. 2007. *Five Year Strategic Enrolment Plan, 2008–2009 to 2012–2013*.

Moore, M., D. Hayward, V. Garcia, T. Thompson, and J. Cash. 2010. *Decision Support: From IR, IE, and Planning to Comprehensive Information Management*. Chicago: 2010 AIR Annual Forum.

Morais, R. 2001. Qualitatively speaking: The end of focus groups. *Quirks Marketing Research Review*. Retrieved March 4, 20 11 from: <http://quirks.com/articles/a2001/20010502.aspx?searchID=115918715>.

Murray, J., and A. Summerlee. 2007. The Impact of problem-based learning in an interdisciplinary first-year program on student learning behaviour. *Canadian Journal of Higher Education*. 37(3): 87–107.

Noel-Levitz. 2009. *Linking Student Satisfaction and Retention*. Coralville, IA: Noel-Levitz. Retrieved February 12, 2010 from: <www.no-ellevitz.com/documents/shared/Papers_and_Research/2009/LinkingStudentSatis0809.pdf>.

Norris, D., L. Baer, J. Leonard, L. Pugliese, and P. Lefrere. 2008. Action analytics: Measuring and improving performance that matters in higher education. *EDUCAUSE Review*.43(1): 42–67.

OECD. *See* Organisation for Economic Co-operation and Development.

Orbe, M.P. 2004. Negotiating multiple identities within multiple frames: An analysis of first generation college students. *Communication Education*. 53(2): 131–149.

Organisation for Economic Co-operation and Development. 1998. *Regards sur l'éducation, les indicateurs de l'OECD*. Paris: OECD.

———. 2008. *Tertiary Education for the Knowledge Society: Volumes 1 and 2*. Paris: OECD. Retrieved November 23, 2010 from: <www.oecd.org/document/35/0,3343,en_2649_39263238_36021283_1_1_1,00.html.

———. 2009. *OECD Science, Technology and Industry Scoreboard 2009: Canada Highlights*. Paris: OECD. Retrieved January 7, 2011 from: <www.oecd.org/document/52/0,3746,en_2649_33703_44265268_1_1_1,00.html.

Orum, J. 2010. *Flexible Pre-Majors: Improving the BC Transfer System for Students and Institutions*. Vancouver: B.C. Council on Admissions and Transfer. Retrieved March 30, 2011 from: <www.bccat.ca/pubs/sr_feb10.pdf>.

Padron, E.J. 1992. The challenge of first-generation college students: A Miami-Dade perspective. *New Directions for Community Colleges*. 80: 71–80.

Palameta, B., and J.P. Voyer. 2010. *Willingness to Pay for Post-Secondary Education among Under-Represented Groups*. Toronto: HECQO.

Parent Commission (Le rapport Parent). 1963. *Rapport Parent, Première partie ou Tome I: Les structures supérieures du système scolaire*. Québec: Les Publications du Québec. Retrieved March 30, 2011 from: <http://classiques.uqac.ca/contemporains/quebec_commission_parent/rapport_parent_1/rapport_parent%20_vol_1.pdf>.

Parkin, A. 2009. Conclusion: From research to action. In *The Price of Knowledge: Access and Student Finance in Canada, Fourth Edition*, edited by J. Berger, A. Motte, and A. Parkin. Montreal: The Canada Millennium Scholarship Foundation.

Parkin, A., and N. Baldwin. 2009a. Persistence in post-secondary education. In *The Price of Knowledge: Access and Student Finance in Canada, Fourth Edition*, edited by J. Berger, A. Motte, and A. Parkin. Montreal: The Canada Millennium Scholarship Foundation.

———. 2009b. *Persistence in Post-Secondary Education in Canada: The Latest Research* (Research Note #8). Montreal: Canada Millennium Scholarship Foundation.

Pascarella, E.T. 1991. *How College Affects Students: Findings and Insights from Twenty Years of Research*. San Francisco: Jossey-Bass.

Pascarella, E.T., and P.T. Terenzini. 2005. *How College Affects Students: A Third Decade of Research*. San Francisco: Jossey-Bass.

PCCAT. *See* The Pan-Canadian Consortium on Admissions & Transfer/Consortium pancanadien sur les admissions et les transferts.

Pike, G.R., and G.D. Kuh. 2005. First- and second-generation college students: A comparison of their engagement and intellectual development. *The Journal of Higher Education*. 76(3): 276–300.

Pintrich, P.R., and E.V. DeGroot 1990. Motivational and self-regulated learning components of classroom academic performance. *Journal of Educational Psychology*. 82(1): 33–40.

Pitkethly, A., and M. Prosser. 2001. The first-year experience project: A model for university-wide change. *Higher Education Research & Development*. 20(2): 185–198.

Pittman, L.D., and A. Richmond. 2008. University belonging, friendship quality, and psychological adjustment during the transition to college. *The Journal of Experimental Education*. 76(4): 343–361.

Pocklington, T., and A. Tupper. 2002. *No Place to Learn: Why Universities Aren't Working*. Vancouver: UBC Press.

Preston, J.P. 2008a. Overcoming the obstacles: Post-secondary education and Aboriginal peoples. *Brock Education Journal for Education Research and Practise*. 18(1): 57–65. Retrieved February 2, 2011 from: <www3.ed.brocku.ca/ojs/index.php/brocked/article/viewFile/248/277>.

———. 2008b. The urgency of post-secondary education for Aboriginal Peoples. *Canadian Journal of Educational Administration and Policy*. Issue 86 (November 19). Retrieved February 2, 2011 from: <www.umanitoba.ca/publications/cjeap/articles/preston.html>.

Priebe, L.C., T.L. Ross and K.W. Low. 2008. Exploring the role of distance education in fostering equitable university access for first-generation students: A phenomenological survey. *International Review of Research in Open and Distance Learning*. 9(1): 1–10.

Rae, B. 2005. *Ontario: A Leader in Learning. Report & Recommendations*. Toronto: Ministry of Training, Colleges & Universities.

Rahman, A., J. Situ, and V. Jimmo. 2005. *Participation in Post-Secondary Education: Evidence from the Survey of Labour and Income Dynamics*. Ottawa: Statistics Canada.

Reay, D., G. Crozier, and J. Clayton. 2009. Strangers in paradise? Working-class students in elite universities. *Sociology*. 43(6): 1103–1121.

———. 2010. Fitting in or standing out: Working-class students in UK higher education. *British Educational Research Journal*. 36(1): 107–124.

Ries, A., and J. Trout. 2001. *Positioning*. New York, New York: McGraw-Hill.

Robins, R.W., R.C. Fraley, B.W. Roberts, and K.H. Trzesniewski. 2001. A longitudinal study of personality change in young adulthood. *Journal of Personality*. 69(4): 617–640.

Romainville, M. 1998. Peut-on prédire la réussite d'une première année universitaire? *Revue française de pédagogie*. 119: 93–102.

———. 2000. *L'échec dans l'université de masse*. Paris: L'Harmattan.

———. 2009. L'estime de soi des étudiants de première année du supérieur en abandon d'études. *L'orientation scolaire et professionnelle*. 38(2): 205–230.

Rose, R. 2003. *Connecting the Dots...The Essence of Planning: The Best of Planning for Higher Education 1997–2003*. Ann Arbour, MI: Society for College and University Planning.

Sadeshi, S. 2008. Gender, culture and learning: Iranian immigrant women in Canadian higher education. *Journal of Lifelong Education*. 27(2): 217–234.

Sanchez, R.J., T.N. Bauer, and M.E. Paronto. 2006. Peer-mentoring freshmen: Implications for satisfaction, commitment and retention to graduation. *Academy of Management Learning & Education.* 5(1): 25–37.

Sauvé, L., G. Debeurme, A. Wright, J. Fournier, É. Fontaine, L. Poulette, and A. Lachance. 2006. *L'abandon et la persévérance aux études postsecondaires : les données récentes de la recherche.* Montréal: TÉLUQ-UQAM. Retrieved March 1, 2011 from: <www.aeteluq.org/mirador/documents/recension_reussite-2005.pdf>.

Sedlacek, W.E. 2004. *Beyond the Big Test: Noncognitive Assessment in Higher Education.* San Francisco, CA: Jossey-Bass.

Seggumba, E. 2010. Interview by Stefanie Ivan. Edmonton, October 11, 2010.

Shaienks, D., and T. Gluszynski. 2007. *Participation in Post-Secondary Education: Graduates, Continuers and Drop Outs, Results from YITS Cycle 4.* Ottawa: Statistics Canada.

Shields, N. 2002. Anticipatory socialization, adjustment to university life and perceived stress: generational and sibling effects. *Social Psychology of Education.* 5: 365–392.

Simonsohn, U. 2010. Weather to go to college. *Economic Journal.* 120(543): 270–280.

Skinner, E.A., and M.J. Belmont 1993. Motivation in the classroom: Reciprocal effects of teacher behavior and student engagement across the school year. *Journal of Educational Psychology.* 85(4): 571–581.

Skolnik, M. 2010. A look back at the decision on the transfer function at the founding of Ontario's Colleges of Applied Arts and Technology, *Canadian Journal of Higher Education.* 40(2): 1–17.

Smith, C., and S. Gottheil. 2008. Enrollment or Enrolment: Strategic Enrollment Management in the United States and Canada. *College and University.* 84(2): 28–38.

———. 2010. *Introduction to Strategic Enrolment Management.* Conference Presentation, Canadian SEM Summit.

Social Research and Demonstration Corporation 2009a. Students from lower-income families more likely to seek post-secondary education as a result of new innovative programming. *News* section, November 30. Retrieved August 4, 2010 from: <http://www.srdc.org/en_news_details.asp?id=27916>.

Somers, P., and J. Settle. 2010. The helicopter parent: Research toward a typology (Part I). *College and University.* 86(1): 18–27.

Spring, J.H. 2009. *Globalization of Education: An Introduction.* New York: Routledge.

SRDC. *See* Social Research and Demonstration Corporation.

Statistics Canada. 2006. *Educational Portrait of Canada, 2006 Census: Highlights.* Retrieved January 6, 2011 from: <www12.statcan.ca/census-recensement/2006/as-sa/97-560/p1-eng.cfm>.

———. 2007. *The Evolving Linguistic Portrait, 2006 Census.* Retrieved on September 26, 2010 from: <www12.statcan.ca/census-recensement/2006/as-sa/97-555/pdf/97-555-XIE2006001-eng.pdf>.

———. 2008a. *2006 Census of Population.* Catalogue No. 97-560-XCB2006036. Ottawa.

———. 2008c. *Canada's Ethnocultural Mosaic, 2006 Census.* Retrieved on September 26, 2010 from: <www12.statcan.ca/census-recensement/2006/as-sa/97-562/pdf/97-562-XIE2006001.pdf>.

———. 2010b. *Table 477-0015: College Enrolments, by Registration Status, Program Level, Classification of Instructional Programs, Primary Grouping (CIP_PG) and Sex, Annual (Number).* CANSIM (database). Ottawa: Statistics Canada.

Summerlee, A.J. S., and J. Christensen Hughes. 2010. Pressures for change and the future of university education. In *Taking Stock: Research on Teaching and Learning in Higher Education,* edited by J. Christensen Hughes and J. Mighty. Kingston, ON: McGill-Queen's University Press.

Terenzini, P.T., L. Springer, P.M. Yaeger, E. T, Pascarella, and A. Nora. 1996. First generation college students: Characteristics, experiences and cognitive development. *Research in Higher Education.* 37(1): 1–22.

The Pan-Canadian Consortium on Admissions & Transfer/Consortium pancanadien sur les admissions et les transferts. 2010. *(Home Page).* Retrieved from: <www.pccat.ca>.

The University of Manitoba. 2009. *Policy on Non-Acceptance of Discriminatory Awards.* Retrieved August 4, 2010 from: <http://umanitoba.ca/admin/governance/governing_documents/academic/370.htm>.

Timmons, V. 2009. *Retention of Aboriginal Students in Post-Secondary Institutions in Atlantic Canada: An Analysis of the Supports Available to Aboriginal Students.* Ottawa: Canadian Council on Learning. Retrieved February 2, 2011 from: <www.ccl-cca.ca/pdfs/FundedResearch/Timmons-ExSum-EN.pdf>.

Ting, S.R. 1998. Predicting first-year grades and academic progress of college students of first-generation and low-income families. *Journal of College Admission*. 158: 14–23.

Tinto, V. 1987, 1993. *Leaving College: Rethinking the Causes and Cures of Student Departure*. Chicago: The University of Chicago Press.

———. 1995. *Educational Communities and Student Success in the First Year of University*. Paper prepared for the Conference on the Transition from Secondary School to University. Melbourne, AU: Monash University.

Toope, S.J. 2006. *Here It Is—It Is Yours*. Installation Address of President Stephen J. Toope as Twelfth President and Vice-Chancellor of The University of British Columbia. Retrieved on March 8, 2011 from: <http://president.ubc.ca/files/2010/04/installation_address_20060929.pdf>.

Torjman, S. 2010. *Barriers to Post-Secondary Education*. Ottawa: Caledon Institute of Social Policy.

Tremblay, L. 2005. La réussite à l'université et l'accès au diplôme. État des connaissances de la recherche institutionnelle hors-Québec. In *L'enjeu de la réussite dans l'enseignement supérieur*, edited by P. Chénard and P. Doray. Sainte-Foy: Presses de l'Université du Québec.

Trescases, U. 2008. *The Role of the Library in the First College Year: The Canadian Perspective*. Presentation at Annual Conference of the Society for Teaching and Learning in Higher Education, University of Toronto, Ontario.

Université Laval (Québec City). 2001. *Politique d'accueil, d'intégration et d'encadrement des étudiants*, CU-2001–100. Retrieved from: <www.bi.ulaval.ca/pdf/accueil_encadrement.pdf>.

——— 2002. *Politique d'intégration des personnes handicapées étudiantes à l'Université Laval*. CA-2002–36. Retrieved from: <www.bi.ulaval.ca/pdf/accueil_encadrement.pdf>.

——— 2004a. *Politique sur l'usage du français*, CA-2004–150. Retrieved from: <www.aide.ulaval.ca/sgc/pid/1871>.

———. 2004b. *Rapport du groupe de travail sur les suites à donner à l'avis de la commission des affaires étudiantes sur la persévérance et la réussite au 1er cycle sous l'angle du recrutement étudiant* .

——— 2008a. *Horizon 2012: Orientations de développement de l'Université Laval*. Québec City: Université Laval. Retrieved from: <www2.ulaval.ca/fileadmin/cabinetrecteur/brochure_horizon2012_3.pdf>.

——— 2008b. *Politique d'encadrement des étudiants à la maitrise avec mémoire et au doctorat*, CU-2008–37.

———. Commission des affaires étudiantes. 2004a. *Persévérance et réussite au 1er cycle*. Retrieved from: <www.ulaval.ca/sg/greffe/Avis/version-1e1.pdf>.

———. Commission des affaires étudiantes. 2004b. *Pour mieux soutenir les étudiantes et les étudiants dans leur projet d'études: persévérance et réussite et aux 2e et 3e cycles*. Retrieved from: <www.ulaval.ca/sg/greffe/Avis/version-2e-3e1.pdf>.

———. Commission des affaires étudiantes. 2006. *L'accueil, l'encadrement et l'intégration des étudiants étrangers à l'Université Laval - Rapport synthèse*. Retrieved from: <www.ulaval.ca/sg/greffe/AvisfinalCAE.pdf>.

———. Commission des affaires étudiantes. 2010. *Les études et la vie étudiante : conciliation-flexibilité-adaptation*. Retrieved from: <www.ulaval.ca/sg/greffe/AvisCAE2010.pdf>.

———. Commission des études. 2006. *Les études à l'Université Laval: Constats et perspectives. Rapport synthèse*. Retrieved from: <www.ulaval.ca/sg/greffe/etudes_constats_et_perspectives.pdf>.

———. Commission des études. 2010. *S'éduquer au monde chez soi: La formation locale à l'international*. Retrieved from: <www.ulaval.ca/sg/greffe/formationlocale_a_linternational.pdf>.

University of British Columbia. 2009. *Place and Promise: The UBC Plan*. Retrieved August 4, 2010 from: <http://strategicplan.ubc.ca/files/2009/11/UBCStrategicPlan.pdf>.

University of Guelph. 2008. *Facts and Figures 2008: Student Quality and Performance*. Retrieved April 1, 2011 from: <www.uoguelph.ca/info/facts2008/student/>.

University of Saskatchewan. 2009. *Achievement record*. Retrieved December 8, 2010 from: <www.usask.ca/achievementrecord/achievement-record-2009.pdf>.

———. 2011. *The University of Saskatchewan Enrolment Plan: Bridging to 2010*. Retrieved March 17, 2011 from: <www.usask.ca/ip/inst_planning/docs/new_EPlanFINAL.pdf>.

University of Toronto. Governing Council. 1998. *Policy on Student Financial Support*. Retrieved August 4, 2010 from: <www.governingcouncil.utoronto.ca/Assets/Governing%2BCouncil%2BDigital%2BAssets/Policies/PDF/ppapr301998.pdf>.

University of Windsor. 2011. *Strategic Enrolment Management Resource Library*. Retrieved March 17, 2011 from: <www.uwindsor.ca/sem/overview/>.

University of Winnipeg. 2010. *The University of Winnipeg Mission Statement*. Retrieved August 4, 2010 from: <www.uwinnipeg.ca/index/hr-mission>.

Usher, A. 2011. *Canadian University Report 2011*. Toronto: The Globe and Mail.

Wallace-Hulecki, L. 2009. *Creating a Sense of Belonging: Strategies for Enhancing Student Diversity and Success*. Greensboro: SEM Works.

Wright, W.A. 2010. Mind the gap: Aligning research and practice in teaching, learning, and educational development. In *Taking Stock: Research on Teaching and Learning in Higher Education*, edited by J. Christensen Hughes and J. Mighty. Kingston, ON: McGill-Queen's University Press.

Wright, W.A., and M.J. Monette. 2010. *Ensemble for Engagement*. Presentation at the annual conference of the Educational Developers Caucus. Thompson Rivers University, Kamloops, BC.

Wright, W.A., M. Frenay, M. Monette, B. Tomen, L. Sauvé, C. Smith, N. Gold, D. Houston, J. Robinson, and N. Rowen 2008. *Institutional Strategy And Practice: Increasing The Odds Of Access And Success At The Post-Secondary Level For Under-Represented Students*. Montreal: The Canadian Millennium Scholarship Foundation.

Zaltman, G. 2003. *How Customers Think*. Boston: Harvard Business School Press.

RESOURCES

Andreasen, A.R. 1988. *Cheap But Good Marketing Research*. Homewood, IL: Dow-Jones Irwin.

Apply Alberta. 2011. *About Apply Alberta*. Retrieved February 8 from: <www.applyalberta.ca/pub/about.asp>.

Bailey, S., S. Kruk, and T. Ogunyemi 2008. *How to Succeed in Math by Really Learning: A Controlled Experiment in Precalculus Instruction*. Presentation at the second annual University of Windsor-Oakland University Teaching and Learning Conference, Oakland University Rochester, MI.

Barnes, N.G. 2009. *Reaching the Wired Generation: How Social Media is Changing College Admission*. Arlington, VA: National Association for College Admission Counselling.

Bartlett, R. 1980. Citizens minus: Indians and the right to vote. *Saskatchewan Law Review*. Volume 44.

Bontrager, B. 2004c. Enrollment management: An introduction to concepts and structures. *College and University*. 79(3): 11–16.

Buissink-Smith, N., R. Spronken-Smith, and R. Walker. 2010. You're doing what? Students' experiences of advice from a New Zealand university. *Higher Education Research & Development*. 29(4): 357–371.

Canada Millennium Scholarship Foundation. 2004. *Aboriginal Peoples and Post-Secondary Education: What Educators Have Learned*. Montreal: Canada Millennium Scholarship Foundation.

Canadian Council on Learning. 2009a. *Post-Secondary Education in Canada: Meeting Our Needs? Annual Report 2008–2009*. Ottawa: Canadian Council on Learning. Available at: <www.ccl-cca.ca/pdfs/PSE/2009/PSE2008_English.pdf>.

Canadian Federation of Students. 2010. *Aboriginal Students: Aboriginal Education*. Retrieved November 23, 2010 from: <www.cfs-fcee.ca/aboriginal/english/campaigns.php>.

Carbone, L. 2007. *The Emotion of Customer Experience*. Minneapolis, MN: Experience Engineering.

Commission Delors. 1996 *L'éducation: un trésor est caché dedans*. Paris: Odile Jacob.

Conférence Des Recteurs Européen. 1997. *Changer l'enseignement supérieur en Europe, un programme pour le XXIe siècle, Cahiers sur l'Enseignement Supérieur*. Strasbourg: Council of Europe.

Conference of Rectors and Principals of Québec Universities. 2009. *Autorisation d'études hors établissement : bilan statistique*.

Conseil De L'europe—Comité De L'enseignement Supérieur. 1998. *Projet de recommandation des Ministres aux États membres sur l'accès à l'enseignement supérieur*. Strasbourg: Council of Europe.

Drolet, D. 2010. Documenting and decoding the undergrad experience. *University Affairs*. August 16. Retrieved March 8, 2011 from: <www.universityaffairs.ca/documenting-the-undergrad-experience.aspx>.

Evers, F., and S. Hall. 2009a. *Faculty Engagement in Teaching Development Activities—Phase 1: Literature Review—Appendix*. Toronto: The Higher Education Quality Council of Ontario.

———. 2009b. *Faculty Engagement in Teaching Development Activities—Phase 1: Literature Review*. Toronto: The Higher Education Quality Council of Ontario.

Finnie, R., S. Childs, M. Kramer, and A. Wismer. 2010e. *Aboriginals in Post-Secondary Education* (Version 11–18–10) A MESA Project L-SLIS Research Brief. Toronto: Canadian Education Project.

Forbes, J.D. 2000. The new assimilation movement: Standards, tests, and Anglo-American supremacy. *Journal of American Indian Education*. 29(2).

Hanson, B. 1995. *Dual Realities—Dual Strategies: The Future of the Aboriginal People's Development*. Saskatoon, SK: Independent Publishing.

Hardy Cox, D., and C.C. Strange. 2010. *Achieving Student Success: Effective Student Services In Canadian Higher Education*. Kingston, ON: McGill-Queen's University Press.

HeavyRunner, I., and K. Marshell. 2003. Miracle survivors: Promoting resilience in Indian students. *Tribal College Journal*. 12(4).

Hossler, D. 2009. Putting students first in college admissions and enrollment management. In *Fostering Student Success in the Campus Community*, edited by J.N. Gardner and G.L. Kramer. Hoboken, NJ: Jossey-Bass.

Karlinski, J. 2010. *Response to Discussion Paper on a Mobile Student Research Framework*. Vancouver: B.C. Council on Admissions and Transfer.

Keeling, R.P. 2004. *Learning reconsidered: A campus-wide focus on the student experience*. Co-sponsored by American College Personnel Association—National Association of Student Personnel Administrators.

Kinzie, J., and G.D. Kuh. 2004. Going DEEP: Learning from campuses that share responsibility for student success. *About Campus*. 9(5): 2–8.

Kuh, G.D., J. Kinzie, J.A. Buckley, B.K. Bridges, and J.C. Hayek. 2007. Piecing together the student success puzzle: Research, propositions and recommendations. *ASHE Higher Education Report*. 32(5). San Francisco: Jossey-Bass.

Macguire, J. 1976. To the organized go the students. *Bridge Magazine* (Boston College alumni magazine). XXXIX(1).

Mandarino, C., and M.Y. Mattern. 2010. *Assessing the Validity of CCSSE in an Ontario College*. Toronto: Higher Education Quality Council of Ontario. Retrieved December 8, 2010 from: <www.heqco.ca/SiteCollectionDocuments/CCSSE_ENG.pdf>.

Morphy, D., P. Dueck, N. Marnoch, and L. Smith. 2010. *Strategic Enrolment Mangement at the University of Manitoba*. Workshop presented at the SEM Summit, Halifax, NS. April 28.

Ontario Universities' Application Centre. 2011. *Background of the Centre*. Retrieved February 8, 2011 from: <www.ouac.on.ca/about/about-background>.

Poole, G., L. Taylor, and J. Thompson 2007. Using the scholarship of teaching and learning at disciplinary, national and institutional levels to strategically improve the quality of post-secondary education. *International Journal for the Scholarship of Teaching and Learning*. 1(2).

Royal Commission on Aboriginal Peoples. 1996. People to people, nation to nation: Report of the Royal Commission on Aboriginal People. *Indian and Northern Affairs Canada*. Volume 1. Retrieved February 2, 2011 from: <www.ainc-inac.gc.ca/ap/pubs/rpt/rpt-eng.asp>.

Smith, C., and S. Gottheil. 2006. Enrollment or Enrolment: The Emergence of SEM in Canada. *SEM Source*.

Social Research and Demonstration Corporation. 2009b. *Report on the Data-Readiness of Post-Secondary Access and Retention Programs for Under-Represented Groups*, Number 46. Montrea: Canada Millennium Scholarship Foundation.

St. John, E.P. 2000. The impact of student aid on recruitment and retention: What the research indicates. In *The Role Student Aid Plays in Enrollment Management*, edited by M.D. Coomes. Sa Francisco: Jossey-Bass.

Statistics Canada. 2008b. *Aboriginal Peoples in Canada in 2006: Inuit, Métis, and First Nations, 2006 Census*. Retrieved February 2, 2011 from: <www12.statcan.ca/census-recensement/2006/as-sa/97–558/pdf/97–558-XIE2006001.pdf>.

———. 2010a. *Education Indicators in Canada: Report of the Pan-Canadian Education Indicators Program*. Retrieved March 4, 2011 from: <www.statcan.gc.ca/pub/81–582-x/81–582-x2010003-eng.htm>.

———. 2010c. *Projections of the Diversity of the Canadian Population, 2006 to 2031*. Retrieved on December 8, 2010, from: <www.statcan.gc.ca/daily-quotidien/100309/dq100309a-eng.htm>.

Statistics Canada and the Council of Ministers of Education, Canada. 2007. *Education Indicators in Canada: Report of the Pan-Canadian Education Indicators Program 2007*. Ottawa: Statistics Canada.

Stonechild, B. 2006. *The New Buffalo: The Struggle for Aboriginal Post-Secondary Education in Canada*. Winnipeg: University of Manitoba Press.

Université Laval (Québec City). 2004c. *Rapport du groupe de travail sur les suites à donner à l'avis de la commission des affaires étudiantes sur la persévérance et la réussite aux 2e et 3e cycles sous l'angle du recrutement étudiant*.

———. 2008. *CIÉRA. Les Cahiers du CIÉRA, No. 1*. Retrieved from: <https://depot.erudit.org/bitstream/003190dd/1/Texte.pdf>.

———. 2008. *Politique d'encadrement des étudiants à la maîtrise avec mémoire et au doctorat*, CU-2008–37. Retrieved from: <www.ulaval.ca/sg/reg/Politiques/Politique_encadrement_maî trise_doctorat.pdf>.

———. *Apprentissage et réussite*. Retrieved from: <www.aide.ulaval.ca/sgc/pid/1075>.

———. *Candidat Étranger*. Available at: <www.futursetudiants.ulaval.ca/admission/admission_au_1er_cycle/candidat_etranger/annee_pre-paratoire/>.

———. *CRIRES*. Available at: <www.ulaval.ca/crires/>.

———. *Le Programme de jumelage des étudiants étrangers*. Available at: <www.bve.ulaval.ca/accompagnement_des_etudiants_etrangers/services_et_activites/programme_de_jumelage_des_etudiants_etrangers/>

———. *Le projet d'environnement numérique d'apprentissage (ENA)*. Available at: <www.ena.ulaval.ca>

———. *Réussir ses études universitaires à l'ère numérique: rechercher et présenter l'information*. Retrieved from: <www.distance.ulaval.ca/fad/cours/EDC-4000>.

Whiteside, R. 2001. Moving from theory to action. In *Strategic Enrollment Management: Revolution*. Ed. Jim Black. Washington, D.C.: American Association of Collegiate Registrars and Admissions Officers.

———. 2004. *Student Marketing for Colleges and Universities*. Washington, D.C.: American Association of Collegiate Registrars and Admissions Officers.